D1046441

FEMINIST THEORY AND
CHRISTIAN THEOLOGY

GUIDES TO THEOLOGICAL INQUIRY

Edited by Kathryn Tanner of the University of Chicago and Paul Lakeland of Fairfield University, Guides to Theological Inquiry are intended to introduce students, scholars, clergy, and theologians to those academic methods, disciplines, and movements that are most germane to contemporary theology. Neither simple surveys nor exhaustive monographs, these short books provide solid, reliable, programmatic statements of the main lines or workings of their topics and assessments of their theological import.

Already available are *Nonfoundationalism* by John E. Thiel, *Literary Theory* by David Dawson, *Postmodernity* by Paul Lakeland, and *Theories of Culture* by Kathryn Tanner. Forthcoming titles in the series include *Hermeneutics* by Francis Schüssler Fiorenza, *Critical Social Theory* by Gary Simpson, and *African American Critical Thought* by Shawn Copeland.

FEMINIST THEORY AND CHRISTIAN THEOLOGY

CARTOGRAPHIES OF GRACE

SERENE JONES

GUIDES TO
THEOLOGICAL
INQUIRY

FORTRESS PRESS / MINNEAPOLIS

For Charis Augusta Parsons Jones
and her future

FEMINIST THEORY AND CHRISTIAN THEOLOGY
Cartographies of Grace
Guides to Theological Inquiry series

Copyright © 2000 Augsburg Fortress. All rights reserved. Except for brief quotations in critical articles or reviews, no part of this book may be reproduced in any manner without prior written permission from the publisher. Write to: Permissions, Augsburg Fortress, Box 1209, Minneapolis, MN 55440.

Scripture translations from the Revised Standard Version of the Bible, copyright © 1946, 1952, and 1971 by the Division of Christian Education of the National Council of Churches of Christ in the United States of America are used by permission.

Cover design: Craig Claeys
Author photo: T. Dagradi

Library of Congress Cataloging-in-Publication Data

Jones, Serene (–)
    Feminist theory and Christian theology : cartographies of grace / Serene Jones.
        p.   cm. — (Guides to theological inquiry)
    Includes bibliographical references and index.
    ISBN 0-8006-2694-X (alk. paper)
    1. Feminist theology. 2. Feminist theory. I. Title. II. Series
BT83.55 J66 2000
230'.082—dc21   00-035365
                                                                      CIP

The paper used in this publication meets the minimum requirements of American National Standard for Information Sciences—Permanence of Paper for Printed Library Materials, ANSI Z329.48-1984. ♾ ™

Manufactured in the U.S.A.   AF 1-2694

Contents

Foreword

Christian theology has always conceived itself in dialogue with other intellectual disciplines, notably philosophy. Such a dialogue has expanded its range exponentially and thereby become more difficult in the pluriform, multivoiced intellectual landscape of contemporary times. Helping theologians navigate an intellectual universe that no one person can now master, or even adequately survey, is one point of the Guides to Theological Inquiry series.

This book on feminist theory and theology is a crucial contribution to the series, each volume of which is dedicated to a topic or method in contemporary intellectual life and its significance for theology. Feminist theology, as it is practiced in the United States today by academic theologians such as Serene Jones, models for theology generally a courageous and creative strategy of theological response to the shifting and variegated geography of the present intellectual terrain. As Jones's book so well demonstrates, feminist theology avails itself of the full range of feminist scholarship in a variety of fields (e.g., literary theory, psychology, and social and political theory) in order better to attend to the concrete specificities of women's lives—their challenges and problems—and to promote, by way of such diagnoses and analyses of women's situations, the flourishing of all. Incorporating the way that feminist scholarship bridges sophisticated academic methods and real-life concerns, feminist theology in Jones's hands reorients doctrines of the human person, sin, grace, and the church in renewed service to the world by remapping creatively the directions for living that such doctrines provide. The book therefore combines an introduction to feminist studies in a variety of fields with both the rich stories of women's lives and a historically sensitive rereading of Christian doctrines (especially in a Protestant vein). The reward, for those interested in constructive theological proposals, is an outline of an exciting new feminist systematics.

—Kathryn Tanner

Preface

A s the subtitle of this book suggests, I undertake the task of "mapping" in the pages ahead. Picking up the cartographer's tools, I sketch for the reader maps of two worlds of reflection, feminist theory and Christian theology. I like the image of mapping because it captures well my intention to lay out central concepts that structure these two worlds and to draw lines that show the interconnections between them. At their best, maps help us figure out the "lay of the land" in areas where we might otherwise be lost; they give us directional guides that allow us to negotiate unfamiliar terrains. I hope these maps provide help of this sort to those unfamiliar with the worlds I explore.

Writing this book has made me increasingly aware of the limits of maps, however. Both Christian theology and feminist theory are worlds of thought that have profound effects upon the people who inhabit their terrains. They are discourses that shape lives, craft dispositions, and form certain virtues of perception and practice; this quality of formation is difficult to capture in the one-dimensional lines of cartographic art. Maps also cannot give one a sense for the fullness and complexity of the lives of the people who live on the streets, hills, and plains they chart. In the chapters ahead, I try to make my maps slightly more multidimensional than usual by stopping occasionally to let their inhabitants speak, to let you see something of the dense texture of their day-to-day existence. The best way to hear these voices, however, is not by observing the markings of my maps from a distance; I suggest, instead, actually using these maps to visit the places I describe.

Having said this, I must also say that writing this book has made me acutely aware of the ways maps can hide or obfuscate dimensions of the worlds they try to order. For example, I spent a good deal of time writing this book in a house that sits on a high-desert dirt road that doesn't appear on any of the marketed maps of the area. Similarly, I am certain that in charting the central concepts that mark the worlds of feminist theory and Christian theology, I have left huge blank spaces in places where there is much more traffic than I had realized. When you find these places, fill them in and be bold enough to redraw the entire map if need be. Do so realizing, however, that maps are never simply open windows to the real; they are just as often blueprints for the "real" that is being formed, the emergent terrain. In other words, maps create just as they are created.

As I have drawn the lines that compose the maps of this book, I have been constantly aware of all these limits. There are countless scholars, friends, neighbors, comrades, family members, and ancestors in the tradition whose work constitutes the terrains traced on the pages ahead but who never actually appear on the map itself. Every sharp black line drawn with my cartographer's tools hides the lives and ideas that give the line its edge. Every cartographic gesture I lay down has been learned and practiced through years of conversation with people who will never be credited for their skillful contribution to this cartographic enterprise. This is particularly true with respect to the countless women who have sat in "women's groups" with me over the years, women whose stories constitute the imaginatively construed Tuesday-night group I describe in the chapters ahead. I hope I have not too dramatically mismapped their tales; when I have, I hope they blame the mapmaker and not themselves. Similarly, there are at least ten years' worth of student voices embedded in the maps I have drawn here. My hope for them is that they, in the communities where they work, are now drawing even better maps than mine.

Over the years, numerous colleagues have read and reread these pages and have steadily tried (often to their frustration!) to sharpen my cartographical skills; and many of them have nurtured in me a healthy sense of feminist adventure when it comes to mapping previously uncharted land. Among them, I thank especially Marilyn Adams, Hazel Carby, Rebecca Chopp, Shannon Clarkson, Sarah Coakley, Paula Cooey, Harlon Dalton, Cynthia Eller, Margaret Farley, Mary Fulkerson, Susan Garrett, the late John Geter, Margaret Homans, David Kelsey, Kris Kvam, Amy Plantinga Pauw, Mary Renda, Rosemary Radford Ruether, Letty Russell, Jone Salomonsen, Miroslav Volf, Jann Weaver, Tammy Williams, and Nicholas Wolterstorff. I also thank my students Barbara Blodgett, Wendy Boring, Shannon Craigo-Snell, Ruthanna Hooke, Kalbryn McLean, and Madhuri Yahlapadi who, along with Marilyn Adams, brought their own brand of "Lux et Veritas" to this enterprise. Patricia Carque, Maria LaSalla, and Alison Stokes gave me the precious gift of their feminist pastoral insights as did Melanie Swenson and Lydia Dixon. Deb and Harry Townshend gave me the gift of Pomfret, and Laura Vanard, the gift of Arroyo Seco—two landscapes that have dramatically shaped my writing. Tracy Swan Tuite and Kate Ott deserve special thanks for ushering this work through its final phases. Kalbryn McLean and Shelly Rambo gave deft form to this book in ways too numerous to name.

This book and its many maps would not exist if it were not for the encouragement and constant guidance of Kathryn Tanner, my editor, good friend, former teacher, and, of course, a brilliant theologian. My sisters Verity Jones, Kindy Jones, Cornelia Dinnean, and Tamara Jones continue to teach me what sisterhood means, and my parents, Sarah Jones and Joe Jones gave me the gift of a feminist spirit from the time I was born. The bright landscapes of Shepard Parsons, both painted and lived, serve as a palate for much of what I say here; he vividly colors my world (and my maps) in so many ways. Because Lynne Huffer and I have intellectually and soulfully dwelled so closely together over the past ten years, I find it difficult to say which parts of this book are mine and which are hers; we map together. And finally, I offer prayers of thanksgiving for the wee soul, Charis Augusta Parsons Jones, whose daily shouts of joy both keep me writing and make me not want to write. If her feminist spirit is any indication of things to come, the future is not only bright; it is intensely so.

1

Mapping Feminist Theory and Theology

My family and friends jokingly refer to the third Tuesday of every month as Serene's "feminist day." After getting my daughter to day care by eight o'clock, I prepare for the afternoon class on feminist theory I teach to seminary and undergraduate students. I love teaching this class; the students' eagerness to learn about recent trends in feminism is inspiring, and their own feminist feistiness keeps me on my toes. After teaching, I hurry to the monthly faculty meeting of the Women and Gender Studies Council. There, our conversations typically focus on how to run an effective academic program, although we also discuss feminist theory. I am the only theologian (and divinity school professor) on the council, and we rarely discuss religious matters, although when the topic comes up, these very secular colleagues listen to me with care and respect. Years of fighting for women in the trenches of the university have built strong bonds of trust among us, and out of these bonds has grown an atmosphere of mutual learning, even about a topic like theology.

After the council meeting, I walk to my local church parish house in downtown New Haven to join a monthly "Tuesday-night women's group" for dinner. We represent a diversity of ages, races, classes, and sexual orientations (to name only a few of our differences), yet a shared history and faith bind us together. We have done many things together over the years, but the most important has been to talk with each other about our lives and faith. We read Scripture and reflect on what it means for us—exhausted women living in the new millennium—to believe in a triune God whose grace embraces us and opens us to life abundant.

As I share in those discussions, reflections on grace intermingle with thoughts about my daughter, my students, my faculty colleagues, and this group of friends. I talk about the feminist theory I have been teaching all day and how it has given me new ways to understand our stories and struggles. I

1

wonder how grace touches us and enlivens us here and now, and how feminist theory might help us see this. To my surprise, my gathered friends always want to hear more, particularly about feminist theory; they want to know about its importance for theology and its effects on understanding God's grace. Though I am the only trained theologian and feminist theorist in the room, the other women have their own expertise concerning matters like gender, God, grace, and the messy complexity of daily living. These women remind me again and again that high theory and local wisdom make wonderful companions.

I offer this description of my "feminist Tuesday" because it sets the context for the reflections that unfold in the pages ahead.[1] My faculty colleagues in Women and Gender Studies make me appreciate feminist theory and its social environment. The folks in my Tuesday-night group force me to think about the applicability of feminist theory to the lives of ordinary women and to struggle honestly with the theological issues it raises. My divinity and undergraduate students help me appreciate the subtlety of play that can exist between theory and theology and the hope to which this gives rise.

In conversation with these communities, this book explains what feminist theory is and illustrates its relevance to contemporary theology. Students of theology have much to learn from feminist theory, I believe. It deepens our understanding of human identity and community and opens up new avenues for understanding the Christian theological tradition and its view of divine grace. I also believe that feminist theory has much to learn from theology, but alas, that topic awaits another time.

Feminist Theory

When I first explained feminist theory to the women in the Tuesday-night group, I had to deal with their fears about the enterprise as a whole. They thought of feminist theory as a specialized discipline carried on by highly trained scholars and analysts, and they felt they lacked the necessary qualifications for doing theory—such qualifications as having a Ph.D. in philosophy, reading French, and understanding the finer points of structuralist semiotics. To them, feminist theory seemed an ivory-tower enterprise with little practical relevance. Yet, as I went over debates in feminist theory, these attitudes quickly changed. They realized that topics feminist theory discusses in highly technical (and sometimes off-putting) terms were immediately applicable to their daily lives. While not engaged in the abstract theorizing of the feminist scholars explored in this book, they realized they already practiced a kind of lay feminist theory when, for instance, they reflected on the conditions of their lives and asked about the role gender plays in them. Suspending their suspicions, they became eager to learn as much as they could from the material I introduced to them.

What is feminist theory?[2] Although women have been engaged in philosophically rigorous reflections on the conditions of their lives for centuries, the term "feminist theory" has a short history. Emerging in the newly born field of Women's Studies during the 1970s in North American universities, the term describes a collection of feminist texts with shared goals, practices, and assumptions. Although focusing on a collection of writings, feminist theory also includes the conversations of women that bring these texts to life. I therefore describe feminist theory as a collection of critical texts and a conversation—and not as a discrete academic field. Feminist theorizing is not limited to a particular discipline but takes place in almost every department of the university (in sciences as well as the humanities) and in many places outside the university (in government policy offices as well as in national women's organizations and local women's Bible-study groups).

What do these texts and conversations share? A number of ideals mark their common aspirations, although they may not always live up to them. First, they share a common goal, namely, the liberation of women. This goal makes these works "feminist": they struggle against the oppression of women and for their empowerment. This commitment is not abstract; it is grounded in political movements that actively seek change. For the earliest feminist theorists, this meant standing in service to the "women's movement."[3] More recently, this commitment has involved linking theory to diverse sites of struggle where women and others seek to overturn oppression, such as national Gay and Lesbian Pride marches, neighborhood rape crisis centers, and international solidarity networks. For this reason, feminist theory often refers to itself as a kind of political practice. Just as one would call forming a tenant organization a form of political action, so, too, feminist theory represents a form of oppositional political action, albeit one with unique tools.

To understand these tools, one must see why feminist theory emerged in the first place, why the women's movement needed people doing research and writing in a mode called theory. From the outset, the goal of liberating women had two aspects. First, feminists sought to identify the various forms of oppression that structured women's lives, and second, they imagined and sought to create an alternative future without oppression. What soon became apparent, however, was that oppression is not always easy to name. In fact, because oppression affects the very way one thinks about oneself and one's world, it is often quite difficult to even see, much less name. Oppression makes itself invisible, distorts vision, and twists thought. Similarly, it is hard to envision new ways of living when everything one experiences is rooted in old, oppressive forms of knowing and acting.

What theory offered to feminists in this context was an opportunity to self-consciously analyze the thought processes involved in naming oppression and imagining a new future. To do theoretical analysis is to analyze thought itself, its assumptions and its rules. Put succinctly, theory analyzes the signposts (orders, rules, assumptions) that structure and direct thought. When feminists "do theory," they look at individual and collective thought processes and ask about the grounding assumptions, orders, and rules that actively but often invisibly contribute to both the oppression and the ultimate flourishing of women. The multiplicity of such assumptions and rules requires feminists to do their analysis at many different levels—language, emotions, physical expressions, institutional forms, economic systems, and so on—and in many different places—at home and in offices, laboratories, synagogues, mosques, churches, courtrooms, and university lecture halls, to name just a few.

In this book, I look at what feminist theorists have discovered about the rules of their various academic disciplines. For example, in the hard sciences, feminist theorists question one of the discipline's traditional Enlightenment assumptions, namely, that science can be and is objective—unbiased, factual, unquestionable. As another example, feminists working in political science and legal studies use theory to suggest that basic assumptions concerning the existence of "the free, property-owning citizen" are not only deeply problematic and illusory but also dangerous. Likewise, in the area of economics, feminists question the assumption that unpaid domestic work and wage labor are fundamentally different species of work. Challenging assumptions like objectivity, freedom, and the division of labor is no small matter, and when feminist theorists do it, the results are monumental and controversial.

These examples of theoretical work may seem far removed from the broader culture and the more common signposts of thought that order our everyday lives. Don't these more common rules and directions need interrogating as well? In answering this question, feminists argue that the assumptions of academic disciplines are mirrored in more general cultural values. I have certainly found this to be the case. For example, when I go to the grocery store, I usually assume (along with scientists) that the label on the cereal box is "objectively true"; I act (along with political scientists) as if I am "freely" buying food for tomorrow's breakfast; and I assume (in concert with economists) that time spent shopping is not "work time" but "leisure time." Using feminist theory, however, I can ask, how might a nutritional label be an advertising ploy, designed to sell the product to women and not just to inform me about facts? I can ask as well: Is choosing cereal a useful way to understand "freedom"? Or similarly, if I need to buy this cereal to eat and have energy for my job, why is the time I spend considered "leisure"? Perhaps because it's "women's work"?

While it may seem trivial, this example makes an important point about the scope of feminist theory's project: this theory reaches into not only the academy but also the most personal dimensions of everyday living. Recognition of this fact has led feminist theorists to point out that many "texts" in our culture participate in feminist theorizing outside the mainstream academic disciplines. In poets and novelists, feminists have often found the voice of critique and reconstruction powerfully articulated on questions of identity, history, and community.[4] Through moving chords of music and song, persons have experienced new sounds and ways of hearing feminist thought. Through the eyes of visual artists and filmmakers, dominant conceptions of agency and space have been creatively questioned and reworked by feminists.[5] While these cultural "texts" are not usually considered feminist theory, they are places where feminists have blurred the borders between the academic disciplines and popular culture to great effect.[6] Along with feminist theory, they share an imaginative and contestatory practice aimed at critiquing thought and its most treasured conceptual markers.

I hope these introductory comments about feminist theory help clarify the subject matter of this book. The book's ideas will become even clearer when, in the course of the chapters ahead, one has the chance to see what feminist theory actually does. To facilitate this clarification, a few more comments are needed to orient readers to the markers that direct and structure feminist theory itself. Not surprisingly, feminist theory, like all thought, has its own rules, grounding concepts, and (often hidden) assumptions. Although changing constantly, they form a loose nexus of assumptions within which feminist theory locates itself.

As I explained earlier, feminist theorists hold that what makes their work feminist is a commitment to participating in the struggle against the oppression of women and for their liberation. Several aspects of this claim clarify the grounding concepts of feminist theory. First, feminist theorists focus on women not because they believe no other group of persons is worthy of critical analysis or because liberating women is the sole key to liberating the world. They do so because women's lives have long been ignored as a subject of critical reflection and because of a sense of urgency related to the present-day harms being done to women. In feminist theory, this decision to put intellectual energies in places where it is needed most is referred to as a "preferential option" for women.[7]

This preferential option for women is qualified, however, by a second feature of feminist theory. Anyone who reflects on women's lives knows that the fate and future of women can never be separated from the fate and future of all persons and of the planet as a whole. Feminist theorists acknowledge this interconnection. Their concern is not only for the liberation of women but for *all* who are broken, physically and in spirit, by the oppressions of our world. Feminists emphasize the inclusive scope of the future for which they struggle by saying: "We are struggling for the liberation of women and *all people*."[8] Feminist theorists know that if women were emancipated, all oppression would not suddenly disappear, and they recognize how women's oppression is intertwined with other forms of oppression, such as racism, poverty, exploitation, heterosexism, ageism, and discrimination against children and the disabled, to name only a few. Appreciating the complexity of interlocking oppressions is crucial to the work of feminist theory, and I return to this topic and treat it at great length in chapter 2.

This discussion of interlocking oppressions and inclusive liberation leads to yet a third clarification concerning the goal of feminist theory. As stated earlier, feminism sees its fundamental task as identifying oppression and changing the social systems that perpetuate injustice. But is this the only thing that drives the theory? As I show in the pages ahead, there is much more to women's lives and to feminist theory than accounts of oppression. There are, for example, the complex dimensions of lives that have survived and flourished throughout the centuries into the present, even in situations of wrenching violence and despair; these lives need to be studied and celebrated. For this reason, the flourishing of women is the subject of constructive feminist analysis and the source of some of its most creative insights. Feminist theorists lift up many different aspects of this flourishing of women—respect for their bodily integrity and creativity as well as social conditions and relations of power marked by mutuality and reciprocity. Feminist theorists also recognize the rich cultural and historical differences of women's experiences in various eras, geographical locations, communities, and ethnicities, differences that are not simply examples of either oppression *or* flourishing. As such, feminist theory tries to hold its analysis of women's oppression in tension with an appreciation for both the flourishing of women and the complex "givenness" of their multiple circumstances. In doing so, feminist theory views women not only as history's victims but as its active agents and ever-engaged protagonists as well.

This brings me to a fourth, extremely important clarification of feminist theory's overall project. Respecting differences in the lives of women requires that feminist theorists listen carefully to the varied experiences of *all* women and avoid too quickly imposing upon them theoretical categories that do not fit. This means attending to women's accounts of their lives *in their own words,* according to their own narratives. This turn to story expands the scope of feminist theory as a whole; in telling and listening to women's stories, we discover new rules, assumptions, and categories of thought that provide new material for feminists both to analyze and critique and to explore constructively and use.[9]

This listening to women's diverse voices is happening in many areas. For example, in womanist thought, African American women are developing new analytic categories appropriate to their historically specific experiences and stories.[10] Latina women are constructing *mujerista* analysis to understand better and describe the unique experiences of Latina and Chicana women.[11] Native American women are giving theoretical form to thoughts and stories that structured their traditions and practices and are critically expanding the scope of our present-day understandings of women's lives.[12] European American women are beginning to see how their experience is not normative for all women but the product of their own heritages. Lesbians are contributing to the feminist conversation as they reveal the dynamics that accompany being women who love women in a culture that privileges heterosexuality. And the growing wealth of theory related to disabled women's lives is expanding the horizons of feminist theory by challenging age-old assumptions about bodies, work, and community. The list goes on as more women claim the particularities of their lives as subjects worthy of theoretical reflection.

This focus on differences among women brings me to a fifth clarification concerning feminist theory's goal of critiquing oppression and advocating the liberation of women. In recent years, the meaning of the term "women" has come under scrutiny in feminist studies. Questions have emerged, such as: Do women constitute a stable group that can be analyzed and liberated? Differences among women seem to make it impossible to speak of ourselves as a single human collective, and yet feminists assume some sort of unity among women. But on what basis is this unity constituted? Does "women" refer to a social class? A biological genus? A historical group? Or is it a meaningless fabrication? To this last question, most feminists answer, No! They insist that the category "women" serves an important political and analytic function in their work. Exactly what this function is, however, remains an issue of debate. The weight of this debate has been felt with particular force in feminist discussions of "identity" and "human nature"; because both terms play a crucial role in feminist theory, I treat them extensively in the next chapter.

One of the most significant effects of this debate over the term "women" is the emergence of the term "gender" as an analytic category for feminist thought. These days, it is not unusual to hear talk of gender studies, gender-bending, or gender-inclusive language. What does "gender" refer to here? In the next chapter, I discuss the term at length, setting it in the context of its development and highlighting its nuances for different theorists. For now, however, a simple definition suffices. *Gender* is distinguished from the term *sex,* which refers to the physiological differences between men and women. In contrast to *sex, gender* refers to culturally constructed systems of meaning that identify various things—persons, ideas, gods, institutions, and so on—according to the binary categories of "women/men" or "feminine/masculine."[13] To capture the dynamic process whereby these categories define and identify things in a given culture, feminists often speak of how things are "gendered" or of "gendered constructions." These terms emphasize the feminist contention that societies and persons create and are created by systems of meaning. These systems are in turn ruled by assumptions about binary gender differences that are not natural but produced by social convention. When one speaks about "gender" or offers a "gender analysis," one is trying to decipher the varied ways in which gendered categories are deployed to create meaning and identity in a given social context.

The contexts of such analysis are quite varied. For example, one can apply gender analysis to a television advertisement for paper towels, noting how gender roles for women and men are enacted in interesting and complex ways around a diner's front counter (where a female waitress in a dress cleans up a spill made by a male truck driver in work pants) and highlighting how the paper towel is given a masculine gender ("tough on stains") just as the spill is feminized ("messy and unruly"). Similarly, in a more traditionally academic context, gender analysis can be used to uncover the dynamic gendered meanings attributed to such philosophical concepts as matter, fluid, chaos, order, mind, body, beauty, goodness, and truth as well as more concrete things like boats, buildings, nations, and leaders. This kind of analysis is important because changing oppressive ways of thinking about the construction of "women" involves unpacking oppressive gendered ways of thinking about *all* reality. As feminist theory constantly reminds us, the gendered assumptions of Western thought run deep in the conceptual bedrock of our language and hence in all of our experience.

One might ask at this point, haven't terms like "oppression," "liberation," and "women" now been so expanded and qualified that the goals of feminist theory no longer make sense? Many of feminist theory's central terms, indeed, are presently up for grabs. This indeterminacy of terms is, however, partially an intended consequence of feminist theory itself, for practitioners of feminist theory enjoy taking a common and seemingly perspicuous term (like "women") and uncovering its hidden meanings and its multiple social functions. They hope this will enable people to determine better when oppressive assumptions about gender are at work in language and thought and when not. They hope, as well, that playing with established meanings will create room for hearing the marginal, the exiled, and the insurgent voices of women discounted by the dominant culture. Thus, in the world of feminist theory, indeterminacy is not always viewed as a problem; sometimes it is seen as a promise of new things to come.

The flip side of feminist theory's sometimes playful view of language and its indeterminacy is its commitment to developing stable, normative criteria for assessing oppression and measuring the liberating structure of a new future. Far from promoting an "anything goes" attitude toward life, many (although not all) feminist theorists develop cultural standards, values, and ethical rules that can be used to make judgments about right and wrong, truth and falsehood, justice and injustice, and freedom and enslavement. Without such normative criteria, a term like "oppression" makes no sense— one needs a framework for naming injustice, and one needs justice to discern when oppression occurs. Similarly, without norms, a notion such as liberation loses its content and meaning—one needs some concept of freedom to imagine what liberation looks like. Should these terms lose their meaning and force, feminist theory would be emptied of the prophetic, emancipatory impulses that drive it. The need for normative criteria does not imply, however, that such norms are easy to discern, much less to justify or implement. In the chapters ahead, I explore models that feminist theorists have developed for sorting through these issues, models that try to hold in tension the feminist commitment to diversity, critique, and playful indeterminacy, on the one hand, and, on the other, an abiding concern to give specific content to terms like "justice" and "truth." In current feminist theory, this tension is most vividly felt in discussions of three specific topics: women's nature, oppression, and community. These are the three themes around which my discussion of feminist theory is built.

One final comment about this broad definition of feminist theory and its rules, norms, and goals. Over the years of my involvement in feminist political action, I have been repeatedly struck by feminism's undaunted predilection for the future. Feminism has always been sustained by the belief that things can get better. This hope is reflected in the theory that comes out of the movement. When a feminist theorist challenges a given social structure, one can be fairly sure that lurking behind her challenge is an imaginative construal of a liberating alternative. Similarly, when a feminist theorist makes normative claims about things such as human nature and the character of justice in gender relations, one can be certain that her argument holds a vision of a better, possible future. To be sure, these images of the future often remain blurry and fragmentary. They are visions that need development and clarification; at the same time, they remain open enough to welcome the emergent insights of each new generation of feminists.

In my experience, these hopes and visions of women flourishing are not usually naively utopian or otherworldly. Rather, they are marked by a pragmatic realism grounded in the experience feminists have gained in years of work to change social systems and reconstruct social institutions. In this sense, the future that feminist theorists imagine is one that has already left its mark, often as a barely discernible imprint, upon the face of history. It is a future that is both "already" and "not yet" present in history. Using theological language, I refer to this predilection for the future as feminist theory's *pragmatic eschatological orientation.* Naming its eschatology thus highlights feminist theory's leanings toward that which is to come. As this book will show, this eschatological dimension of feminist theory crucially shapes my understanding as a Christian feminist of the relation between feminist theory and theology.

Feminist Theology

The purpose of this book, as I said earlier, is not simply to introduce feminist theory; I want also to illustrate its relevance to Christian theology and its many traditions. This second task is the most distinctive contribution of this project: there are a number of general introductions to feminist theory, but few written specifically for persons with theological interests and faith-related questions.[14] In the pages ahead, readers should exercise their own expertise in making everyday theological judgments. Just as the theoretical portions of this book need to be tested against the readers' practical experiences of being women and men in today's world, so too the theological reflections I offer here need to be measured against the lived experiences and traditions of persons who seek to know God truly and to live faithfully.

Given the breadth of topics covered by feminist theory, I could bring this theory into productive conversation with any number of theological questions, themes, figures, doctrines, or schools of thought. For example, it could be used to open up new avenues of exploration in fields such as Christian ethics, biblical studies, church history, preaching, and pastoral care.[15] Likewise, it could be applied to such traditional Christian themes as the cross, salvation, the nature of God's providence, and the ever present problem of evil and suffering. It could be used as well to throw new light on social issues with which today's Christians struggle—the environmental crisis, reproductive rights for women, the intransigent injustices of racism, and the increasing poverty of most of the world's population. At the same time, it could also assist in clarifying more ordinary tasks like teaching a child to look at art, deciding which hymns to sing on Sunday morning, and figuring out what the church should do with an unexpected estate gift. As stated earlier, feminist theory deploys its analytic tools upon even the most minute details of our cultural thought processes; no topic is too insignificant or too preciously important—from communion cups and old hymnals to abstract doctrines and wrenching existential questions—not to benefit from conversations with feminist theory.

In this book, however, I touch on only a fraction of these many topics. I bring feminist theory into conversation with my own field: Christian feminist systematic theology informed by doctrines of the Reformation traditions. Although limiting the conversation in this manner leaves out many voices and theological issues, it allows me to explore in detail how feminist theory can inform the thought patterns of one particular tradition. In my experience, feminist theory is most illuminating when applied to a *particular* system of thought and *specific* imagistic patterns of reflection. This sharp focus allows feminist theory to show its relevance to the complex weave of ideas and images that constitute a tradition. One can then appreciate the subtle ways feminist theory informs theology, often with the turn of a phrase or the twist of an image. Such a sharp focus also has the practical advantage of engaging a discrete (but not isolated) theological tradition that continues to shape people's lives in specific and discernible ways.

How might one define the narrowed field of feminist, constructive, systematic theology in the Reformation tradition that I bring into conversation with feminist theory? As the women in my Tuesday-night group continually remind me, the technical language of theology can be as off-putting and inaccessible as the language of feminist theory. To avoid this, let me offer brief definitions of five facets of the arena in which I work as a feminist theologian: "Christian theology," "feminist theology," "constructive systematic theology," "doctrinal theology," and "Reformed theology."

Let's first explore what it means to say I engage in "Christian" theology, and then second, what it means to call this Christian thought "feminist." When I refer to the theological sections of this book as "Christian theology," I situate this project within the work of a long line of theologians who have shared in the critical task of helping the church reflect on its present-day witness and practice to see if it continues to be faithful to the revelation of God manifest in Scripture, tradition, and the ongoing life of the Christian community. Using this definition of theology highlights the "churchly" or ecclesiastical character of my feminist theology. Far from being a disinterested academic enterprise criticizing Christianity from the outside, my Christian feminist theology locates itself within the Christian faith and attempts to serve and strengthen the community from inside. This form of feminist theology is therefore responsible to Christian faith communities as its audience and contextual judge. This means I have to ask: Would what I'm saying make sense to people who sit in church pews on Sunday morning? Does it make a difference in their lives? Does it deepen faith? Does it help us to pray? Does it assist the church in serving God's purposes of liberation? This communal grounding affects the uses to which I put feminist theory—I make feminist theory do "church work."

This does not mean, however, that this form of theology is a compliant and unquestioning servant of the church. For centuries, theology's position vis-à-vis Christian community has been restless, uneasy, challenging, and critical. With this posture toward the church, my work in feminist theology once again shows itself firmly planted in the soil of a Christian theological tradition that sees its task not as a simplistic reiteration of the community's traditional and present-day beliefs but as a contribution to the church's ongoing process of self-examination and reform. One must rigorously test conventional practices and beliefs to see whether they have remained true to their purposes or have become distorted by complacency, arrogance, the temptations of power, and the unrelenting passage of time. In doing so, theology helps the church see with renewed clarity the comprehensive theological vision that grounds and centers its faith.

This brings me to the most important feature of the Christian theology I undertake: its commitment to exploring the central truths of the Christian message. While centuries of experience have taught the church that this message is never static or unambiguously self-evident, Christian communities found their identity upon a firm belief that a divine truth or vision beckons the community to an ongoing covenantal relationship with God. I too make truth claims about the reality of God and the nature of the gospel. This affirmation of faith roughly follows the story of Christian faith told in Scripture and unfolded in the classical creeds. It begins with the affirmation that God calls the world into being and seeks to be in loving relationship with it. Creation, in the mystery of its freedom, however, turns from God in sin. God nonetheless continues to seek relationship with God's creatures, a seeking vividly embodied in the history of Israel, in the New Testament community, and in present-day communities of faith. Although not treated with much depth here, at the heart of my theological reflections also lie the affirmations that in Jesus Christ, God reconciled the world to Godself and redeemed humanity from sin and that this triune God calls us to abundant life in community and promises to dwell with us here and now and in the world to come.

This short summary of "the Christian message" is hardly a developed theological confession. It simply serves to orient the reader to the general features of my theology. In the chapters ahead, only a few of these themes will be clarified and expanded; others will be left underdeveloped. By asserting that these are "truth claims," I also leave a number of epistemological issues hanging, such as: What do I mean by truth? As my analysis of both feminist theory and theology will suggest, I am at heart a critical realist.[16] I believe there is a "fact of the matter" about ourselves, the world around us, and God, but I also hold that we do not have unmediated access to these facts.[17] This critical realism is explored briefly in the next chapter, but this is not primarily a book in theological epistemology.

Having said this about the "Christian" nature of this enterprise, what does it mean to say that this is "feminist theology"? Like many terms used in this book, "feminist theology" means different things in different communities. For some people, it immediately calls up negative images of angry women destroying the church with pagan rituals. For others, it evokes more positive images, such as a round banquet table where feminist theology "happens" as women gather, from all corners of the world, to celebrate creation and to praise the God of life and liberation, singing and feasting on the "bread of hope" and the "cup of salvation."[18] Even for those with positive images, however, the term "feminist theology" means many things. Sometimes it refers to the broad movement of feminism in the church; at other times, it describes a highly intellectual enterprise undertaken only by professional theologians. "Feminist theology" can refer, as well, to any type of feminist "spiritual" thinking about God, be it by a Muslim Imam, a Baptist organist, or a New Age poet.[19] In these contexts, "feminist theology" can name anything from the liturgy of a healing ritual to a formal treatise on matriarchal symbols.

What are we to make of this diversity? "Feminist theology" as an official title has a relatively short history (although the history of feministlike theological reflection is quite long).[20] Like feminist theory, its roots are in the women's movement of the late 1960s and early 1970s in North America. In places ranging from church-basement Bible studies to women's consciousness-raising groups, feminist theology emerged as a grassroots challenge to traditional views of women's role in religion and society. In its earliest stages, few distinctions were drawn among Jewish feminist, Christian feminist, and post-Christian contributions to the movement's critiques of women's oppression. Similarly, the distinction between feminist theory and feminist theology was less important then. In fact, the most treasured texts of early feminist *theory* were texts written by women theologians and philosophers of religion: Mary Daly's *Beyond God the Father* and the essays collected by Carol Christ and Judith Plaskow in *Woman Spirit Rising: A Feminist Reader in Religion*.[21] Also, in these early years it was often in religious studies departments that Jewish, Christian, and post-Christian feminist theologians and philosophers of religion introduced the topic of feminism to the curriculum of college campuses. This same heritage continues in many present-day college classrooms where the cutting edge of womanist and *mujerista* theology cuts across the usual boundaries separating theory and theology.

When I use the term "feminist theology," I work within this broad tradition of reflection, but I focus on the Christian tradition. Feminist theology in this context, therefore, does not represent the theology of every woman who reflects on her spiritual journey and her beliefs about God and the world. Nor does it represent Jewish, Muslim, and post-Christian feminist theologians and feminist philosophers of religion, all of whom play an instrumental role in feminist theology in North America. Instead of representing all religious reflection undertaken by feminists, I focus here on distinctly Christian themes.

What makes this specifically Christian theological enterprise "feminist"? It takes a special interest in the lives of women, their stories, their hopes, their flourishing and failures, and their multilayered experiences of oppression. This kind of feminist theology brings these lives and experiences into the drama of the Christian message and explores how Christian faith grounds and shapes women's experiences of hope, justice, and grace as well as instigates and enforces women's experiences of oppression, sin, and evil. The term "feminist," then, locates the distinctive interests of this theology. It is a theology that articulates the Christian message in language and actions that seek to liberate women and all persons, a goal that Christian feminists believe cannot be disentangled from the central truth of the Christian faith as a whole.

What does this mean in concrete terms? Let us look for a moment at how the term "feminist" adds to my previous description of theology as a communal, self-critical, and truth-seeking enterprise. When feminist theology claims the church as its audience and practical judge, it particularly attends to *women* in the church, a group that centuries of theologians have failed to include in their church audience. Feminist theology also listens to women who have been harmed by the Christian community or who have left the church, for these women are able to identify, often with painful clarity, the most broken and twisted places in church life for women. This commitment to listening extends as well to many voices with no confessional connection to Christian faith and practice, whose insights illuminate what it means to be "women" and "men" in other cultures and other times—for example, a feminist atheist in France, a Buddhist activist in Sri Lanka, or a Jewish rabbi in Los Angeles.

Being "feminist" informs, moreover, how this theology grapples with the self-critical and reforming task of Christian thought. Feminist theory plays a particularly important role here. Its principal function, you will recall, is to analyze how gender constructions inform our most basic thought processes. This same kind of analysis can be used to explore the gendered character of Christian rules of thought. Feminist theory provides critical methods for analyzing terms such as "sin," "human nature," "Christian freedom," and "the Holy Spirit." By exploring these terms, feminist theory helps us better understand how cultural constructions of gender have affected the development of Christian thought and practice over the centuries into the present. As we shall see in the next chapters, the revelations about gender and women that emerge from these explorations are often startling and disturbing; they show how deeply the oppression of women is embedded in the most innocent-seeming habits of Christian thought.

At first glance, this enterprise of bringing women's lives into theological focus and analyzing gender constructions in church doctrine and practice appears straightforward. Anyone with a commitment to the church, a willingness to take women's stories seriously, and an openness to critical thinking about gender assumptions can do it. And this is true to a certain extent. Feminist theologians include women like my mother, who challenged traditional assumptions about gender by becoming the first woman elder in our local church in the 1960s, and my friend who last year organized a Bible study for incest survivors in New Haven. They include the young student who on Sunday mornings belts out "she" every time the hymnal reads "he," just as they include the quiet, elderly accountant who sits in a front pew of my church with the woman she loves and finds great comfort in the reading of the psalms. They include many women in communities across the country and around the world who are transforming not only their own lives but the lives of the church and the broader society, as they think critically and creatively about gender, women, and the dynamic truth of the Christian faith.

Having said this, if I were to ask the women I mentioned to identify a feminist theologian, they would not point to themselves but to the books on feminist theology they were handed by a friend or in an adult education class. Unfortunately, by pointing only to the work of these women, they miss the opportunity to affirm their own roles in feminist theology. Still, they are partially correct in identifying official "feminist theologians" as the ones who write these books. There is a group of feminist scholars who have developed highly respected reputations for their work in the fields of religion and theology. One can find their books on the shelves of any good theological library, and some of these women have names well known enough to elicit nods of recognition in places ranging from Enid, Oklahoma, to Bangalore, South India—names like Russell, Ruether, and Schüssler Fiorenza. The new generation of professional feminist theologians in North America includes too many names to list.[22] Most hold teaching positions in theology on university, college, and seminary campuses, and most are active in local communities of faith. They represent different ages, races, and Christian traditions, and yet they share a high level of academic training and a commitment to using this training to advance the cause of women. Like the women in my local church, I point primarily to the work of such women when I use the term "feminist theology" in the chapters ahead.

In light of the account of feminist theology offered here, what does it mean that this theology explores doctrine? Given the rather rigid and authoritarian connotations of the word "doctrine," many feminist theologians hesitate to use it to describe the focus of their work, preferring instead terms like "faith claims," "theological models," or "Christian themes," because they capture the lively and creative character of the liberating faith feminists confess. Some feminist theologians, however, like me, have chosen not to forgo the term "doctrine" altogether but to breathe new life into it by redefining its conceptual contours and its social function.

When I use the term "doctrine" in this book, I refer to topics that regularly appear in the history of Christian theology and play a normative role in the shaping of Christian faith. In Western Christianity, the list includes the doctrine of God (Trinity), Creation, Human Nature, Sin, Christology, Incarnation, Redemption (Atonement), Pneumatology (the Holy Spirit), Soteriology (the Christian Life), Ecclesiology (the Church), and Eschatology (the "last things"). Given their normative roles, doctrines are often described as communally inherited teachings that serve a regulatory function in the life of the Christian community: they regulate beliefs by setting out the broadest parameters of what Christians do and do not believe.[23] Another way of putting it is to say that doctrine provides the basic outline of the theological drama within which the Christian life unfolds.[24] Through images, concepts, arguments, and story lines, doctrines provide the Christian community with a sketch of the arena where faith is shaped and lives are crafted. In concert with the definition of the term "theory" I offered earlier, one might say that doctrines consist of the signposts (rules, orders, assumptions) that direct and structure Christian thought and action.

Feminist theologians move beyond traditional views of doctrine, however, by insisting that, as life-shaping dramas, doctrines do more than simply provide Christians with propositional statements or static rules. Doctrines serve as imaginative lenses through which to view the world. Through them, one learns how to relate to other persons, how to act in community, how to make sense of truth and falsehood, and how to understand and move through the varied terrain of life's everyday challenges. Viewed this way, doctrines are the conceptual arenas in which character is shaped or personhood is crafted.

Doctrines shape not only individual identities but the identities and practices of entire communities as well. In community, these person-shaping concepts are reshaped and passed on to new generations. Hence, these doctrines give specific form and shape to collectives of people—determining the tenor and pace of their actions and interactions as well as defining the nature of the institutions and power relations that mediate the character of their public life.

As the theological arenas within which faith unfolds, doctrines thus serve as the "concepts we live in" or "inhabit" both individually and communally, and as such they touch and shape all aspects of the Christian life, from the most intimate relations with family and friends to public commitments. Contemporary theologians use different images for this particular understanding of doctrine; some describe doctrine as a language game, others as a cultural logic or an imaginative lens. In this book, I use two images to capture the character of the forming power of doctrines. The image of theological dramas suggests that doctrines function like loose but nonetheless definitive scripts that persons of faith perform; doctrines are the dramas in which we live out our lives. The image of landscape suggests that doctrines construct an imagistic and conceptual terrain within which people of faith locate and interpret their lives and the world around them. This terrain is marked by signposts that classical theology identified as the central doctrines of the faith.

From my perspective, this view of doctrine is crucial for the central task of feminist systematic theology. Doctrines play an enormous role in mediating the gender relations that structure our lives and the multiple levels of oppression that restrict the flourishing of women. Feminist theology recognizes this and concentrates on identifying the ways doctrines do so. Feminist theology does so by looking at the drama of a given doctrine like the Trinity and asking: What views of women are embedded in this drama? How might a person whose character is shaped by the Trinity live as a woman in today's world? Would having the Trinity as the conceptual drama within which a woman lives make a difference in how she responds to gender roles? And, perhaps most important, does the landscape of the Trinity promote the full liberation of women and all persons? Is it a doctrine that situates the community within the drama of God's emancipatory will for creation? There is no one answer to these questions, just as there is no single feminist theological opinion about the liberating force of doctrines like the Trinity. In the following chapters, I explore the multiple levels at which feminist theory informs the theological analysis of such questions.

As with "doctrine," feminists hesitate to use the word "systematic" to describe their enterprise because it evokes images of tightly calculated, closed conceptual systems. Such images hardly seem conducive to the feminist project of exploring the often invisible nature of women's oppression, gender constructions, and the life of faith. Feminist theologians know that purportedly comprehensive conceptual systems inevitably exclude things—and in many cases, those "things" are related to women. As such, feminist theologians remind us how exclusions are embedded in any discourse that presumes to "cover it all."[25]

These concerns about the potentially exclusionary nature of systems have led feminist theologians like me to conceive "systematic" theology differently. The term "systematic" highlights the need for theology to be internally coherent and practically viable. This means theologians must tell the Christian story in a language and with images and doctrines that hold together as a whole. A theology holds together if it takes the various strings of the Christian message and weaves them together in a manner that avoids internal contradictions and demonstrates the mutually supportive character of its parts. For example, a systematic theologian would be troubled by an account of the Christian message that affirms both that God creates the human body as good and that the pleasures of the body having to do with women are inherently bad or sinful. The task of putting the different parts of the Christian message together into a coherent whole is not unlike the task of the feminist theorist who looks at the structure of our cultural thought processes and tries to see how it all fits together, how it works internally, and where its weak points might be.

Feminist systematic theology also identifies "fitting connections" between doctrine and concrete actions in the Christian community. This means at least two things. First, feminist systematic theology asks whether the church practices what it confesses. It asks, for example: Does it make sense—is it coherent—for a Christian community to confess that by the grace of God, women and men are fully equal and yet leave the community's decision-making power in the hands of men? Second, feminist systematic theology requires that doctrinal dramas be tested in the concrete lives of women. It asks, for example: What happens when a battered or raped woman looks upon the sacrificed, tortured body of Jesus on the cross? Is the cross a celebration of victimhood and abuse or a condemnation of sin and the violence of the powerful? While there is, again, no one answer to such questions, feminist theologians insist that if the lives of women are taken into consideration when interpreting doctrines and church practices, new and challenging insights promise to emerge.

The last feature of my feminist systematic theology is its distinctive focus on doctrines central to the Reformation. I focus on these traditions, particularly in their Calvinist form, not because I think they are unusually suited to feminist theoretical reflection but because their doctrinal dramas and landscapes are familiar to me. I have long been interested in John Calvin and

Martin Luther and their ongoing roles in shaping Protestant communal identity in contemporary North American culture. Their Reformation theological vision, I believe, continues to fund the identities of Christian communities such as my Tuesday-night women's group. As such, exploring the thought of Calvin and Luther from a feminist perspective allows me rethink patterns of reflection with deep roots in Christian traditions and a continuing presence in today's faith communities. The hope is that such exploration will assist these communities in making informed decisions about the doctrines, practices, and beliefs they embrace—whether to reconstruct them or consider them unfaithful to the Gospel story.

Like most theological traditions, Reformation ones are doctrinally rich; they cover all the major doctrines I listed previously. In this book, I am especially interested in those related to divine grace and to the role they play in our understanding of individual and communal identity. I look at what these traditions say about faith and the dynamic process by which divine grace judges, frees, and envelops believers. I also look at the doctrine of sin and explore the traditional Protestant claim that graced believers nonetheless remain sinners caught in patterns of thought and action contrary to grace. I explore as well the doctrine of the church, asking what it means to be part of a community marked by this double logic of grace and sin. While these three topics—faith, sin, and community—are not the whole of Reformation thought, they allow one to peek inside the systematic web of beliefs that constitute this particular strand of Christian reflection.

Cartographies of Grace

Having defined the two main topics of this book, what remains to be explained is how I relate feminist theory and feminist theology to each other. As the subtitle of this book suggests, I find the image of mapping to be a useful metaphor in describing this relationship. Taking up the role of cartographer, in the pages ahead I lay feminist theory over the terrain or landscape of Christian doctrine to see how the lines of theory might map the contours of theology. I like the image of remapping because it captures well the fact that feminist theory's principal contribution to theology lies in analyzing and reorienting the conceptual markers that Christians use to describe the terrain of their faith. The cartographical metaphor makes clear feminist theory is concerned not so much to reconstruct the terrain of faith as to provide markers for traveling through the terrain in new ways. In the chapters ahead, I hope the reader will come to better understand what this remapping involves and to appreciate how feminist theory can be respectful of the tradition it maps while displaying formerly unseen dimensions of its landscape.

A second metaphor I use for the relationship between feminist theory and theology follows from the idea of doctrines as scripts or dramas. As I discussed earlier, doctrines can be understood as sets of performative directives that define the possibilities and boundaries of appropriate Christian identity and behavior. Christians and Christian communities can be said to "perform" these scripts when, in faith, they try to follow their rules and directives. Doing so involves some individual and collective improvisation. To enact a dramatic role, one has to make the script one's own while recognizing that one does not own it—the script has its own logic from which the actor improvises. In this process of improvisation, feminist theory suggests to us new performative possibilities. As it remaps traditional doctrinal terrain, it allows Christians to find new ways to live (enact) their knowledge of the reality of God's grace.

In the following chapters, I remap and improvise by moving back and forth between the worlds of theory and theology, each time pairing a theoretical concept with a theological theme. In chapter 2, I discuss a current debate in feminist theory over the character of "women's nature." In chapter 3, I use this conversation to remap the doctrines of justification and sanctification. In the fourth chapter, I discuss feminist theory's multifaceted understanding of women's oppression, and in the fifth chapter, I use this theory to reorient the doctrine of sin. I continue this pattern in the last part of the book when, in chapter 6, I explore debates in feminist theory over the nature of community and then, in chapter 7, use them to remap features of the doctrine of the church. In this process of remapping, I bring feminist theory directly into contact with some of the Reformation traditions' most treasured themes and thinkers. As such, this process of remapping is fraught with tension, because these themes and thinkers are incontestably oppressive in their views of women and yet they tell a Christian story filled with emancipatory possibilities.

The reader will no doubt begin to recognize in each of these chapters those places where my own story, in both its theological and feminist theoretical dimensions, enters the picture. My story, too, is filled with its tensions. I write this book as a woman with the status and power afforded by a position at an elite institution, and yet I have felt the awkward smiles and silent dismissals that accrue to the body of a pregnant scholar in a masculine world. I speak in this book as a U.S. citizen with forty years of experiencing the protection and the economic advantages of being white in our racist nation, and yet I remain deeply haunted by the violence known by my Cherokee great-grandmother more than a century and a half ago. I do theology as a person of faith who celebrates her roots in the Christian Church (Disciples of Christ) and the United Church of Christ, and yet I am wrenched by the abuses our language, our theology, and our church perpetrate against women and gays.[26] I enter this theological-theoretical conversation as one who finds the scholarly world as potentially dangerous as it is life-giving, and I believe that both bold normative visions and a robust respect for history and difference are necessary for the liberating struggle that lies ahead. Standing in these tensions, I offer this book as a contribution to that struggle and its many participants.

2

Women's Nature?

There is not the least doubt that women are by nature maternal
and men are not and that it is the essence of the maternal
attitude toward life to be sensitive to the needs of others and to
retain the miracle of creation and the miracle of love.
—Ashley Montagu, *The Natural Superiority of Women*

One is not born, but becomes, a woman.
—Simone de Beauvoir, *The Second Sex*

I recently served on a ministerial search committee that was debating
whether a woman should be hired as the next pastor. No specific candidates had yet been considered; the discussion was about hiring a woman "in principle." Should calling a woman be a priority since we had never had a female pastor? Or should we simply call the best candidate, male or female? As we debated these questions, revealing comments were made about what a woman minister is and is not.

In support of hiring a woman, some members suggested that women ministers are more nurturing and pastoral than men; that women are good listeners and excellent teachers of children; and that a woman's more intuitive spirituality would bring a sense of God's "feminine side" to our worship. Some members also argued that we needed female role models in the community, that the pastoral presence of a woman "makes a difference." On the other side, several members asserted that women have soft, high voices, which people in back pews cannot hear; that they usually do not have enough experience to be senior pastors; and that the congregation was simply not ready for such a radical change. A few committee members even argued that having a female minister "makes a difference" in a negative way, although it was hard for them to say exactly how. One member put it succinctly: "It's just not the same."

This church conversation reflects just one of the many ways debates over "women's nature" have taken shape in Western Christianity over the centuries. As the comments suggest, assumptions about what women are, and should be, are built into our theology and church practices. These assumptions consist of deep, often unexpressed images of "woman" and what it means to be Christian and female. They run so deep that the simple statement "It's just not the same having a female minister" receives knowing nods from even those who support hiring a woman. These images and assumptions are, in fact, so basic to a Western view of the world, they structure thinking about God and humanity even when gender is not under explicit consideration.

Many of these images of women's nature are found in our scriptures, confessions, creeds, and liturgies. They also show up in many of Christianity's most valued theological writings. From the time of the early Christian apologists, theologians have asked about "woman": Is she fundamentally or essentially different from man? Is she created by God to be more nurturing, loving, motherly, and intuitively spiritual than man? Perhaps because she can bear children, she understands embodiment and the cycles of life and death in ways that men cannot imagine. Does she therefore have a uniquely close relation to God? Or, negatively, is she weaker than man? Was she created to help and follow him? Or do her bodily cycles make her more powerful than man and hence more connected to sin, more responsible for the fall, more prone to wander from the path of true faith? Is she thus less capable than man of bearing the image of God? And, perhaps most important, can God bear her image? Can God be metaphorically figured as a woman?

In this chapter and the next, I explore the insights that recent feminist theologians and theorists have offered concerning women's nature. At their center lies the essentialist/constructivist debate. This debate wrestles over the origin and character of our understandings of women's nature in particular and of human nature in general. It asks: Is being a "woman" the product of nature or nurture? Put another way, does "womanhood" express an inborn, natural, female disposition or follow from socially learned behaviors? This question cuts to the heart of the pastoral search committee's debate over a female minister; it also sits at the center of the many conversations about sexual difference taking place in workplace meetings, in public-policy discussions, and perhaps most important, in daily conversations between family, friends, and neighbors. The pages ahead explore how the essentialist/constructivist debate developed in the nontheological world of feminist theory.[1] With this secular debate as backdrop, I turn in the third chapter to its implications for feminist theology.

The Essentialist Side of the Debate

It is late Monday afternoon, and my class on feminist theory begins with a conversation about women's nature similar to that of my church's search committee. We are discussing Hélène Cixous's essay "The Laugh of the Medusa."[2] Several students recount how strange they found her writing. They express surprise at the essay's unusual genre; its mixture of abstract, nonlinear prose and fragmented poetic reflections challenges their assumptions about what "theory" is. They also express surprise at the essay's bold thesis—that women, because of their embodied reality, have a fundamentally different way of knowing and being than men. Because of this difference, Cixous argues, women need to break free of male forms of writing and reclaim a genre that reflects their unique embodied perspective. Women need to "write their bodies," connecting with their feminine erotic pulses and nurturing motherliness. Women must morphologically "write in white ink" with their milk.[3]

As the class sorts through this idea, different reactions surface. Some women say that they deeply resonate with Cixous's descriptions of "womanhood" and "woman's writing."[4] They feel excluded and silenced by men's ways of speaking and knowing, especially in the classroom, and Cixous's book gives them permission to claim their distinctive voices and to speak loudly, without apologizing for the fact that they do not sound like men.[4] Several of these students identify with Cixous's descriptions of "woman" as having a "cosmic libido," as "spacious singing Flesh."[5] Some class members also like Cixous's descriptions of their internal "mother nature."[6] For these students, Cixous opens up dimensions of womanhood that patriarchal thought has long excluded, and in doing so opens onto new forms of seeing, doing, speaking, and writing—each with the potential to revolutionize Western thought.

Some class members, however, do not find Cixous's text liberating. They feel excluded by her analysis of womanhood. They find her descriptions of motherhood alienating, her evocation of women's bodies more fantastic than realistic, and her call for women to "write with their milk" ridiculous and marginalizing. As one student remarks, "Cixous tells me to celebrate the very characteristics that patriarchal society uses to oppress me. That sounds more like a prison than an open door." Another student feels uncomfortable about Cixous's mother image because, "my mother was far from nurturing." And another sums up by exclaiming, "Cixous's just an *essentialist!* And I don't like it."

With the claim that Cixous is an "essentialist," the class breaks into passionate, fast-paced arguments. Some students exclaim that, yes, she is an essentialist but not the old-fashioned oppressive type. She is a *feminist essentialist,* and that is good because women need to reclaim their essential identities before they can overturn oppressive, patriarchal ways. Other class members argue that ascribing a specific "nature" to women is inevitably oppressive because it recapitulates old stereotypes about male and female differences. A few others, however, are not quite sure what "essentialism" means, much less whether they think it's a positive thing. One such student finally explains to the rest of the class, "There seems to be a whole vocabulary at work here about 'essentialism' and its related concepts and I need some explanations before I can jump into the argument." I welcome this comment because, in the field of feminist theory, no single term is more used and less defined than the term "essentialism." Let me define the term and explore its related concepts—such as sexual difference, gender, and gender binaries. This groundwork will help clarify why all feminist theorists reject the old essentialisms of Western culture but some, nonetheless, feel the need for a new, reworked, feminist essentialism.

Defining Essentialism

To unravel the multiple meanings of "essentialism," it is best to start with the term's classical roots. These roots go back to ancient Greek philosophers who classified "things" according to inherent and unchanging qualities or "essences."[7] These essences were considered the fundamental and indispensable properties of persons or objects and thus constituted their most basic or core identity. In contrast to accidental properties that may vary over time, essential properties were thought immune to historical forces; they inhere in an object naturally and cannot be attributed to culture or convention. Essential properties are thus *universal* in that they must be present in all instances of the object. Take the "essential identity" of a table. It consists of the properties that are necessary to its being a table—ones present in all instances of "table." These essential attributes might include having a flat top and sitting on legs. In contrast, its "accidental" attributes—its color, the kind of material it is made of, its age, general condition, and number of legs—can change without changing the table into something else.

What happens when "essential identity" applies not to objects such as tables but to a group of persons defined as "women"? Classical philosophers offered a rather interesting list of women's "essential traits."[8] Some were strictly *biological*—for example, the "hystera" or uterus was described as an empty receptacle awaiting the male "energy" necessary for procreation.[9] Some were dispositional—such as female "hysteria," a state of disorientation and anxiety caused by the womb's proclivity to wander around a woman's body seeking the stabilizing force of male intercourse. Other traits were offered as well, traits that have come to be associated generally in the West with things "feminine"—passivity, instability, emotionality, and nurture.

The oddity of much of the Greek account makes clear that perceptions about women's nature change dramatically over time. Each generation adds to and subtracts from the list. Feminist theorists such as Cixous join in when they come up with accounts of female "essences" rooted not in male philosophers' opinions about the "other sex" but in women's experience. Disagreement exists, however, among feminist theorists about the character of these essences. But all agree on one thing: most traditional views harbor deeply problematic patterns of thinking about women and gender. So, before exploring the new feminist essentials, let us look at the central features of the older, more problematic patterns of thought. By identifying them, we will see more clearly which of them continue to the present day and how they might be challenged.

The first aspect about these traditional patterns of thought is that they have not always been precise or logically consistent. In many of classical philosophy's most renowned texts, comments on women's nature are sparse, ill organized, and often drawn from popular opinion rather than from the "reasoned logic" devoted to other topics. Although often put forth with great zeal and certainty, few grounds are offered in their support. Sometimes "women's nature" receives only a passing mention, leaving one to infer from the broader argument what her "essence" might be. Some classical texts even treat the topic of "human nature" or "man's nature" without specifically mentioning women's nature at all. Does this silence mean the author has no position or only a passing interest in women's nature? Feminist theorists respond that silence often speaks loudly of very definite positions. Classical texts sometimes say little about "woman" because they assume she is automatically included under the broader category of "man." This assumption means that "women's nature" is defined according to the standard of "man's/human nature"—a standard that includes no reference to women's experiences. Women are also left out because, for some, they simply did not exist as subjects for philosophical reflection: they either were not human or, more often, their subordinate social position placed them outside the philosopher's frame of reference.

Feminists note something else as well: traditional texts that *do* discuss women's nature frequently speak not only of "essentials" but of "universals." For this reason, "essentialism" and "universalism" are interchangeable terms in feminist theory. Defined most broadly, essentialism/universalism refers to any view of women's nature that makes universal claims about women based on characteristics considered to be an inherent part of being female. The notion of universality highlights the all-pervasive scope of essentialist claims about women's nature, namely, the belief that features of womanhood cover women's lives in every place, age, and culture without exception. If one is an essentialist or a universalist, then one usually believes as well that these universal features constitute an unchanging core of womanhood—hence the idea of the "essential woman" or the "universal feminine."

This belief in an unchanging core of womanhood signals two additional features of essentialism: its naturalism and determinism. Essentialist views of women historically appeal to a "natural state of affairs" as the basis for claims about universal features. These features are believed to be inherent in all women, meaning that they are not produced by cultural training, learned conventions, or social expectations but are natural. They are "inborn," "innate," "native," "instinctual," or "presocial." Essentialists believe these natural, universal essences constitute "the authentic woman" or "the true inner woman." This language carries determinism with it. Determinism assumes that the so-called essential or true woman is not an abstract ideal that women should try to model; the "essences" or "universals" describe what women inherently *are*, whether or not they choose to acknowledge it. As natural traits, these essences therefore are believed to determine what a woman can become as she moves into her future.

Traditional forms of essentialism have some other interesting features that feminists highlight. One is the role sexual difference plays in defining women. Feminists note a tendency to define the essential core of womanhood by its "difference" from the essential nature of manhood. This tendency is often correlated with the belief that a fundamental biological difference between men and women undergirds human society. Tied to this belief is the further one that sexual difference predetermines how men and women relate to each other. They are biologically oriented toward each other (hence, they are essentially heterosexual). Anyone reading the daily paper realizes that the claim of innate differences between the sexes is not limited to the past; it continues today in research projects on heart disease, talking styles, stress levels, voting patterns, and child-rearing practices.

Feminists refer to another recurring pattern of essentialist thinking as "the sex-gender scheme."[10] As mentioned earlier, the sex-gender scheme is a tendency in Western thought to identify sexual difference with both biological/physiological dimensions (sex), and dispositional/psychological and social characteristics (gender). Greek thought reflected this tendency. In Plato's day, women and men were distinguished biologically by their reproductive organs (that is, the woman's hystera), and then dispositionally by such attributes as their emotions (that is, the woman's proclivity to hysteria). Today, the biological "universals" supposedly connected with the female sex range from her distinct chromosomal structure and hormonal makeup and cycles to the structures of her brain, heart, and nervous system. Correlative dispositional gender traits are equally diverse: in behavioral studies of gender, women are described as more relational, nurturing, and emotional than men, while also less mechanical, self-confident, and individuated than their male counterparts.

As feminist theorists chart how these patterns of sexual difference and the "sex-gender scheme" function in Western culture, they note their many forms. To get a sense of the variety, look not at a classical text or a formal study of sexual difference but at the casual assumptions about men and women that people make over coffee with friends or as they watch children on the playground. People often refer to differences between men's and women's natures as if they were opposites: women are relational (connected) and men are autonomous (independent). Women and men are also differentiated by complementary traits: women are emotional and men rational, or men are assertive and women receptive. In another variation on this binary theme, men and women are placed in hierarchical relation: men are physically superior to women, or women are emotionally more developed than men. The relationship between the sexes is also defined by absence or lack: men experience a castration complex because they have a penis, whereas women, because of an anatomical absence, suffer from penis envy. In other cases, difference is a matter of degree: women are *better* with children, or men have *more* technical aptitude. As these examples show, essentialist thinking about women assumes male essences as well. Feminist theory examines such popular assumptions about gender and sex and tries to discern the relational logic of male and female differences.

Feminist theorists also trace how these dualistic patterns (also called "gender binaries") describe things other than actual men and women. In the introduction, I illustrated this point with a paper-towel commercial where the masculine towel is depicted as tough on stains and the feminine spill as messy and unruly. To get a general sense of how freely and often gender binaries are used to describe the world around us, look at this frequently cited list of dualities:

> male/female
> culture/nature
> straight/curved
> reason/intuition
> public/private
> humanity/nature-animality
> production/reproduction
> subject/object
> self/other
> mind/body

civilized/primitive
good/bad
master/slave[11]

Using this list, one can ascribe a gender—and hence a set of binary relations—to every element in daily life, from paper towels to a prayer over dinner or a late-night newscast about war in Eastern Europe.[12] I return to the topic of gender and language throughout this book, but I raise it now to highlight again an important point about gender binaries, essentialism, and discussions of women's nature. When one describes various things according to a gendered logic of essentialized thinking about women and men, the things being gendered frequently seem "universally," "essentially," and hence "naturally" gendered. For example, it is often assumed that differences between public and private spheres or distinctions between civilized and primitive societies are as historically inevitable as "natural" differences between men and women. When essentialized categories function this way, the whole world begins to look not only gendered but naturally dualistic and often hierarchical.

Feminist Responses to Essentialism

Given this description of the character and pervasiveness of sex/gender binaries, it should not be surprising that feminists find this type of essentialism problematic. Their resistance is easy to understand. They question essentialist naturalism because it makes women's historical subordination to men seem like a natural fact rather than a cultural product. Feminists also challenge the determinism of essentialism because, in a world full of gender "givens," it is hard to imagine radical social change in support of women's full equality with men. Feminist theorists also note that, in these schemes, women's nature is often defined only as "the other" to men's nature and is reduced thereby to a function of masculine identity. Women thus have no identity of their own. Moreover, attributes that have traditionally passed for the "essentials" of women's nature, feminists point out, are often the projections of a culture that depends upon notions of sexual difference to justify its division of labor. Finally, feminists argue that these views of women's nature are simply not accurate: they fail to describe the complex reality of women's (and men's) lives.

In the next section, I explore more fully these critiques of essentialism. It is important to note now, however, that some feminist theorists (such as Cixous) also defend essentialism, albeit in a feminist version. On what grounds? These "feminist essentialists" admit that many aspects of the traditional sex/gender binaries are false and oppressive to women, particularly such value-related binaries as good/bad and master/slave. They approve, however, of some others—binaries such as straight/curved or reason/intuition. The historic problem with these binaries, they claim, is not that male and female were distinguished but that the masculine was valued over the feminine. In response, they argue that present-day feminists need to celebrate and perhaps even privilege feminine distinctiveness.

As an example of this positive use of essentialism, recall my church search committee. When several committee members argued for hiring a woman, they made statements like "women do this . . . ," "women are always . . . ," and "women are just like that." They asserted, for instance, that women are more nurturing, intuitively spiritual, and better with children than men are. They may simply have meant that most women have been socialized to behave in these ways. Their comments, however, probably reflected the deeper belief that women exhibit these traits because of their inherent nature. One does not have to be a student of Plato or an avowed sexist to believe that essentialism makes sense of the lived differences of experience.

There are other reasons universal claims about women's nature are attractive to feminists. As the feminist movement has demonstrated, identifying universals in women's experience can serve a positive political function. On the pastoral search committee, essentialist arguments were garnered *in favor* of hiring a female pastor: a woman would bring a new spirit of nurture, care, relationality (connectedness), and feminine spirituality to a job too long held by clergymen not disposed to "womanly" qualities. This positive form of the essentialist argument hopes that women will bring new ways of acting and new insights, values, and commitments into areas historically dominated by men. If women are finally no different—essentially—from men, hope is more difficult. Furthermore, if feminists could identify universal characteristics shared by diverse women around the globe, these universals would provide common ground for worldwide political movements and networks devoted to the liberation of women.[13] They could serve as the basis for a common women's vision that articulates and defends what is truly good for women (and all people) in a world that has hitherto silenced and oppressed women.[14]

Perhaps the most famous and popular form of feminist essentialism is Mary Daly's work, which articulates and celebrates the unique experience and perspective of women.[15] According to Daly, patriarchal male paradigms of the world have dominated women's experience, an experience with the potential to revolutionize our present-day forms of knowing and acting. Daly is often referred to as a "biological essentialist" because she suggests that the source of women's revolutionary way of being rests "within them" as part of their embodied distinctiveness. She generates images and vocabularies that value the uniqueness of women's bodies—something, she argues, that is desperately needed in a culture that ignores and undervalues the specificity of women's physical experiences.[16]

Daly is not the only feminist theorist who makes biological sexual differences the starting point for emancipatory projects, however. A number of recent works on mothering argue that women's reproductive capacities and childbearing activities provide them with a unique perspective—a perspective more peaceful and nurturing than competitive and aggressive male interactions.[17] This kind of thinking is clear in New Age women's spirituality that helps women reclaim and celebrate their "feminine essence" by focusing on both the physical and spiritual dimensions of women's unique sexual and soul power.[18]

Another form of feminist essentialism sets its universalizing roots not in women's bodies but in the human developmental process. Often referred to as "psychoanalytic universalists," these feminists admit the role cultural expectations play in the construction of gendered identity but insist on the important, universal influence of roles of "mother" and "father" in a child's psychological formation. This universal process of development, they argue, needs to be understood by feminists in order to help families avoid harming their children with ill-conceived notions of gender. While few feminists have not benefited from its insights, this type of essentialism has its critics. It does not always allow for cross-cultural differences in child-rearing practices, and the assumption that identity formation occurs in a triadic nuclear family (mother, father, child) ignores the varied shapes of family life.

The Constructivist Side of the Debate

It is another Tuesday afternoon, and as I leave my feminist theory course, I encounter a student in the hall. "Professor Jones, I need to talk to you about the material we read this week. I feel my whole world is being turned upside down, and I'm very confused by all this 'constructivist stuff.'" The set of her jaw and the furrow in her brow tell me she's serious, and I soon learn why. The student is personally—and not just abstractly—wading into the murky, turbulent waters of the constructivist side of the feminist debate on women's nature. Her identity as a woman is being swirled and seemingly dissolved, and she feels as if she is standing on quickly shifting, unstable ground as a feminist and a person of faith.

The reading that provoked this reaction is Judith Butler's *Gender Trouble: Feminism and the Subversion of Identity*, a text with a strong defense of the claim that "gender," "sex," and "woman" are neither natural facts nor essential/universal features of personhood but rather are effects of the dynamic play of culture and convention.[19] For Butler, the "essences" and "universals" of essentialism are "fictions," "fables," "inscriptions," "phantasmic constructions," and "illusory grounds" falsely passed for "the real" and "the natural" over the centuries. Being a woman or a man is therefore not the expression of a natural predisposition or a biological fact; gender identities are better understood as "performances" in which one puts on the "drag" of culturally generated gender/sex/body assumptions and thus enacts (or is enacted by) socially inscribed roles and positions. Butler thinks this is true not just for the categories of sex and gender but also for the varied identities we perform over a lifetime, such as race, ethnicity, and age. She concludes that there is no "ready-made subject" nor "foundational self" available to ground discussions of women's nature. There are only multiple discourses positing shifting "selves," all of whom are always and already performing in "drag."

Defining Constructivism

Butler's position is not new to Western discussions of human nature. Constructivism goes back, as essentialism does, to the age of Plato and Aristotle. It has a rich and diverse history in contemporary feminist theory as well. Butler echoes Simone de Beauvoir's famous statement in the 1950s—"One is not born, but becomes, a woman"—as well as Monique Wittig's more recent assertion that because lesbians reject heterosexual codes, "they are not women."[20] What these theorists share is a profound appreciation for the constitutive role of nurture or socialization in the construction of "women." Feminist constructivism can be defined as a theory that focuses on the social, cultural, and linguistic sources of our views of women and women's nature. Feminist theorists do not always use the term "constructivism" precisely, however. In most cases, use of the term makes the general point that supposed eternal verities of women's nature are historically and culturally variant and, consequently, that gender is "formed" rather than "given."[21]

Feminist constructivists explain that this formation process happens in myriad ways. As children grow, they learn to see the world in terms of the gendered categories and meanings that language makes possible. This occurs in schools, courts, hospitals, workplaces, churches, synagogues, and mosques as well as in the family. In each institution, children learn to behave as "girls" and "boys" by following certain gender codes. The force that language and institutions exert over the years to shape them into "women" and "men" is heavy and persistent; the process consists not just of soft directives and subtle hints. Its scope is so pervasive and its weight so enormous that no individual or community escapes its power. Because these forces constantly shift, however, the making of gendered persons takes many forms, and outcomes are never entirely predictable.

Feminist theorists often refer to the constitutive role played in this process by culture or cultural constructs. Feminist constructivism is itself a form of "cultural constructivism." By "culture," feminists usually mean the entire system of symbols, languages, beliefs, actions, and attitudes within which persons live and learn to organize and make sense of their world and actions.[22] According to Hazel Carby, culture consists of "lived, imaginative constructs," which persons and communities inhabit and through which they experience the world.[23] Echoing the definition of "doctrine" I offered in chapter 1, this view of culture emphasizes its all-embracing scope: culture consists of the endless and often subtle patterns of knowing, feeling, acting, and believing—the web of meanings—in which we live.[24]

This definition of "lived, imaginative constructs" has several features. To call cultural constructs "imaginative" means that they have been creatively generated out of the ongoing struggle of communities to interpret their worlds. They are human artifacts, not pre-given, natural facts; we have crafted them, sometimes over the course of centuries, sometimes in response to a single event. We shape them through the workings of our imaginations. "Imagination" refers to the vast world of our conceptual capacities and not to "fantasy" in a narrow sense. "Constructs" are thus imaginative lenses through which the world, ourselves, our relationships, and even our faith come into view and receive shape and significance. While one may shift cultural frames over one's life or even live in a number of different imaginative frames or cultural constructs at the same time, one can never know anything outside them, because these constructs are what make knowing possible.

Another dimension of this definition is its description of these cultural constructs as "lived." The category "imaginative" might mistakenly suggest that these constructs exist "only in our heads." One avoids this danger by describing these constructs as "lived." They quite literally *construct* the material reality of our lives both at the level of individual actions and lifestyles and at the level of institutions and social structures. As an example from my own life, look at just one way that culturally constructed, "imaginative" views of gender are lived and are thereby material realities. I am going to a Wednesday faculty committee meeting to discuss the appointment of a guest lecturer for the next academic year. Entering the room, I notice I am the only woman along with four other men. I make these gender identifications using codes my culture has taught me to read—codes embedded in things like clothes, posture, tone of voice. My wearing lip gloss and a silver hair clip codes me as the lone woman, and their coats and ties code them as men. By wearing this "drag," we all perform gender roles that are materially evident (and clearly not just "imagined").

As the meeting progresses, I worry about how forcefully to make my opinions known, and I feel increasingly insecure about the legitimacy of my perspective. Could this be another way in which I inhabit the gender/cultural constructs I have been taught since childhood—by experiencing self-doubt, feeling out of place, and thinking I am not meant to speak in a "man's world"? Probably so. Sitting in the room, I feel uncomfortable in the large leather chairs that are so deep my feet do not touch the ground. Someone bought these chairs years ago because they fit the purchaser's image of a male academic's body size—a decision based on cultural assumptions about gender and the academy. Those assumptions feel very real as my back gets sorer. The committee is deciding between a junior-level, African American woman in church history and a well-established, Anglo American man in biblical studies. Although race, gender, and rank never explicitly enter the conversation, the committee votes to invite the biblical scholar. The "cultural constructs" of the committee members make him appear the better scholar. With a sore back, with feelings of frustration for not having spoken more, with lips in need of more gloss, and the knowledge that once again the figure occupying our lectern will be senior, white, and male, I leave the meeting quite aware that "cultural assumptions/imaginative constructs" are not just "ideas" but the very institutional materiality within which I live. I leave feeling, knowing, and concretely seeing the reality of cultural/gender constructs.

Weak vs. Strong Feminist Constructivist Views of Women's Nature

Based on this description of constructivism, it may not be clear why my student felt so disoriented by Butler. After all, in contemporary North American culture, it is a broadly accepted fact that one's social environment affects everything from the type of religion one practices to the ice-cream flavor one prefers. Are feminist constructivists saying anything new or radical? At one level, no; they simply develop the logic of a fairly commonplace insight about the intimate relation between identity formation and social context. They often, however, push beyond this broadly accepted position; these "stronger" claims are what my students find troubling.

Before discussing this strong version of constructivism, let us examine the more common and "weaker" constructivist position. The popular claim that "culture shapes gender identity" is often softened by the idea that culture begins with "raw material" of a biologically sexed and genetically predisposed woman or man. This raw material is "the essential self" of the "sex-gender scheme." The environment works upon a preexisting self with certain natural limits, such as being female, Native American, short, and of average intelligence. While admitting that culture can profoundly affect the identity that emerges from this raw material, "weak" constructivists insist there are unalterable bottom-line givens—such as being female. Like the clay of a potter, the raw material of personhood can be formed by culture into different figures, but it never ceases to be clay.

Feminist theorists in recent years have gone beyond weak constructivism at several levels. Theorists such as Butler argue that culture so profoundly determines human beings that no point beyond convention (no "Archimedean point") exists from which to ascertain what is "nature" (the clay, the raw material of personhood) and what is "nurture" (the potter, culture) with respect to sexual difference. They are making a claim here about how profoundly culture determines how we know and interpret human nature. They are thus making an *epistemological claim* (from the Greek *episteme,* meaning "knowledge") about the relation between gender categories and our knowledge of the natural. They argue that because social contexts so profoundly mediate our experience of the world, we are incapable of ascertaining what is "natural," "given," or "essential." Apart from heavily gendered cultural rules about sexual binaries, identifying the truly natural is impossible—particularly given that the category "natural" is itself a construct.

How might constructivists of the weaker variety respond? They assert that while culture profoundly contributes to our perceptions of differences between men and women, the raw material of male and female bodies is more than a cultural construct: it's biological; it's chromosomal; it's genetic; it's real! Science can therefore measure it and prove it; objectively speaking, men and women are *by nature* different. Faced with this response, strong constructivists such as Butler argue that, *at an epistemological level,* culture so disposes one to see the human body in terms of sexed differences that science cannot help but identify and analyze biology in gendered terms. Science measures and analyzes sexed differences as if they were self-evidently natural because it looks at bodies through the lens of Western cultural conceptions of gender.

To illustrate this point, strong constructivists ask us to imagine living in a culture where another set of identifying characteristics marks the raw material of personhood, for instance, a world where the color of one's hair is as important as our present-day emphasis on one's sex. In such a world, science would generate an elaborate and seemingly objective apparatus for evaluating the significance of hair as the raw material of personhood. The cultural construction of "hair color" would thus function as a mediating lens through which human bodies would be measured and interpreted. In such a world, the significance of hair color might be raised to such a level of cultural importance that our present-day cultural emphasis on sexual difference would appear insignificant or irrelevant to discussions of human nature. Although one may be looking at the same bodies in this imagined world and our present one, framing the body through a different interpretive lens significantly alters the differences we claim to "know."

As my student indicated, moving into this strong constructivist terrain can be quite disorienting. After all, it seems a straightforward, empirical fact that women and men are biologically different—and that hair color is less significant than sex in shaping personhood. Seeing culture as the origin of sex and gender is troubling because it seems to imply that women do not exist apart from one's cultural proclivity to identify them as such. This suggests, further, that the people we confront each day are only cultural constructs and, hence, that bodies as "matter" do not really matter. If strong feminist constructivism were to lead to such conclusions, it would seem to undermine the possibility of talking about the material realities of women's lives.

Few feminists, however, endorse such an antirealist and relativistic account of constructivism. Most strong constructivists point out that recognizing the cultural limits of knowledge need not imply that the material world does not exist; it implies only that one's cultural perspective profoundly predetermines the significance one gives to it. For this reason, feminist constructivists often heartily support scientific research on women and gender in the hopes it will help interpret the world and the place of women in it in new and useful ways. They remind us, however, that such research on women should be treated like all generalized views about people: not as findings about purely natural facts but about the diversely structured play of gendered culture and its interpretive lenses. They remind us as well that this "diversely structured play of culture" often produces "facts" deeply oppressive to women. For this reason, strong feminist constructivists are epistemologically skeptical about naturalized claims concerning women's nature—that is, they recognize the limits of knowing and are suspicious of perspectives that ignore or pretend to have overcome such limits. They are also ontologically agnostic—that is, they remain uncommitted (but suspicious) on the question of the real status of sexual difference.

General Features of Feminist Constructivism

In order to understand how feminist theorists analyze the gender codes of culture, one must understand a few additional features of constructivism. The first is its peculiar view of the "human subject" and the "self." For feminist constructivists, "selves" are no longer assessed and measured by universals but are viewed as dynamic products of vast cultural forces. To emphasize this, feminists refer to the self not as a stable entity but as a kind of "site," "terrain," "territory," or "space" through which cultural constructs move, often settle, and are frequently contested and changed. This emphasis on the dynamic character of personhood does not imply there is no self pulling together the varied forces of culture in any given moment. A self exists, but not one that, from moment to moment and place to place, remains the same. Constructivism conceives of persons as fluidly constituted; as webs of discourses, agendas, attitudes, relationships; and hence as more messy, unstable, and open-ended than essentialists' discussions of human nature allow. For this reason, feminist constructivists are often described as de-centering the subject—which means that, by removing those central anchors called "essentials," they acknowledge the shifting complexity of forces and histories that constitute our ever changing identities.[25]

A second feature of feminist constructivism follows from this de-centering of the subject; this feature directly challenges an "additive approach" to women's identity.[26] According to an additive approach, if one wants to describe a particular woman, one takes as the baseline her gender and then adds to it such layers as race, class, geographic region, and sexual orientation. For example, in the additive model of identity, a woman like my neighbor Carmen might be defined first as a "woman" and second as "Latina." She might be further described as a "mother" and then as a "social worker" and "middle-class." By not commenting on her sexual orientation, this description assumes she follows the "norm" of heterosexuality—an example of how unstated identifying descriptions can be as strong as the spoken. According to the additive model, Carmen's identity is then calculated by adding up, in careful order, all these different "lived, imaginative constructs" that make her who she is. Each is viewed as a stable entity in itself—as if, for example, when Carmen is said to be a "mother," the meaning of "motherhood" is self-evident, stable, and clear to all.

Viewed from the perspective of the constructivist's de-centered subject, Carmen's identity appears, contrary to the additive view, as a site where multiple "lived, imaginative constructs" simultaneously converge.[27] Once the notion of a well-ordered, additive self is abandoned, it is easier to see the particularities and peculiarities of Carmen's life. She can be described as a "place" where many cultural discourses intersect and where each of her identifications is shaken up, redefined, and enacted by Carmen in various ways. For example, what constitutes being a woman in her Mexican hometown may be different from what I, as an Oklahoman, learned about womanhood in early childhood. When this difference is combined with the dynamics of being "Latina" in Connecticut instead of "Hispanic" in Texas, and "middle-class" in New Haven but "upper-class" in Mexico, Carmen may well seem quite different from the woman assumed in the static additive model with its one definition for each feature. Furthermore, Carmen's identity is no longer derivative from a standard model of "woman." When the self is a site where multiple constructs course with persistent force, such static standards seem illusory.

With this de-centered understanding of personhood comes a third feature of feminist constructivism: its view of agency. When the self is described as a "site" or "space," what role is left for human freedom? Some feminists have argued, against constructivists such as Butler, that turning persons into "spaces" occupied by multiple languages, institutions, and histories makes them passive recipients of their culture rather than engaged protagonists. Persons begin to look like mechanical products of their environment, and the possibility of self-determination and intentional action is lost. If this is the constructivist picture of personhood, then feminists are right to be concerned, for they have long affirmed the importance of promoting women's agency and have resisted the notion that women are inactive recipients of other people's desires, projects, and meanings. A careful reading of feminist constructivism, however, reveals a more complex picture—one suggesting that women have sometimes less and sometimes more agency than one might imagine.

To see why women have *less* agency than one might imagine, look at the overly agentic view of woman that constructivists contest. This highly agentic woman, for example, appears daily on television commercials and in so-called professional women's magazines; she is the emancipated woman who, by strength of will, fights off sexist forces of cultural expectation and makes it in a "man's world" of corporate success and power. Feminist constructivists wisely point out that this is a tremendous burden of agency for women to bear, one that often prevents them from appreciating the force that culture does exert on their lives, in both oppressive and emancipatory ways. In other words, an overly agentic view of the self and social change eclipses the dynamics by which culture "enacts" women.

On the other side of the agency question, however, constructivists such as Butler are careful to say that women are not *incapable* of actively and intentionally participating in processes of cultural formation. They protect the notion of agency by saying that, unlike essentialism's subject, "woman" is shaped not by inevitable traits but by "imaginative" products of human community and can therefore be contested and changed. Resistance to determinism, according to feminist constructivism, does not require stepping outside of culture and seeing things in the critical light of pure reason. They advocate, instead, an "implicated resistance," one that is never completely free of the constructions it contests but with enough critical distance from them to challenge the status quo and envision alternatives. The vague and underdeveloped character of this defense of agency is acknowledged, even celebrated, by constructivists. To say more about "agency"—to make it into a stable structure or calculate its universal form—would be to step onto the terrain of rock-hard essences that constructivists avoid.

Given their rejection of universal structures and essential qualities, how do constructivists describe the shape of women's lives? This question brings me to yet another feature of constructivism: "localized thick description." Instead of offering a single description of "womanhood," constructivists analyze the varied cultural constructs shaping specific groups of "women." Constructivists do not clearly define what constitutes a "group of women." It could be a collection of women who live on a single block in New Haven or who ride daily buses in New York. It could be a group of charismatic Appalachian women church leaders, a gathering of first generation Asian American grandmothers who cook together, or a collective of "drag queens" in New York who problematize the dominant culture's definition of what a "real woman" is.[28] The subject of constructivist study could also be an individual woman's life (including reference to her many constitutive communities) or the lives of women in a given nation-state or continent during a particular historical period. One could also give localized descriptions of "representations of women" in classical literature or the image of the "witch" in Puritan piety in order to ascertain how a given culture produces and disseminates its views on gender. Constructivists want the discrete parameters of one's analysis to be named and localized in specific historical and social contexts so as to avoid the illusion of universality. By establishing a localized scope of analysis, one more fully attends to the particularities of a given situation or person and refuses essentialist analyses with a global frame of reference.

By attending to the local, feminist constructivists generate thick accounts of women's lives. "Thick" means two things.[29] First, it indicates that localized descriptions are composed of many layers. For example, when I reflect, in a constructivist mode, on the women who live on my block in New Haven, I immediately do a quick economic analysis of the incomes of different households and the tax structures of their properties. I think as well about the history of this block, particularly in terms of the fast-changing ethnic makeup of the city as a whole. I reflect further on the social functions of the different family configurations in each household and on the psychological dynamics that seem to play into their child-rearing practices. To make my analysis thicker, I also think about how the women on the block describe their own lives, the stories they tell about who they are, the loves and hates they harbor, and the hopes and fears that drive them. Descriptions of this sort are often referred to as "bricolage" (a French word meaning "something constructed by using whatever comes to hand")—a term high-lighting the often ad hoc, diverse character of thick descriptions.[30] Like loosely constructed stone walls, such descriptions are made up of differently shaped pieces of insight and analysis that rarely fit together tightly yet give the appearance of solid artifice.

This multilayered analysis is also "thick" in a second sense. My account of women neighbors is not unbiased or value free; it is "thickly layered" with my own cultural presuppositions and therefore not transparent to these women's lives. Consider the questions I bring to my neighborhood situation—questions of economic location, familial patterns, and ethnic history. My posing of them is rooted in years of academic training in contemporary social theory. Yet most women on my block do not share this background; they have not been formed by the culture of the university as I have. Their descriptions of their own lives, therefore, are different from mine. Whose description is correct? According to constructivists, both are legitimate and neither is correct. Both are legitimate because each reveals something about the one doing the describing as well as the one being described and hence reflects our different "lived, imaginative constructs." Neither is unambiguously correct because there is no single, "correct" description of a situation, person, or community; there are only shifting sites where diversely constructed selves are rendered meaningful and, in turn, render meanings.

Responses to Feminist Constructivism

As with most topics in feminist theory, feminist constructivism has both strong advocates and critics. Feminists cite several elements in its favor. One is its ability to combat one of essentialism's most dangerous side effects: a "wall of inevitability" or "don't mess with nature" syndrome in politics. Recall that feminist theory was inspired from its inception by a vision of human community in which women were not oppressed. This vision presupposed that radical social change is both possible and necessary and that change will cut deeply into our conceptions of the normal and the possible. The counterclaim is that such change is impossible because the present order of male and female relations reflects a "natural state of affairs." Feminist theorists have had to argue vigorously against this deep sense of inevitability. One of the best tools for doing so remains a constructivist view of "women" that shows how thick essentialist stones are made not from solid rock but from the humanly constructed, porous material of culture. Constructivists argue we are free to chip away at these stones and thereby open up space for new forms of human community.

Feminist theorists also find constructivism useful because it can account for diversity in women's lives. What woman has not felt that she is not living up to a cultural model of "essential womanhood" because her *sense* of self, her lifestyle, or her community does not fit essentialist claims about women? She may be African American in a racist culture or a lesbian living in a country where "heterosexual white womanhood" defines the "essential woman."[31] She may be labeled "right-brained" (reasoning) in a culture that thinks women should be "left-brained" (feeling); or she may have no desire for children in a culture where maternal instincts are considered as natural as the desire to eat and sleep. A constructivist approach can be liberating in such situations because it allows one to appreciate the different ways women are shaped by their contexts. In doing so, it allows one to ask critical questions about the particular cultural standards of "natural womanhood" that have been imposed on women. Complex questions such as Who in this culture benefits from essentializing a standard of white, heterosexual womanhood, and How is this view of woman disseminated, promoted, and enforced? Or simple ones such as Why are all the teachers at my child's day care women? Or Why are their salaries so low? . . . It's hard to imagine a more important job.

These two reasons for favoring constructivism offer a glimpse of the perspective constructivists take toward the world. They are skeptical about views of women that invoke universals and inevitability. They find differences among women as interesting as the similarities. And they interrogate the cultural logic and power relations that undergird sexual differences and the seeming inevitabilities that structure women's lives.

The positive aspects of constructivism, however, have occasioned some of its harshest criticisms. Feminists worry about the political effect of celebrating the fluid, fragmented character of women's identity at the very moment women are arguing that their identity has been overly fragmented by the dominant culture.[32] They also worry that although constructivists defend agency, the logic of constructivism might lead to a cultural determinism even more oppressive than the determinism of essentialism. Women can appear to be nothing more than victims of a sexist culture. Further, feminists point out that for the purposes of political organizing, one needs descriptions of women's lives that bring people together *across* lines of difference; one needs a rhetoric of commonality. Constructivism does a good job investigating the particular and the indeterminate in the lives of women, but has a more difficult time with the general and the decisive, both of which play important roles in political movements for social change. Finally, critics worry about constructivism's leaning toward moral relativism. If no single description of women's lives is correct and all are equally valid, what standards are available for assessing harm or the nature of justice and injustice in women's lives? Don't we need normative standards for assessing what is good and bad? Questions such as these have led some feminists to advocate a middle ground in the feminist constructivist/essentialist debate: strategic essentialism. To this third option, let us now turn.

Strategic Essentialism

At midsemester, my feminist theory class reads a series of essays by the French feminist theorist Luce Irigaray. Like Cixous's, her writing style is unconventional, a mixture of poetic allusion and philosophical analysis. My students have trouble figuring out which side of the essentialist/constructivist debate she belongs to. From her earlier works, they get the impression she is a strong constructivist. In her later works, however, she sounds like an advocate for essentialism. Can she really be both? they ask. I suggest she can, but it is an awkward place to be. At this point, however, the students have learned that awkward places can be interesting, and the lively conversations we have about Irigaray witness to this.

The class first looks at some of Irigaray's early essays in *Speculum of the Other Woman.* Here, Irigaray uncovers the hidden gender story of Western philosophy and psychoanalysis: the story of "phallocentrism."[33] By doing a feminist midrash on classic texts such as Plato's *Republic,* Irigaray shows that Western thought patterns define the "true" or the "good" by referring to their opposites—what is not true (false) and not good (bad). Irigaray further illustrates that in Western thought, we typically ascribe to the former (the true and real) a masculine identity and to the latter (their opposites) the space of the feminine. In this way, the feminine is put in the untenable position of being defined according to the needs of the masculine; as she states it, the feminine becomes solely a function of masculine desire. According to Irigaray, this leaves "women" in the fragmented cultural space of having no identity apart from the "men" they were constructed to define. Irigaray thus leaves her reader with the impression that her feminist constructivist sensibilities run deep. She leaves the reader, as well, with a clear sense that this gender story (she calls it "phallocentrism") is not only disturbing but dangerous for women.

The class next discusses a later work, *An Ethics of Sexual Difference,*[34] in which they encounter a different Irigaray. Adopting a posture that is more positive and seemingly essentialist than her earlier position, Irigaray gives vivid descriptions of what women (and men) need to become in order to relate to each other in a manner that does not reduce women to a function of male desire. She provocatively depicts "woman" as needing to be *enveloped* in a structure of identity that enables autonomy and thereby contests the fragmenting relationality that Western discourse has imposed upon

her. As she poetically describes it, "woman" needs to "adorn" herself in garments of her own desires rather than wear the clothes of men's desires. She
needs to "become herself." Irigaray also suggests that God plays a role in this
adornment, as the one who authors the space of her becoming.

Irigaray then adds an equally vivid account of woman's need to remain
connected to the world. Rather than allow her to rest secure but isolated in
her envelope, Irigaray sends woman on a journey toward "the other"—much
like an envelope traveling through the mail toward its destination. The purpose of woman's envelopment is not simply to enclose her in her own desires
but to give her sufficient definition to meet and be met by "others" in a play
of "wonder." We experience wonder when we encounter someone truly different and differentiated from us, and we embrace this other with an openness that is made possible because of our adorned differences. This double
ethic of envelopment and wonder becomes, for Irigaray, a normative
description of "essences" worthy of woman's embodiment. It describes the
space in which she flourishes—a space of bounded openness.

The class now returns to Irigaray's place in the essentialist/constructivist
debate. Some like her early, critical work but find her later vision hopelessly
reductive. Others like her vision of envelopment and wonder. It seems to be
what North American women standing on the edge of a new millennium
need to further their struggle. Still others argue for something in-between.
They applaud Irigaray's early critiques of gender constructions; they agree
with her that "men" and "women" are products of deeply phallocentric patterns of thought and action. But they also applaud her later, more essentialist
work because it offers what present-day, socially constructed "women" need
in their struggle to contest phallocentric patterns of thought. While they realize Irigaray's essentials are social products and hence implicated in the very
language these essentials contest, the students find them pragmatically compelling. Although the students in this third group are not initially aware of it,
they are defending what feminist theorists call "strategic essentialism"—that
"awkward third option" in the essentialist/constructivist debate.

Defining Strategic Essentialism

I have so far explored two sides of the ongoing feminist debate over gender
identity. To highlight the central points championed by each, I emphasized
the radical difference between them: the essentialist believes in gender fun-
damentals, and the constructivist is suspicious of them and searches for the
social roots of our varied experiences of gendered personhood. By focusing
on the differences, I tried to capture the passion of the debate. Although I
looked primarily at academic positions, I also described ways in which each
side finds expression in everyday, nonacademic thinking about women.

Whenever one finds oneself thinking, "Women always do this . . . ," or "Men never do that . . . ," then one is engaged in essentialist thinking about gender. Whenever one responds to a popular view of womanhood with the exclamation "I am not like that!" or "My mother never acted that way!" then one has stepped onto the path of constructivist social critique.

I also showed why each position makes sense from a feminist perspective, and why, in everyday discussions, many people (feminists included) spend time in both camps. Often in the course of a single conversation, I make the two observations "Women always . . ." and "I'm not like that. . . ." I may be simply inconsistent and confused. Some feminist theorists argue, however, that it is preferable to spend time in both camps, in a position somewhere in-between, a position known as "strategic essentialism."[35] The position goes by other names as well: normative constructivism, pragmatic utopianism, and pragmatic universalism. This in-between position applauds constructivist critiques of gender but feels nervous about giving up universals (or essences) altogether. While its proponents respect the hard questions posed by the debate, they believe that the divide between essentialists and constructivists fails to capture the complexity of daily experience.[36]

To understand the roots of strategic essentialism, recall my previous discussion of the relationship between feminist theory and feminist activism. Feminist theory has always understood itself as serving larger movements for the liberation of women and all persons. Feminist theory has its roots in a practical concern to support and encourage concrete political struggles on behalf of women. Because of this activist orientation, feminist theory must answer these questions: How do our theories actually function when used by people involved in struggles for liberation? Are they helpful? Or are they problematic—maybe even irrelevant? Feminist activists and theorists have recently posed these questions to both essentialists and constructivists. One mark of strategic essentialism is its commitment to offering pragmatically useful answers.

When a strategic essentialist asks the question Is there an essential character to women's identity or is it a product of culture?, she does so from a distinctive angle. The issue of practice comes to the fore. The strategic essentialist is a "pragmatist" or "functionalist," because she uses "practical effect" as the measure of theory. Instead of relying on rigid principles (either constructivist or essentialist), she asks: Will their view of women's nature advance the struggle for women's empowerment? She also makes calculated, "strategic" decisions about which universals or essentials might work in a given context and which might fail. The almost militaristic emphasis on strategy highlights the fact that she is *not* a disinterested observer of other persons' practices and theories. She is a politically engaged analyst studying the practical effect of views of women's nature so as to craft ones that are emancipatory and life-giving.

What view of "women" is pragmatic and useful? Strategic essentialists give no single, unchanging answer. The claim that women are "by nature" more nurturing than men may be oppressive when used to argue that women are not tough-minded enough to be good political leaders. The same view, however, may be emancipatory if it brings women's nurturing sensibilities into public politics in order to challenge patriarchal views of power, hierarchy, and control.[37] In another example, the constructivist rejection of universals is liberating when it exposes the racism and classism embedded in falsely essentialized notions of white womanhood. When used to argue that violence against women is culturally defensible, however, it no longer serves emancipatory ends.[38]

The strategic essentialist's task is also complex because in determining what is "emancipatory," she must make strong normative judgments. As the name "strategic essentialism" suggests, a feminist theorist in this camp finds positive value in making essentialist claims about human nature in general and women's nature in particular. She pragmatically values essentialism because she believes people simply cannot live without a view of human nature that includes "essentials" or "universals." Further, she believes that constructivism alone cannot sustain ongoing movements that require not only collective action but also normative visions of human nature and the human good.[39] Both points will be explored in chapter 6, but a brief elaboration of them now is needed.

With regard to the first claim (that it seems impossible to live without "universals"), a strategic essentialist notes, in concert with the constructivists, that language systems, cultural forms, traditions, and social organizations that persons inhabit inevitably consist of conceptual rules (imaginative constructs) that make sense of the world. These rules usually include normative views about the nature of human persons. While it is certainly possible to analyze and critique these views (as a constructivist would), one does so *not* by stepping outside of all language and culture and adopting a "view from nowhere," but by stepping into a cultural space shaped by an alternative set of normative views. When this occurs, old and oppressive "essentials" about human nature and gender may be critiqued and discarded, but only insofar as new or different rules about human nature are simultaneously adopted. In the parlance of feminist theory, pure critique is impossible. Note, too, that the principal difference between the strategic essentialist and the constructivist is that the constructivist is usually content to offer localized thick descriptions of constructed rules and essences, whereas the strategic essentialist elaborates the normative meaning and power of these universals with respect to the flourishing of women.

In addition, a feminist strategic essentialist argues that "essentials" serve an important political function.[40] Anyone who has participated in a feminist political battle recognizes the importance of an alternative view of "what women are." Simply criticizing oppressive views of women's nature does not get very far. Likewise, shouting out that "women exist only as a social construction" probably guarantees the struggle will die before it gets off the ground. Putting all of one's energy into elaborating the particularized differences between women with no reference to commonalities makes effective collective action difficult. Yet, if a movement lifts up an alternative, unifying image of "women" that is believable and compelling—even if this image is admittedly only a universal *ideal*—then it is likely to make a good start. This normative imagining, in its universal or essential form, provides a regulative ideal. Such ideals involve a "utopic essentialism"—they are utopian visions that, by breaking open the present, imagine humanity anew.

At an even more concrete level, a strategic essentialist supports the practical importance of essentialism by reflecting on the fact that "universals" about human nature abound in the most common tasks. Take, for example, the complicated process of raising a child. One constantly calls upon some normative view of human nature to make child-rearing decisions. For instance, if I believe that lesbian relations are *not* essentially unnatural and can be good and fulfilling, I will not raise my daughter to expect that she will find joy in adulthood only with a male companion. If I believe women are essentially agents capable of making decisions, owning their bodies, and crafting their own lives, then I will encourage my daughter to think for herself and take on responsibilities. While I am trying hard to do these things, I also recognize how her own growth and development challenge my deepest, often unconscious convictions about human "universals." Her delight in dancing teaches me to view the human body in more expansive and imaginative ways, just as her surprisingly early inclination to hit her cousins challenges my lifelong view that human beings are inherently peaceful and nonviolent. I offer this example not as a normative feminist vision of parenting but as an instance of strategic essentialist thinking in one of its most deeply personal and yet most profoundly political forms.

This in-between position is different from the essentialisms discussed earlier. Recall that the most significant difference lies in the degree to which strategic essentialism stays open to critique and hence continually revises its "universals." Revisions may be prompted by a number of things: the "universals" may no longer serve feminist emancipatory ends or be intelligible to the community that holds them; they may come into direct conflict with other, more important "universals"; or they may be "essentials" that historical and cultural reflection disproves. When "in use," they may also prove not to be universal but exclusive. A strategic essentialist therefore keeps one foot in the constructivist camp; she remembers that all "universals" are inescapably marked by context. A healthy dose of constructivist suspicion, along with an emphasis on feminist practice, thus keeps strategic essentialism from assuming the fixed positions associated with traditional forms of essentialist reflection.

As one example of this revising of universals, look at how discussions of women's sexuality and feminist sexual ethics have evolved over the past forty years. In the women's liberation movement of the early 1960s, emancipated women embraced "free love" as a central step toward the liberation of women and humanity as a whole. In the language of essentialism, the liberation call was for women to give into their "natural sex drive" and thereby throw off the shackles of repressive views of monogamous sexual ownership and constrained feminine sexuality. As the movement evolved, however, it realized that "freeing one's natural sex drive" was not what it appeared. This view of "essential sexuality" made it culturally permissible (even liberating) for men to claim unlimited access to women's bodies. What had once passed as a feminist "liberating essential" came to seem instead a constructed oppression.

In response, the women's movement revised its rhetoric of sexuality by shifting to "essentials" emphasizing a woman's ownership of and control over her own body and pleasures, as in the famous book *Our Bodies, Ourselves*.[41] While this image of autonomous ownership served an important political function in a society seeking to control women's bodies, it was not long before it, too, was challenged. Lesbians contested the heterosexist assumptions of this feminist rhetoric about embodiment, and women of color raised questions about the classist and racist assumptions in "universals" of "property" and "ownership."[42] Language of sexuality thus began to shift once again to include such universal principles as "agency," "the erotic," "difference," and "relationality." These terms were recently challenged again by feminist debates over such topics as butch/femme relations and the moral status of lesbian sadomasochism.[43] In each of these conversations, competing views of "essential human nature" and "sexual universals" play a normative role—as, for example, in the debate over the nature of pornography: Is it a product of innate sexual desire or constructed relations of power and social control? Likewise, there remains a lively sense that "universals" on each side are deeply shaped by culture and should stay open to radical revision and reconstruction. If these two moments—the universal and the critical—remain together, then strategic essentialism will likely mark future conversations about sexuality as well.[44]

As this brief example suggests, contemporary feminism is a history of shifting essentials; strategic essentials are constructed anew for each generation of activists and new terrain of struggle.[45] As to present-day "strategic essentials" that mark the terrain of North American feminist reflections, I have already mentioned a few: agency, embodiment, relationality, and difference. A quick glance at the Women and Gender Studies section of any bookstore reveals numerous volumes devoted to these normative values and to others, such as Irigaray's ethic of envelopment and wonder. To appreciate the full range of feminist reflections on these matters, however, one needs to look to the religion section, where one finds the writings of feminism's oldest and most experienced "strategic essentialists"—the feminist theologians. Let us now turn to their world of discourse and explore the further lessons that feminist theology and theory have to teach.

3

Sanctification and Justification:
Lived Grace

If she is to be able to contain, to envelop, she must have her
own *envelope*. Not only her clothing and ornaments of
seduction, but her skin.
—Luce Irigaray, "Place, Interval"

Wonder goes beyond that which is or is not suitable for us.
—Luce Irigaray, "Wonder"

On a Wednesday night near the end of the semester, I sit in a local coffee
shop with three divinity-school students from my feminist theory class.
Disheveled piles of books and coats surround us, and the air is crisp with the
excitement of early winter and the energy of good conversation. We have
gathered to talk about how feminist theory relates to pastoral work in local
churches and the community. The discussion crackles with humor, passion,
and an abundance of ideas as we move from topic to topic—from worship
and preaching to ministerial counseling and political action, and even to the
broader topics of women's nature, gender, and God. Having spent the semester immersed in the world of high theory, the students express delight at moving back into the more familiar world of theology. They all agree, however,
that the world of Christian doctrine no longer looks the same.

As one student explains: "Feminist theory has given me a new road map
for driving through an old theological neighborhood. I still recognize the
place, but I now see things I missed before, and even the most familiar terrain looks different." The other two nod and offer vivid descriptions of how
feminist theory has affected the theological landscapes of their faith. They
describe how feminist critiques of essentialism have made them painfully
aware of Christianity's centuries-old role in promoting oppressive views of

subordinated womanhood as if they were natural, innate, and divinely sanctioned truths. And they recount how these images have left scars not only on the bodies of countless past generations of women but on their own bodies as well.[1] They also tell, however, how feminist theory helps them see other traditional theological landmarks in a positive, new light. Far from driving them away from faith, theory has led them to a deeper and ever more expansive understanding of God and of themselves. In this newly mapped theological landscape, they excitedly explain, there are surprising sights to behold—surprising both in beauty and in liberative power.

As I move in this chapter from the world of theory into theology, recall the image of remapping laid out in chapter 1. It captures the complex nature of this shift. Remapping reminds us that feminist theory seeks not to generate a static set of principles but to analyze the signposts of our thinking. In the previous chapter, I explored how feminist theorists do this with "women's nature." In this chapter, I take those insights and lay them over the landscape of theological doctrine in order to see how it looks when feminist theory charts its contours. To understand what I mean by "theological landscape," recall my description of doctrine in chapter 1. Christian doctrine is not a world of strict principles and static beliefs. Rather, doctrines are lived, imaginative landscapes, which persons of faith inhabit and within which their Christian identity is shaped. As my student's image of remapping suggests, feminist theory's task here is neither to destroy nor to create this landscape—for that is not the purpose of a map—but rather to give new perspectives on its signposts and mark new pathways into its varied terrain. While this exercise most certainly involves painful visits to some of Christianity's most ruinous views of women, feminist theory can also help us map paths to more hopeful views.

In the pages ahead, I undertake this remapping by exploring two doctrines used in classical Protestant thought to depict what a person's nature looks like when it is transformed in faith by the grace of God. According to Luther and Calvin, the person of faith is described as "justified" and "sanctified" by grace. The classical doctrines of justification and sanctification explore this twofold process of transformation; they describe how the sinner is forgiven by God and called to new life. I have chosen the landscape of these two doctrines as the terrain to be remapped by the feminist discussion of women's nature because these doctrines also discuss human nature, albeit from the distinct perspective of our "graced (redeemed) nature" in Christ. I have chosen them also because little attention has been paid in the Protestant tradition to applying justification and sanctification to the lives of women.[2] Feminist theory helps us think about this application. Although it admittedly knows little about the Christian notion of grace, its insights into the character of women's identity are profound. Feminist theory thus offers to theology a new "cartography of grace." [3]

Feminist Theology as Eschatological Essentialism

Let me start this remapping with a general comment about why the feminist theology I offer here is more methodologically at home with strategic essentialism than with either straightforward essentialism or strong constructivism. In the world of Christian faith claims, normative claims about human nature abound. This is as true for contemporary feminist theologians as it was for sixteenth-century Reformers or first-century Apologists. To engage in the business of theology is to explore who we are as created by God and called to live in relation to God. Although exploring our identity as creatures of God involves an ongoing interpretive engagement with Scripture, tradition, and present-day experience, it also seeks to identify the truth of the matter about God and humanity. For a feminist theologian like me, this truth is articulated in claims such as: all persons are loved by God; our bodies are part of God's good creation; we are all fundamentally determined by our relationship with God and neighbor; and violence, slavery, and injustice (oppression in any form) fundamentally contradict God's will for humanity in creation and cut against our basic human orientation. These are universal claims about the nature of our status before God—"*all* people are loved by God." They are also normative claims about how humanity is called to live in relation to God—"slavery contradicts the will of God." Similarly, they are essentialist claims about the nature of the human person—"God-relatedness is a determinant feature of our being." Hence, they place this feminist theology on the essentialist side of the debate.

Commitment to universal claims about humanity, however, is held in tension with another set of feminist theological claims on the side of constructivism. As feminist theologians well know, essentialized theological views of women's nature and sexual difference have been used historically to diminish rather than promote the humanity of women. Whether such Christian universals about women's nature were generated out of arguments from natural law, Scripture, or ecclesiastical teachings, the results have been devastating.[4] The effects of oppressive essentializing are also felt within feminist theology itself where European American feminists have poured their own experiences into a universalized model of womanhood that discounts differences among women.[5] Feminist theologians thus have good practical reason to be suspicious of essentialist and universalist positions and to use the tools of constructivism to uncover the cultural and political origins of "universals" passed off as God's truth.[6]

There are also distinctly theological reasons for leaning toward the constructivist side of the debate. At the heart of the Christian doctrine of creation is the affirmation that difference is good, that diversity finds its origin in a divine delight in difference.[7] This affirmation supports feminist worries about the restrictiveness of the sex-gender scheme; the complex, highly differentiated world that God calls into being can fruitfully sustain a variety of sexual and gender identities. For this reason, feminist theologians find constructivism's attention to difference and particularity compelling and essentialism's drive toward sameness and universals constraining.

Tied to this affirmation of diversity and particularity is the feminist theological recognition of the fundamentally finite character of life. Feminist theologians affirm, along with Christian theologians in general, that finitude imposes certain epistemic constraints upon us. As creatures marked by time and space, we cannot see this diversity of creation in the fullness of its glory—we can't see it as God sees it. We see through the glass darkly: our history marks us; our language holds us; our communities form us. We engage the world through the thick particularity of our lived conditions. Recognizing the epistemic limitation of finitude, theologians share constructivism's affirmation of "epistemic skepticism." There is no unmediated access to "reality."

Moreover, as I illustrate in chapter 5, feminist theology takes the doctrine of sin seriously. Having suffered the devastating effects of lived, imaginative constructs that harm women (and that women use to harm others), feminist theology affirms that sin—a fundamental fault line running through humanity—twists thought and distorts the vision of humanity. As such, feminist theologians have strong reasons to affirm the constructivist's hermeneutic of suspicion regarding essential claims about gender and sexual difference. Although there are essential truths to be had in faith, feminist theologians do not trust that we rightly grasp them given our finitude *and* the corrupting power of sin in the world.

Closely related to this affirmation of the epistemic limits of sin is the feminist theological affirmation of the power of grace, the reality of hope, and the possibility of true conversion. At the heart of feminist theology lies the belief that God wills that women (along with all people) flourish, and that, as people of faith, Christians are called to follow God's will and seek out conditions for that flourishing, all the while recognizing the limits of sin and the need for the Holy Spirit. Feminist theologians thus affirm that God's grace has transformative power. They believe that human beings can be converted, changed, redeemed, reborn, remade. Thus, women's oppression in the broader culture (as well as in the Christian tradition) can be altered, new being is possible, selves and communities can be truly recrafted in grace.

This predilection for a remade future resonates well with the constructivist affirmation that identity is constructed and changeable. It similarly resists the essentialist tendency to build a "wall of inevitability" around the conditions of human existence.

For the feminist theologian, this hope appears most concretely in her reconstructive work on the language and images of theology (doctrine); just as oppressive theological views of women have constrained women's lives, so too, the feminist theologian believes, a liberative theological perspective on women can be freeing. The hope that reworking theology might open new ways of being for women is tied to a recognition that doctrines, as forms of "lived, imaginative constructs," have the capacity to shape the identity and character of their adherents in positive as well as negative ways. If feminist theologians did not believe in this constructive and emancipatory power of doctrine (and the potential for people to be remade in Christ), then they would not engage in the transformative, prophetic work of theology.

These four theological affirmations—creation's diversity, human finitude, the power of sin, and the remaking potential of grace (and the power of doctrines to facilitate that work)—lead feminist theologians to find feminist constructivism resonant with their theological commitments. Feminist theologians also appreciate constructivism's facility for generating "localized thick descriptions" of women's lives. Feminist theology needs such descriptions to understand how specific theological images, doctrines, or linguistic forms function in different communities of women.[8] For example, feminist theologians need to be aware that reworked images of Mary speak more powerfully to Irish Catholic women in Boston than to Caribbean Moravian women in Kingstown. Similarly, in constructing Christian doctrines, feminist theologians need to be aware that images of the broken body of Jesus on the cross may be violent and abusive to a battered woman in the United States, whereas in Guatemala they may serve to remind a mother that God grieves the loss of a child to political torture and military repression.[9] Localized thick descriptions thus help feminist theologians understand the overdetermined contexts within which their doctrines operate.[10] Such descriptions also allow feminist theologians to think about relations of power and the character of culture as they think about the function of doctrine.[11]

Having noted the constructivist leanings of feminist theology, let us remember that as feminists are busy celebrating diversity, acknowledging finitude, confessing sin, proclaiming the power of grace to transform lives, analyzing contexts and power relations, thinking about social change, and seeking conversions, we are also trying to speak the truth of the matter about women's nature and God. We converse with Scripture, traditions, and ecclesiastical experiences that constrain what we say about humanity. There are theological truths that feminists believe are so fundamental to the life of faith that, while we may recast, reconstruct, and even revolutionize them, we may not finally relativize or dismiss them. The doctrines that feminists construct for use in the varied contexts of women's lives are articulated from faith claims that are by no means considered tentative or culturally relative. To the contrary, these claims are bold, normative, and powerful enough for persons to stake their lives on. For feminist theology to be as life-transforming and life-enhancing as it claims to be, it must be committed to such truths and to their enactment in the lives of women and men.

How does one strike a balance between these two sides of the feminist theological project—the normative universalist and the constructivist? By following a path similar to the strategic essentialism described earlier—a path between willingness to stake a claim and openness to constant revision and challenge, between belief in universal truth and recognition that we are radically constructed and constrained in our ability to know that truth objectively. This is a path theology has followed many times in the past. As feminist theologians engage in this process, we therefore do so in the good company of both feminist theorists and previous generations of Christians. For this reason, I earlier referred to feminist theologians as "feminism's oldest and most experienced strategic essentialists"—a title that we have won by our long years of speaking not only behind lecterns and podiums but also from pulpits and in pews, where revelatory truth and prophetic critique are required side by side.

Standing between normative truth and prophetic suspicion, feminist theology has developed a form of strategic essentialism that I call "eschatological essentialism."[12] Feminist theological discussions of women's nature are rooted decisively in a theological vision of an already/not-yet future—a vision of God's will for a redeemed humanity where all persons live in right relation to God and one another. This normative perspective looks ahead to a model of identity yet to be realized and not back to models of personhood that remain rooted in an essentialized nostalgia for the natural and the given. Such theologizing shapes the present by touching our daily lives with its vision of redeemed humanity as the goal of faithful living in this moment.[13] It is thus a boldly pragmatic universalism in that its truth cannot be disengaged from its ongoing transformative power. Just as it does not hesitate to use the language of "sin" and "brokenness" to speak about the injustices and alienation it resists, eschatological essentialism, because of this same sin, recognizes the need for constant revision and critique of the vision it proclaims. Further, eschatological essentialism uses the religious language of "salvation" and "grace" to describe the liberation it announces and the divinely given character of that emancipation.

In describing feminist theological anthropology as eschatological essentialism, I prefigure much of what will follow in my discussions of lived grace, sin, and church. This description also moves us into the doctrinal world of justification and sanctification. To that topic, let us now turn.

Lived Grace: Remapping Justification and Sanctification

When my students reflected that night in the coffee shop on the many ways feminist theory has remapped the terrain of their theology, one topic they continually returned to was the life of faith. More specifically, they kept coming back to the question: How has feminist theory opened up my understanding of what it means to be a woman of faith—to be a person who distinctly identifies herself as "Christian" in a world where many different constructs compete to define her?

As the students and I struggled together to find images and words that might throw light on this question about "faith identity," we moved deeper into the dramas of feminist debates over women's nature, on the one hand, and theological treatments of "the doctrine of the Christian life" (lived grace), on the other. We discovered surprising similarities between these two dramas—between what feminist theorists say about women's nature in the essentialist/constructivist debate and what Christians say about faith identity in the images of justification and sanctification. These similarities are not rooted primarily in a shared analytic framework—the two discourses depend on different tools of analysis and use different vocabularies. Rather, the likenesses are most apparent when one situates "woman" in the middle of these two discursive fields and traces how the dramatic forces of each define "her" identity. In the language of doctrine, this means asking, How might the doctrine of justification and sanctification craft the faith character of the woman who inhabits it? In the parlance of theory, this means exploring how a strategic essentialist like Irigaray might describe the principal contours of the feminist subject. As I show in the pages ahead, it is in the conversational play between these two questions that the constructive work of feminist theological remapping takes shape.

A Reformation Map

Let me begin unfolding this new feminist theological map by looking back at an older one: the map of the traditional Protestant views of "justification" and "sanctification." Although both terms have a long history in Christian theology, it was not until the sixteenth-century Reformation that they were brought together as *the* primary metaphors for describing how a person comes to faith or, better stated, how God comes alive to persons as the creator and redeemer of their lives. According to Luther and Calvin, this event of faith is grounded in God's merciful reestablishing of the divine-human relationship destroyed by human sin. When this happens in a believer's life, the now faithful sinner is "converted," and what follows is a life committed to praising God and acting in accordance with God's will. The terms "justification" and "sanctification" describe two aspects of this transformation.

Most important to Luther was justification. (He devoted very little attention to sanctification, a point to which I shall return shortly.)[14] The term "justification" comes from the Latin *justum facere*, which means "to make just," and is commonly translated from the Greek as "to pronounce just." According to Luther, "justification" describes what God does to redeem humanity in Jesus Christ: God "justifies" the sinner.[15] Drawing on the metaphor of juridical adjudication, Luther uses the image of a courtroom. His account unfolds as a three-part drama.

The story begins with God as a judge looking down upon a defendant found guilty of sin and awaiting punishment. The defendant is humanity, and the crime is turning away from God and arrogantly conforming life to destructive human desires rather than to the divine will manifest in the law.[16] To portray the complexity of this sinner's crime, Luther places himself in the role of defendant. The sinner awaiting judgment is not only the person who has boldly flouted the law; the sinner is also a person like Luther himself, a former Augustinian monk, who has devoted his life to "following the Law" but who has repeatedly failed to fulfill it. In his repeated failures, Luther describes himself as being "crucified by the Law." The law beats him down by constantly lifting up his woeful inadequacy. Try as he might, he cannot do what he believes the law requires of him. This dire situation is a "bondage of the will." The harder the sinner asserts his will in an attempt to accomplish the law and win God's favor, the more he exhibits the root of humanity's sin—a misguided desire to save himself, to make himself God. In trying to merit God's approval, humanity fails to see that divine grace must be given, not earned.

Luther then narrates a second courtroom scene. Here, the drama takes a surprising turn. The Divine Judge looks upon this sinner and decides, because of Jesus Christ, to reverse the deserved verdict and forgive the crime, thereby offering radically new life to the guilty. In legal terminology, this act of divine mercy involves the "imputation of righteousness" to an otherwise unrighteous humanity. The term "imputation" emphasizes that through this verdict, the sinner puts on an alien righteousness in faith—a righteousness not belonging to the sinner by nature or by right but belonging to Christ, who has transferred God's mercy to the guilty party. The righteousness that comes from this imputation springs not from human nature but from a free act of God, who redefines the terms of personal and collective humanity. When this righteousness is imputed to humanity, it frees the will from its bondage, not because the will no longer asserts itself but because God has decided against punishment. Through an act of divine forgiveness, God sets the will free to pursue a life not filled with fear of divine reprisal but empowered by grace.

Luther's courtroom drama of justification does not end with forgiveness. In a third scene, the sinner hears this divine verdict pronounced through the proclamation of the gospel in the community of believers (the church). In hearing the word, the sinner comes to faith and knows that he is saved by a grace not earned but imputed through Christ. In the light of faith, the sinner now understands himself to be living under a double determination: guilty of sin, which is destructive, and yet also loved through a grace that is empowering. Luther thus describes the person of faith as *simul iustus et peccator*—"simultaneously justified and sinner." To put on such an identity is to inhabit a space in which one stands as both the judged and the loved. It is to live in a drama of divine action where the self is constantly pronounced sinful and yet continually redefined according to the grace of a divine forgiveness offering new life. In this tension, the justified sinner/saint is freed to live joyfully, praising God. This person has a spontaneous desire to please God and to love one's neighbor, not as a way of earning grace but out of gratitude for the wonderful things God has done.

Let us turn now to justification's companion in Reformation accounts of lived grace: sanctification. Developed more fully by Calvin than by Luther, this doctrine describes a lifelong process in which the justified sinner is empowered by the Holy Spirit for service to neighbor and faithful obedience to God. From the Latin *sanctifactio,* sanctification literally means "the process of becoming a saint" or "becoming holy," which for Calvin is the ongoing aim of the Christian life—a struggle ever upward toward Christian perfection. Also referred to as "regeneration," the term draws on organic metaphors of growth, process, and developmental change. According to Calvin, this growth toward God is forever incomplete in this life because of sin, but this incompleteness never eclipses the importance of the real transformation that occurs in persons who know themselves to be loved and forgiven in Christ. Thus, in contrast to justification, where the sinner is made righteous by an external judgment and an imputed, alien righteousness, in divine sanctification, God initiates real, internal transformation. The believer's life is materially (not just juridically) remade.

To elucidate the precise character of this transformation, Calvin turned to Scripture. A holy life rests in following the Law of Moses, which not only judges (crucifies) us, as it did for Luther, but also gives positive direction. Like a teacher, the Law (in its third use) provides concrete instructions for faithful living. Sanctification rests as well in the life of Christ, which Christians are called in faith to put on or to "imitate."[17] This process has two features, mortification and vivification. When "mortified," believers come to see their sinfulness and turn away from it. They "die." When "vivified," mortified believers are reborn and given new being in Christ. They "live again." In both instances, sanctification refers to that ongoing moment in the formation of Christian identity in which the old is cast aside and believers are given new structure and direction and a new standard for measuring their actions day by day. In his account of this remaking process, Calvin emphasizes the role that the church plays in providing sanctifying structure and direction for believers. The church is like a mother who tenderly cares for her children, the community of believers; she teaches and disciplines them as they advance in their ability to follow the Law. Through its practices and beliefs, the church gives defining edges and concrete form to the believers it holds.

Let me conclude this overview of the old doctrinal map by returning to my earlier question: What sort of faith identity might emerge for a person who inhabits these two doctrines? In short, when persons of faith stand in the conceptual space carved out by these metaphors, they are pulled by two sets of dramatic forces. On the one hand, each stands as *Luther's justified sinner*—the one whose worldly identity has been judged harshly by divine law and yet radically opened by divine forgiveness. Standing in the space of justification, one is thus "converted" by both coming "undone" (crucified) and being "forgiven." The old script of one's identity is revealed as a prison, a place of sin, and upon this identity is placed (imputed) a new center of graced identity marked not by nature but by a divine relationship in which God's forgiveness authorizes the sinner's agency anew. On the other hand, each person of faith also stands as *Calvin's sanctified believer*—one whose life has been re-created and redirected toward the goal of praising God and living in just and faithful community. Standing in the space of sanctification, the one whose identity has been "undone" and "forgiven" is now given normative contours, disciplines, laws, and ethical directives within which to become a concretely new person in Christ. Thus, in each of these ways—as the judged and absolved defendant and as the regenerated and redirected initiate—the believer who occupies the space of the Reformation doctrines of justification and sanctification stands as one dramatically crucified, opened up, and redefined by God's call to the life of faith.

A Feminist Strategic Essentialist Map

While many contemporary readers will find these traditional doctrines to be not only out-of-date but disturbing, I hope that readers have begun to notice similarities between this older map and my map of the women's nature debate in feminist theory. To bring these similarities into clearer focus, let me look briefly at the map of feminist theory in its mediating form as strategic essentialism and quickly review how it defines the forces shaping the identity of "woman." Recall that there were two principal moments in strategic essentialism's analysis of gender and women's identity: the normative (essentialist) moment and the critical (constructivist) moment. How is "woman" defined in the play of these two dramatic dynamics?

The constructivist side represents the moment of radical critique in feminist theory, calling into question the varied naturalizing assumptions about sexual difference and female nature that have ruled Western thought for centuries. The feminist constructivist challenges such essentialist views not because there are no differences between men and women, but because it is impossible to theorize or know such differences apart from the constitutive, gendered lens of culture. In this moment of radical critique, the constructivist also reminds us that these "imaginative cultural constructs" of gender are shaped by concrete relations of power and material interests that oppress women. The constructivist is therefore concerned to nurture a healthy suspicion for the varied ways our daily discussions of "woman" and "women" reflect not "facts" but vested interests—interests that often enforce a hierarchical order in our notions of sexual difference. Thus, in its suspicious, critical mode, feminist strategic essentialism destabilizes the sex-gendered subject by dissolving its seemingly natural moorings and exposing the dangerous politics hidden in it.

Feminist constructivism offers us a second moment of reflection on the question of women's identity. The constructivist views the person as profoundly relational and fluid. She sees women (and men) as sites or positionalities where multiple axes intersect to form identities that are constantly shifting and reconfiguring. In the space of this de-centered subject, no universal standard or naturalized essence exists by which to measure what is "normal" for women. No guiding principle establishes a stable order for the varied coursings of the cultural constructs, institutions, and persons that shape us. Instead, there is a celebration of the indeterminate, of differences, of the messiness of women's identities that surfaces when the legislative powers of normality and order flee the scene. The constructivist appreciates as well the analytic productivity of localized thick descriptions of women's lives. In these descriptions, she traces the complex social and personal forces (including race, class, sexuality, and age) that give shape to the particular persons that we are always becoming. Here, then, in the second moment of feminist constructivism, the concept of "woman" is shown to be both profoundly open and radically relational.

This dismantled and open-ended constructivist subject is expanded, however, by the strategic essentialist to include insights from the other side of the debate. From a strategic angle, one is concerned how our views of women actually function in various contexts and communities. The strategic essentialist thus asks about the pragmatic politics of our visions, and she ventures the guess that in the context of feminist political activism, essentialist or universal claims about women and about justice can be used for emancipatory purposes.

Two universalizing moments thus enter the strategic essentialist's reflections. The feminist in this third camp asserts that we live in a culture that either renders women invisible or reduces them to a fragmented function of their relations to men. One cannot leave women here; that would only replicate an oppressive definitional logic. Instead, women must collectively develop ideals that serve as a containing space or an essential core of personhood, ideals that, when inhabited, enable women to become resiliently visible. This woman-defined space should be one that allows women to be more than the relations that fragment them.[18] The strategic essentialist also talks about the value of asserting an emancipatory vision of a just and caring society. Here, discussions of women's nature blend into broader discussions of social organization and ethics (a topic for my last chapter). The normative vision that arises from such discussions is one in which the oppression of women is vanquished and the flourishing of women is celebrated as an ongoing reality. At both of these levels, then, the feminist strategic essentialism reconstitutes an emancipated subjectivity for women. Since the strategic essentialist keeps one foot in the constructivist camp, however, her reconstructed vision of identity remains conscious of the power relations and cultural forms that undergird it and is therefore open to ongoing critique and revision.

What kind of woman inhabits the space of this strategic essentialism, which sees the value of universals but is also convinced by the critical openings of constructivism? This woman would find the dismantling of essentialism to be liberating and would understand the constitutive role played by culture and power in her view of women's nature. Yet, because of her vision of essential personhood, she would also feel empowered to move through the world with a coherent sense of herself as an embodied agent committed to living in just relation to others. In short, this woman is both the destabilized subject of constructivism and the reconstituted agent of feminist essentialism. She is the woman whose identity feels the pull of two dramatic forces: she is continuously undone and remade, disarticulated and redeployed; she is radically relational yet centered and directed.

A Feminist Theological Map

Thus far I have sketched the landscape of the Reformation doctrines of justification and sanctification and asked: How might this particular doctrinal terrain shape the Christian identity of the person who inhabits it? I have also re-sketched a map of the strategic essentialist's approach to the question of women's nature by asking: What are the dramatic forces that shape the subjectivity of "woman" when she inhabits this pragmatic space between essentialism and constructivism? With these two discussions in place, we can now move to feminist theology. This third field brings together the two former discussions by using feminist theory to deepen, expand, and sharpen the metaphors of justification and sanctification. In doing so, it stands at the intersections of theory and theology and of faith and feminism.

I begin my feminist theological reflection by asking: What dramatic forces might shape Christian identity in a feminist account of these doctrines?[19] Or, stated differently: How might the story of Christian conversion to new life in God look through the eyes of feminist theory? What sort of Christian subject would a feminist language of faith create? These questions, of course, bring us back to the theme of this and the preceding chapter, women's nature—but they do so in a new way. Now interrogated is the shape of their nature in a Christian theological landscape where faith identity provides the basis for our answer.

Let us begin where Luther did by looking at the doctrine of justification. What happens when the Christian feminist subject is situated in this discourse? When "woman" inhabits this story, she finds herself judged by a God who is imaged in distinctly male terms: he (God) is the mighty tribunal patriarch of Roman law. She will fit the role of the defendant insofar as she identifies herself as part of Luther's masculine subject. Although Luther no doubt meant to include woman in his account of "the sinner," his conceptual focus on man suggests that she is only guilty and saved by association. Luther's story leaves no place for her specificity as "woman."

In addition to these obvious gender limits to the classical story of justification, feminist theory makes us aware of other, perhaps more serious problems confronting woman when she enters this tale. Recall that in Luther's story of justification, the first scene in the courtroom drama depicts God as wrathfully "undoing" (crucifying) the subject. The arrogant unbelief of the sinner who has defined himself according to his own desires is judged harshly by God's verdict of "guilty." The Law reveals the sinfulness of the subject's narcissistic self-understanding—a self-understanding exhibited most vividly in his desire to save himself. By using such imagery, Luther designed a doctrine of justification that, in its first moment (the first use of the Law), moves against its inhabitant with harsh, judgmental force. The pretensions of self-definition and pride are broken, and the arrogant defendant is positioned before God as deservedly "fragmented" and "lost." According to Luther, this first gesture is necessary so that arrogant subjects might recognize their inability to save themselves and admit their complete dependence upon divine grace.

Let us pause and look at this initial undoing gesture from the perspective of feminist theory. Feminist theory asks: What happens to the woman who enters this tale having spent her life not in the space of narcissistic self-definition but in a space of fragmentation and dissolution? What happens to the woman Irigaray has described as "without garments of her choosing"—the woman who, in contrast to the man in an impenetrable container of his own making, lives without containment, without an envelope to hold her? How might this first stage in the justification narrative affect her?

Feminist theory helps us see the negative effects of using Luther's account of God's dismantling wrath for woman's encounter with God's grace. Recall Irigaray's fuller description of the state in which woman finds herself. Her reality is marked by a double problem. First, she does not have "skin" (an envelope) of her own; she exists without independent self-definition because she has been constructed by Western discourse to be radically fluid, to be a space that is always receiving—she is *in* her relationship, to a fault. Second, because of her lack of internal self-definition, she has no boundaries to defend against the onslaught of a culture that also wishes to define her (in her fluidity) according to an economy of masculine desire. When her fluidity is given form, she exists to define "him." According to Irigaray, her clothes thus become garments of his pleasure. Her few borders are a function of her use value to another. In this sense, she is not allowed to be truly other to man. She is merely an extension of his arrogance; she defines his being without having being of her own. She is simultaneously uncontained and reductively other contained.

What happens if feminist theology places this woman in the position of the sinner before God in Luther's courtroom drama? First, feminist theory helps us realize that this woman suffers from an illness different from Luther's classical sinner. Her sin is not one of overly rigid self-containment; her brokenness lies in her lack of containment, in her cultural definition in relation to others. Instead of an overabundance of self, the source of her alienation from God is her lack of self-definition; she is too liquid, she lacks skin to hold her together, to embrace and envelop her. She lacks the structuring boundaries that allow her to be an other in relationship to God in faith. She thus enters Luther's courtroom as a defendant already unraveled by the world, undone by falsely inscribed relations of power. She comes not with a robust self that needs to be dismantled by the wrath of the Law but as a de-centered subject whose lack of self is her prison. She comes before God not as a defendant caught in the bondage of the will; she comes as one whose will has been diluted in her many relations. In an ironic twist, one might say her will could benefit from bondage, for in its present state, her agency has dissolved into the fluid motions of her relations.

What happens when this story of God's "crucifying" wrath meets this woman? There are two possibilities. The wrath may simply "miss the mark" with her. She may be unable to relate to it, unable to see herself in the mirror of this story. She is therefore without a story to initiate her into grace. Or, she may identify with Luther's sinner and take upon herself a script designed for the prideful sinner. Already suffering from an excess of humility and a debilitating lack of self-containment, she is made by God's grace to recapitulate the dynamics of her oppression and self-loss. When Luther's God meets this woman, he potentially reenacts the cultural unraveling she already knows too well.[20] This entrenches rather than challenges the worldly definitions that surround her. Rather than a conversion narrative that opens into transformation and new beginning, the story that meets woman here is the story of a shattering she knows all too well—more like sin than the freeing act of divine mercy.

What might be done to narrate conversion in women's lives more meaningfully? The story of God's judgment and mercy should, I think, be told in reverse—starting with sanctification and its rhetoric of building up instead of with justification and its initial language of undoing. With sanctification at the beginning, the first word to meet the woman who enters the doctrine of the Christian life is one that constructs her, giving her the center and the substance she needs to become the subject then judged and graciously forgiven.[21] This inversion does not replace or destroy the logic of justification; narrating the story of a sturdy and resilient new creation before turning to the moment of dismantling and forgiveness simply allows the most problematic aspects of justification (its first de-centering moment) to be tempered. By changing the order of the two doctrines, the feminist theologian affirms, in concert with the strategic feminist theorist, that for women the normative moment is politically and pragmatically crucial. The feminist theologian is thereby able to proclaim, from a Christian perspective, that as the author of those defining essentials, God desires to empower and liberate women rather than to break what little self-confidence they have.

What might such a reconstructed feminist doctrine of sanctification look like? Here, the stretch from feminist strategic essentialism to feminist theology is not far. The doctrine of sanctification serves as a powerful resource for articulating the strategic essentialist's recommendation that we envision ideals as a "containing space" or an "envelope" of identity that fragmented women can inhabit and thereby use to claim their embodied agency. Believers are invited to inhabit a space where God's grace nurtures and forms persons, thereby enabling them to become agents responding to God's love, empowering them to move "in body" toward perfection, and calling them to conform themselves to an eschatological vision of gracious wholeness and holiness.

Let us look closely at how woman might inhabit this terrain of sanctification. First, note that in the traditional Christian view of sanctification, the metaphors of growth and regeneration are implicitly ones of action, of becoming, and of change. Consequently, the woman who inhabits this doctrinal terrain is neither passive nor fragmented but is set in motion and directed toward a goal. In this manner, sanctification provides doctrinal grounds for a logic of identity that counters views of woman's nature that undermine her agency. Here, she is not only an agentic subject but an agent shaped by her mission to love God and live in just relation to neighbor. Second, in the doctrinal space of sanctification, *materiality* and *embodiment* are explicitly affirmed by the growth metaphor: to be shaped by the Law and to grow in Christ, one must be an agent of a body that is as particular and as substantive as the body of the Christ. In this regard, "the Law" and "Christ" serve as women's space of containment—although these two terms also need to be remapped along similar feminist lines. The important point here is that woman cannot inhabit the space of this sanctifying reality and still remain invisible or effaced. When she enters this territory, she is given flesh and bone as her embodiment is affirmed and her agency is instantiated. She is, in short, given an envelope of grace to contain her. Because its intention is her ultimate flourishing, she can be said to have, in grace, a skin of her own (and God's) best desires. She is clothed in grace.

Third, the dramatic force of sanctification, like the force of feminist strategic essentialism, is eschatological. The woman created in the space of this doctrine is the embodied agent struggling to become the ever shifting essential woman of the *future*. She does not look behind her to ossified descriptions of her nature to direct her life; rather, she looks ahead, toward an emancipatory future where her identity is defined as "graced." What does it mean to be a woman of faith whose essential identity rests not in her nature but in God's grace? It means, in part, that the container that embraces and holds her—stopping her from dissolving into her relations or becoming a subordinate function of gendered binarism and hence masculine desire—comes to her from beyond, as an unmerited gift of divine love. How might she live in such a gracious space? Her nature is now defined according to the grace-given virtues of the Christian life: faith, hope, and love. While this invocation of the virtues may seem an ambiguous affirmation of feminist identity, its promise is its ability to convert the language of "women's nature" into a language of "becoming." In the space opened up by this reorienting gesture, women are invited, moreover, to write new scripts of faithful living—scripts more appropriate to their shifting contexts than the oppressive essentialisms that have long constrained them. Not by being undone but by enjoying the pleasure of flourishing in the containment of divine life, they begin a lifelong journey of faith, moving toward a perfection that resists falsely gendered versions of the self. As I shall later illustrate, this containment is communal in character; its shaping force lies in the space of Calvin's mother church or, better from a feminist perspective, in the community of faith adorned in freedom.

In using phrases like "woman's undoing" and "her container, skin, and envelope," I have stepped into the realm of essentializing claims about an ideally constructed "woman." Universalizing gestures are warranted in this particular doctrinal context because the dramatic function of sanctification (in both its traditional and feminist forms) is to provide the person of faith with the structure and direction needed to follow the path of the Christian life. This structuring occurs through normative gestures that instantiate the subject—not just as an abstraction but in the concrete materiality of everyday life. From the perspective of the strategic essentialist, these bold gestures are necessary if women are to combat social scripts that define them as silent, passive, or invisible, or as pure relationality. There are, however, two important limits on this discourse. Recall that for the Reformers, sanctification was not a process destined to be completed in this life. It was an ongoing struggle in constant battle with sin. Also recall that strategic essentialists hold these bold visions of womanhood in constant tension with an awareness that such truths are communally constructed and hence shaped by workings of culture and power. Thus, in both theology and theory, this structuring moment calls us to return to the place of critique and deconstruction.

How might one bring these critical moments into a feminist theology of the Christian life? How might one write a theological script for women in which they are given a positive space to inhabit but also are called to self-critique and collective revisioning? The tradition provides us with an answer, albeit one in need of significant feminist reinterpretation; it provides us with that doctrine that dismantles and undoes as well as forgives—the doctrine of justification. Having first constructed a sanctifying space for women, let us return to this favored doctrine of Luther.

When we revisit justification from this reordered feminist perspective, a number of issues come to the fore. First, the deconstructive character of justification gives the feminist theologian critical leverage against the stultifying weight of traditional views of women's nature. It exposes the role that sin plays in humanity's attempts to define and control the world by measures of our own making. These sinful measures include the construction of gendered categories and the binarism of sexual difference, which are placed upon women as defining marks. When implicated as sin, these marks are exposed as a prison enclosing persons in a controlling logic of identity where hierarchy is assumed, multiplicity of difference is denied, and transformation and new becoming are contrary to nature and hence impossible. Is this sin as "original" as the sin Luther envisioned when he spoke of God judging our unrighteousness? Answering this question and further developing the relation between women's oppression, gender, and the Christian doctrine of sin form the content of the fifth chapter.

What does it mean for women to inhabit the space of a doctrine of justification where God's judgment dismantles the gender measures that define and order our lives? For some, it may come as a moment of exhilarating emancipation—they are now empowered to try on new and different identity constructions in the imaginative space of faith, hope, and love. For others, it may feel disorienting and disturbing to lose naturalized gender categories as the anchor of their self-understanding. It is important, then, to reaffirm how the doctrine of sanctification positions one firmly in the reconfigured space of identity grounded in God. In both cases, new possibilities are opened by the absolving force of a justifying act of the Divine, who seeks to establish new relation by breaking the hold of our falsely defining measures of personhood. Justification means forgiving the sins of constructions that bind us, so that, through God's mercy, we may be opened to the crafting work of the Holy Spirit. For women formed by restrictive conceptions of gender, this act of person-crafting forgiveness signifies new life.

Recall constructivism's two principal contributions to a theory of "woman." Its critical function—that of exposing the illusions of falsely inscribed gender "truths" that have patterned women's lives for centuries—is captured above in the discussion of sin. Its alternative view of personhood—persons as relational and fluid subjects—is captured by the doctrine's notion of imputed righteousness: the new identity one puts on in Christ. To rethink this dimension of the doctrine of justification from a feminist perspective, remember the constructivist notion that "gender" is best described not as a "nature" but as a "performance." In God's merciful decision to forgive the sinner, God does not give us a new nature but allows us to "play" (perform) an identity that is not ours by right but is a gift. We are invited to put on—as in a performance—an alien righteousness, one that is Christ's, not ours, an identity laid upon us because of God's decision to reestablish relation with us. Conversion to faith is when one is forgiven because of God's imputation of an alien righteousness, a performative conversion in which we receive a new role, one that calls us to live as those who are loved by God. One effect of this is new vision: we begin to see that the usual way of doing things is itself a series of performances—performances that, in sin, we have raised to the status of essential truths. God challenges the "as usual" quality of the roles we had formerly played in our brokenness—the "as usual" performances of the old gender binaries of sexual difference—and offers a new performance, one in which women become performers of Christ's imputed righteousness.

How do women enact this new performance? Again, the answer turns us back to feminist theory and the constructivist discussion of identity as relational and fluid. In the story of justification, the space of mercy and absolution defines the new person in exhaustively relational terms: her identity as righteous results from God's decision and not from an inevitable nature. We cannot help, then, but understand woman, in all her dimensions, as a relational subject, opened by God to relation in God and thereby opened by God to the world of her relations. Is this the constructivist's de-centered, fluid subject? Yes, but only partially, for in the space opened by conversion, relation is not the product of a culture that relentlessly constructs but is the gift of the God whose grace opens all to interactive *co*-existence. Through divine forgiveness, the self is also reauthorized to move through the world as an agent, a self responsible for the actions it initiates. We see, therefore, how justification as well as sanctification forms a space within which women's agentic identity is reconfirmed and created, ever anew.

Lastly, if in sanctification women are wrapped in graced envelopes that give them defining borders, could it be that in the doctrine of justification we meet women in the moment Irigaray describes as "wonder"—the moment in which the envelope is sent on a journey toward the other, a journey that finds its end in its opening? According to Irigaray, wonder happens when two who are truly other meet and, in an embrace that respects difference and defining borders, resist the temptation to make their love a function of sameness. When God, in an act of unmerited love, imputes to woman the identity "forgiven," God meets her as truly "other" and does not reduce her to a function of God's desire. While woman cannot, as a finite creature, respond with a wonder as pure as God's, God's grace still authorizes the terms of her lesser wonder. The wonder she knows in receiving God's grace in justification opens her to neighbor and God. As the envelope now traveling through history toward the other, the justified believer meets the world with a wondering self both contained and opened.

Let me close with a final word about feminist theory and the doctrine of justification. In both Calvin's and Luther's articulations of the justified Christian life, although we may be forgiven, we remain sinners—a position summarized in their famous "saint and sinner." What does this mean for the woman who enters the imaginative space of this doctrine? Perhaps it is a reminder of the "implicated resistance" described by feminist constructivists. As feminists, we can never claim to have extricated ourselves from the cultures we so vigorously critique. Our cultures continue to construct us as we continue to challenge them—for even our challenges grow out of the constructions themselves. Recognizing this limitation, feminist activism avoids an arrogant triumphalism that cries: We have finally gotten beyond culture, beyond gender, beyond all oppression. It adopts instead a realist's posture, yearning for a new future and working for a new day while struggling with the limits of the present and the inevitable brokenness of the future vision itself. Does this posture not echo the sound of Luther's "saint and sinner"? To live in the space of justification—to be a woman absolved and opened to relation—is not to be freed from the constraints of culture and history. It is to live in Christ forever poised on the edge of a promised land: she smells the milk and honey of the new world to come but remembers that the ground beneath her feet remains dry and in need of tilling.

4

Oppression

A discourse may poison, surround, encircle, imprison
or heal, liberate, nourish, and fertilize.
—Luce Irigaray, *Parler n'est jamais neutre*

Social inequality is substantially created and enforced—
through words and images. Social hierarchy cannot and does
not exist without being embodied in meanings.
—Catharine A. MacKinnon, *Only Words*

The Tuesday-night women's group at my local church begins each meeting by sharing tales of the struggles and joys of our individual lives. We listen carefully to each woman's story. Sometimes the stories are uneventful reports of daily life; sometimes they are filled with joy; and sometimes they are full of the frustration and pain of being a woman in our contemporary world. In these last stories, the theme of women's oppression reverberates as a constant refrain.

Although seldom used by us, the term "oppression" captures the tone and texture of these tales. One elderly woman in the group tells of her battle with declining health and her sense of becoming "invisible" with the death of her husband. A Caribbean woman tells of her struggles with immigration, racism, and unemployment. A middle-aged secretary at the local university relates her decision to join the clerical worker's union and go on strike. From one of the younger women, we hear the story of childhood incest; from her best friend, who recently came out as a lesbian, we hear of her ongoing battle with addiction and depression. The stresses of raising children, families falling apart and reconfiguring, bills not getting paid, and physical ills going unattended—in the midst of all these stories, we hear, again and again, about the shattering of our fragile self-confidence and the fragmentation of our often hard-won sense of centeredness.

The theme of women's oppression is not the only theme that regularly surfaces in these stories, however. As a Christian group, we also use the language of "sin" to speak about the brokenness of our lives. At first, "sin" was a difficult term for us: its relation to Eve and to women generally in traditional Christian beliefs has a mixed history, and our sense of fragility and fragmentation as women has often been exacerbated by a theology of sin that tells us we are bad and shameful. Over the years, however, we have begun to find comfort and strength in the fact that the Christian tradition demands serious reflection on the depth to which persons can "fall" in their brokenness and their participation in the breaking of others. For this reason, the doctrine of sin now plays an important role in our discussions.

In the next two chapters, I explore insights that recent feminist theorists and theologians bring to conversations like this one about women's oppression and sin. As with the topic of women's nature, there is not one position but many on these matters, reflecting the diverse locations and commitments of the theorists and theologians who hold them. Unlike the topic of women's nature, these positions do not divide neatly along lines of a central debate; they move off in many directions. Exploring this area means, then, covering a broad sweep of disciplines within feminist studies—economics, political science, sociology, and psychology as well as history, literature, and cultural studies. This sweep of fields suggests that reflecting on women's oppression requires tools of analysis as diverse as the topics raised by the women in my group—topics ranging from health-care policy and immigration law to childhood incest and women's lack of self-confidence. Exploring these topics thus allows us to see why feminist theory is, by necessity, a radically interdisciplinary endeavor.

I begin the dialogue between theory and theology in this chapter by discussing what feminist *theorists* say about the nature of women's oppression. I offer a general definition of oppression and delineate its common features. Next, I look at recent attempts to demystify feminism's well-known enemy "patriarchy." I then build on Iris Young's description of five forms of oppression in the day-to-day workings of North American culture.[1] Although these "five faces of oppression" do not exhaust the complexities of women's lives (there are no doubt more "faces" to add to the list), they serve as a useful grid for locating a diversity of perspectives. Readers should use their own experiences of oppression and brokenness to judge the appropriateness of this grid, for, unfortunately, oppression is a reality that has made experts of us all.

In the next chapter, I again move into the world of Christian theology and offer a feminist interpretation of sin. Like the previous discussion of justification and sanctification, I use feminist theories of oppression to remap the landscape of this traditional doctrine. My discussion highlights the exciting promise and the potential hazards of traditional views of sin for women's lives. It illustrates how feminist theory deepens and expands Christian theology's ability to address the concerns of women and hints at ways Christian theology challenges and enriches feminist theory's ability to engage women in our complex and ongoing struggles for emancipation.

General Features of the Feminist Theory of Oppression

At the end of our storytelling in the Tuesday-night group, we spend time drawing connections among our tales. Although sometimes a woman's story is so painful that silence is our only response, we usually have a lot to say. The woman struggling with immigration finds comradeship with both the elderly widowed woman's and the young lesbian's feelings of invisibility. The secretary who has "no voice" in her workplace hears familiar reflections on "the loss of voice" from the young incest survivor and the Caribbean woman. In these moments, we sense our common problems and feel part of a common struggle. Defining this commonality, however, is difficult, for our individual lives are quite different, and the harms we suffer resist simple classification.

In contemporary feminist theory, the term that sums up these problems, harms, or injustices is *women's oppression*. Broadly defined, "women's oppression" refers to dynamic forces, both personal and social, that diminish or deny the flourishing of women. As this definition and our conversations suggest, strong similarities weave through the stories of harm told by women. These resemblances are often where feminist theorists start in mapping the destructive contexts within which women live. This definition, however, is also sufficiently open-ended to allow for differences among women and to incorporate the complexities of women's experiences—recent feminist work insists that the specific forms of oppression in women's lives are multiple and, for this reason, we need many theories of oppression. In fact, women's oppression requires theories as diverse as women's identities.

In my Tuesday-night group, for example, this diversity is apparent—both among the women and within individual women's lives. We need theories of economic exploitation to understand one woman's decision to go on strike for a better wage and yet other theories about sexual violence to come to grips with the damage done to the woman struggling with childhood incest. We need one set of tools to think through the racism suffered by one member and quite another (albeit interconnected) set of theories about labor distribution to understand why she faces chronic unemployment. For the mothers, we need theories about the traps our culture lays for women who raise children; for the woman who experiences a loss of voice, we need theories about invisibility; for the woman in her seventies, we need theories about gender, dependency, and health; and for the lesbian, we need theories about compulsory heterosexuality and its relation to her ongoing struggle with depression. In the next section of this chapter, I explore more closely several of these forms of women's oppression by drawing on what Young calls the "five faces of oppression."

Before turning to Young, however, let's take a look at some of the similarities that run through feminist accounts of these varied oppressions. In order to map these differences, feminists make a first, very basic distinction between women's material oppression and cultural oppression. We find several examples of this distinction in the stories above: on the one hand, the oppression that keeps a woman in an underpaid job and doing unpaid domestic labor and, on the other, the oppression that makes a woman feel invisible or dismissed in a church board meeting. To understand the first kind of oppression, one must analyze how jobs and wages are distributed across gender lines—one must do materialist analysis. To understand the second, one must examine how a particular culture perceives and devalues women's voices—one must do cultural analysis. If one focuses only on the material, one misses the complex ways in which systems of value harm and exclude women. If one focuses only on the cultural, one misses the concrete, institutional ways that relations of power shape our corporate life. Although distinct, these levels of oppression also entail one another. For example, for the woman struggling with her immigration status, it is almost impossible to disentangle the harms of racism from the economic harms she suffers. Feminist theory therefore both distinguishes these two forms of oppression and then complicates this distinction by tracing the complex dynamics of their interactions.

Tied to this distinction is a second dimension of feminist theories of oppression: the insistence that we trace relations of power and domination. Although both terms have a long and complicated history in feminist thought, how feminists use them at a general level is easy to see. Feminist theory asserts that one must attend to the power dynamics that shape social worlds. It further asserts that power is *not* something that may or may not be present. Rather, it is ubiquitous; it permeates all aspects of our interactions with other persons and with institutions and ideas as well.[2] Feminists add that among these numerous relations of power that constitute women's lives, some are best described as relations of domination. In relations of domination, women occupy the subordinate place in the power dynamic and therefore experience diminished control over their lives.[3] While relations of domination are often ones in which men, because of their privileged social positions, have control over women, domination can also exist in relations between women and, even more important, between women and broad social institutions and cultural forces.

This last point brings me to a third feature of feminist discussions of oppression. One of the greatest challenges for feminist theory is to hold together an appreciation for both the collective/institutional and the individual/personal character of oppression. With respect to oppression's collective character, feminists point out that relations of domination are embedded in large social forces that constrain "collectivities" of women. For example, the woman who struggles with immigration faces constraints not because of any individual character flaw or idiosyncratic life experience, but because, like other women of her background, she is a "Caribbean woman." The woman on strike against the university is out on the picket line not because of a personal problem with the college administration, but because she, like her co-workers throughout the university, faces a structural injustice related to her institutional position as a low-salaried clerical worker.

In both cases, recognizing oppression's collective character also allows us to see that injustice is not solely the product of individuals' malevolent intent to "oppress"; it is the product of larger institutional and social forces—as in the case of the clerical worker who had positive relations with her boss and his managers but nonetheless felt her work environment was discriminatory. It is not helpful to associate oppression solely with intent, because the injustice here is a partly unintended effect of institutional forces.[4] As suggested in chapter 3, these institutional forces take many forms—from cultural rules that regulate how women are to sit, dress, and smile to policy regulations that require women to return to work after only six weeks' maternity leave with no support for child care. Seeing the collective and institutional character of oppression is important because it allows us to better understand forces of harm in our lives. Recognizing these impersonal dimensions of oppression stops women from trying to figure out what we as individuals may have done to deserve injustice. As my Tuesday-night group would attest, the tendency of women to take personal responsibility for social and institutional injustices can be quite debilitating.

Having said this, feminists affirm that the personal does, however, play a role in dynamics of domination. In feminist theory, this personal dimension is described in two ways. First, broad and historically grand social forces constrain and harm women in personal and even intimate ways—ways that cannot be summarized in grand theories but await articulation in specific stories of individual lives. When feminists say that "the personal is political," they are saying that what happens in the bedrooms, kitchens, workstations, and interior dialogues of women must be included in theories of oppression. It is often in these intimate and mundane settings that oppression exerts its most exacting and particularized grip. If oppression were depersonalized, we would not be able to see how specific forms of oppression function on a day-to-day basis; we would also ignore the mundane places where women can challenge their oppression, encourage resistance, and enact social change.

Second, feminist theorists insist that although large cultural forces are involved, individuals' intentions and actions *do* work to oppress women, and thus individual (and not just large institutions) must be held responsible. They argue that men and women must be held morally accountable for their active participation in oppressive structures lest we lose sight of human agency in perpetuating social injustices. In the Tuesday-night group, holding the oppressor morally accountable is most salient in the case of the woman struggling with childhood incest. Her adult offender was personally responsible for abusing her—although he was also abused as a child and although larger social forces that give power to men and impose silence on women were at work. By stressing the agency of sex offenders, feminist theorists make space for moral discourse within the framework of talk about institutional injustices.

Feminists argue that it is also important to affirm the agency and personal responsibility of the victims of oppression as well as the perpetrators. Although the young incest survivor was clearly *not* responsible for the harm done to her as a child, she is responsible, as an adult, for her healing and for preventing the same harm from being done to others. This affirmation of her responsibility and agency helps the incest survivor battle the sense of helplessness and fear that originated with the abuse. By embracing her ability to act and to resist, she also works to prevent further abuse—by confronting her abuser, by speaking out about incest at a local rally on violence against women, or by making it through another day without being consumed by fear or harming herself. It also involves recognizing in herself patterns of behavior that could be harmful to others. For example, her past history of falling silent in situations of abuse may prevent her from protecting her own children. Affirming her responsibility thus becomes a way of breaking a cycle of oppression from one generation to the next.

This discussion is tied to a fourth general feature of feminist theory's discussion of oppression: its *engaged* character. In an earlier chapter, I discussed at some length the feminist challenge to epistemological objectivity, particularly with respect to "knowing" essential human nature. Feminist theory makes a similar affirmation in its reflections on injustice: far from engaging in a disinterested, objective, ahistorical enterprise, feminists who theorize women's oppression do so from the inside. They theorize it at the same time they stand in it—as inside experts. This position on the inside has both advantages and disadvantages. On the positive side, persons who best understand the complex workings of oppression are often those suffering from it. The recently widowed woman in our Tuesday-night group points out that the flaws in the health-care system are most apparent to the persons for whom the system does not work. She reminds us that to understand discrimination against the aging, one has to view the world through "an old body"—with declining strength and an increasing sense of dependency—in a society that holds youth and independence in highest value. Her place on the inside gives her privileged access to knowledge about oppression. Feminist theorists refer to this as the epistemological privilege of the oppressed.[5]

On the negative side, however, feminists recognize that harms done to women by oppression are real and can be emotionally and physically damaging. This damage can affect one's ability to analyze the oppression from which one suffers. In our Tuesday-night group, the young woman who wrestles with drug addiction attests to this. When in the depths of addiction, she says she cannot analyze the social dimensions of her oppression because her tools of analysis are so disabled. Her limited ability, however, does not mean for feminists that her voice has no place. Feminists argue that one must listen to the emotions, pain, and often inchoate speech of the oppressed—for it is here that one meets oppression face to face, in all its brokenness and loss. But feminists also avoid romanticizing such voices by acknowledging that the damage of oppression runs deep. Feminist theorists thus hold in tension their desire to listen to oppression from the inside with an acknowledgment that harm can diminish one's capacity to carry out such analysis.

Related to this is a fifth dimension of feminist theories of oppression: the role played by feminist visions of "women's wholeness." In previous chapters, I stressed the importance of having in feminist theory a bold vision of what life without oppression might be like—a vision I referred to as feminist theory's "eschatological moment." My opening definition of oppression invoked this vision by referring to "the flourishing of women." As I have explained, this vision functions as a yardstick against which the pains of the present are measured and critiqued. In theories of oppression, this measurement serves as a "regulative ideal," allowing one to assess the present against standards of justice, wholeness, and in the case of my definition, "flourishing."

Articulating this vision is challenging because it is always in a state of flux. Women's flourishing means something different to my Tuesday-night group than it meant to the first women's group that gathered in the church in 1772. Within the present-day group, the vision also shifts from person to person. For the woman on strike, flourishing means being treated like a professional woman, capable of offering her co-workers creative leadership and solid decision making. For the Caribbean woman, it means being surrounded by generations of her family, all in good health and receiving the education they desire. For the woman who struggles with addiction, it is simply another day without a drink or drugs. What does this diversity suggest about feminist theory's eschatology? Just as there is no single model of true womanhood or true oppression, so too there is no one image of full flourishing in feminist theory. But articulating visions of the future is not finally an exercise in cultural relativism: it is strategic essentialism at its best.

A sixth general feature of feminist theories of oppression is their practical character. By "practical" I mean that feminists want their theories of oppression to work for the good of women's lives. Theories do this when they illuminate what women already know quite intimately but have not yet theorized. In the Tuesday-night group, we know when this happens because one can see women having "aha" experiences—"Aha, that's what's happening." Theories also work practically when they empower action for change. In the Tuesday-night group, the woman on strike against the university relies on theories of women's economic oppression that insist upon the possibility of social change. She believes a wage increase and greater participation in the decision-making processes in her office are possible. If she held to a social theory that claimed low wages for women were inevitable and that her "lack of voice" was necessary for an efficiently run office, she would never have decided to go on strike. While such a theory might shed light on certain dimensions of her plight, it would not meet the feminist pragmatic criteria of emancipatory social engagement—because again, feminists analyze the oppressive conditions of women's lives to better engage in the process of change.

These remarks bring me to the end of this section. Before moving on, however, let me summarize the features of oppression I have listed. I first suggested that the harms and injustices that diminish the flourishing of women are multiple and interrelated. I then explained that they are often a function of relations of domination. Such relations, I argued, constrain women not just individually but collectively, and they are frequently institutional in character. I then explained that oppression has personal dimensions as well. Individual oppressors need to be held personally responsible for harms they do, and women need to be affirmed in their ability to contest their oppression responsibly. I explored next the eschatological character of theories of oppression, arguing that feminist critique relies on a vision of women flourishing. This vision serves as a pragmatic yardstick, measuring oppression as well the shape of the future.

A phrase that captures the eclectic and shifting character of the feminist theories just described is "theories on the move." When reflecting on the messy complexities of women's lives, one needs agile tools of analysis. One needs theories that can travel to the many sites of women's oppression and be adapted or reconfigured to fit constantly shifting situations. Feminists thus favor theories that are never finished but keep moving across the varied terrain of women's lives. Theories on the move not only travel horizontally across our histories, they propel us forward as well, toward an emancipatory future. They are theories that travel before us, holding out a vision of the wholeness toward which the struggle for women's liberation is moving. To use a term from my discussion of strategic essentialism, they are theories that mark the horizon of "women's becoming" by denouncing the forces that diminish our lives and calling us ahead to a future where we flourish.

Demystifying Patriarchy

In the early years of the contemporary women's movement, one could not sit through a feminist discussion of oppression without hearing repeated references to "patriarchy." The term derives from the Latin *patriarchia*, which means "rule of the father," although in the popular feminist lingo of the time, it more often meant "the rule of men over women." Even more broadly, "patriarchy" referred to the enormous web of economic, political, social, and religious regulations that enforced the domination of women by men throughout the ages. Using a single word to describe this grand web of oppressive forces served the rhetorical function of suggesting that male domination had a long history and stretched across national and cultural boundaries, touching every facet of life. As such, the term "patriarchy" invoked a sense of the enormity of the struggle ahead by identifying the enormity of the history that had bound women for centuries. In such a context, it was not enough to win the right to vote or to change the laws on rape; the struggle for liberation had to reach farther and cut deeper.

The word has had a varied history since.[6] Like many feminist terms, it means different things to different theorists. Recent theorists have made a concerted effort to use it more precisely. They worry that if used as a broad umbrella to cover all forms of women's oppression, "patriarchy" hides the multifaceted and constantly shifting character of the injustices suffered by women over the centuries and around the world. One especially dangerous implication of the assumption that patriarchy is responsible for women's oppression everywhere is the idea that oppression results from a universal desire of men (the patriarchs) to dominate women.

Feminist theorists contest this view of universal male domination on several grounds. First, this view can mistakenly suggest that men are biologically predisposed to subjugate women. As I argued earlier, this biological essentialism entraps men and women in natures that appear inevitable. It is then difficult for people to imagine the possibility of radical social change. Moreover, if the real culprit is a monolithic, ahistorical force, individual men (and women) cannot be held responsible for the harms they do. Second, when men become the sole focus, it is easy to overlook how broad institutional and cultural forces harm women quite apart from the intentions of individual men. Placing the full weight of oppression on the shoulders of an often demonized caricature makes it difficult to see the domination of women as something structural. Third, feminists contest this monolithic view of patriarchy because it deflects attention from the effects of racism, classism, heterosexism, and ageism on the lives of women. When male domination is the sole culprit, these dimensions of women's experiences are underestimated and the complexities of women's lives are ignored.

What stricter definition of "patriarchy" do feminists now offer? Feminists return to the Latin meaning, "rule of the father," and explore how "fathers ruled" in the classical Roman and Greek world. The Hellenistic social system maintained the sovereignty of male heads of household over wives, children, slaves, and all other dependent persons in the familial sphere.[7] This social system gave women no legal status as citizens, restricted their rights of inheritance, and dramatically constrained the scope of their social power.[8] The hierarchical order of the household also extended to Hellenistic culture and religion, a culture where male citizens ruled the polis and ordered the lives of women, slaves, and children.

Against the backdrop of this analysis, feminists look at how women's oppression today may be both different from and similar to Greco-Roman patriarchy. Attending to the differences means, for instance, that feminist theologians should avoid suggesting that "father rule" took the same form in Hebrew scriptures as it did, say, in the Middle Ages or in the early modern nation-state. While in each of these historical contexts men were dominant and women subordinate, the form and content of their relationship changed dramatically. In the social world of the Hebrew scriptures, men ruled as tribal leaders whose power was mediated through a complex weave of kinship ties different from those of the Roman overlord. In the Middle Ages, the relationship between men and women was structured according to a feudal organization quite distinct from the Roman city-state.[9] In the early modern nation-state, further differences arose with the emergence of social institutions such as the nuclear family, a capitalist mode of production, slavery in the Americas, and the Renaissance humanists' distinct reconceptualization of gender differences.[10]

Having noted these differences, feminists quickly note that there are similarities between periods as well—similarities such as the standing restriction of women's legal rights. Attending to these similarities remains important because it suggests clues for uncovering the roots of present oppressions. But one will not find a single, easily identified, transhistorical thread called "patriarchy" that winds through all these periods and ties them neatly together. The forces that oppress women are historically variant and institutionally mediated and not, as the term "patriarchy" suggests, the product of a great, universal conspiracy of men against women.[11] Demystifying the "myth of universal male domination," however, does not hide the sobering fact that the domination of women by men reaches back for centuries, nor the painful reality that some men have intentionally oppressed women for their own benefits. It only redirects attention away from explanations of oppression that are too simplistic and turns attention instead to the more politically pragmatic task of identifying the various institutional formations, social practices, and cultural constructions that undergird women's oppression in our present context.

Five Faces of Oppression

Iris Young describes "five faces of oppression" in contemporary North American culture: exploitation, marginalization, powerlessness, cultural imperialism, and violence. Each is well known to the women in my Tuesday-night group and probably to most women in our culture. Most women in the United States, however, are not familiar with the vocabulary Young and other feminist theorists use to describe them or with the wealth of historical and sociological research upon which feminist theorists draw for their analysis. The value of these theories rests on their abilities to illuminate women's experience of oppression while encouraging struggle for a different future. With this in mind, readers are encouraged to use their own experiences of oppression to measure these theories. These categories are not meant to be exhaustive, nor are they *all* meant to apply to every woman. For some women, all five forms of oppression will be familiar; for others, only two or three. Still others will not find their oppression named at all. Whatever the case, measuring these theories against our stories keeps feminist theories of oppression "on the move."

Oppression as Exploitation

> The injustice of social *exploitation* consists in social processes that bring about a transfer of energies from one group to another to produce unequal distributions, and in the way in which social institutions enable a few to accumulate while they constrain many more.[12]

When the clerical worker in our Tuesday-night group decided to join her local union and go on strike against the university, she was primarily concerned about her low wage and lack of job security. She was also, however, troubled by an administrative chain of command in her office that gave her little control over how she did her work. Moreover, she had recently taken on the responsibility of caring for her elderly mother at home, and her husband's job prevented him from helping with housework. When she added up her labor on all these tasks, she was working a sixty-five- to seventy-hour week and still felt financially strapped. She was exhausted, and her hard work was not paying off in either economic advancement or more leisure time. Although she did not explicitly name it as such, she was experiencing exploitation.

The statistics her union presented her with gave her exploitation a clearer and more broadly institutional face. At the time she joined the union, women in the United States were making approximately fifty-nine cents for every dollar that men made for the same work. Most women in the United States were also putting in an extra six or more hours a day at home, doing jobs such as housecleaning, food preparation, caring for children, and shopping—all unpaid work necessary to keep their households going and the economy moving. Her union compared these statistics to global patterns of labor distribution and economic power. The numbers were sobering: women's work encompassed approximately two-thirds of the world's work hours (both paid and unpaid); women received one-tenth of the world's wages; and they owned only a hundredth of the world's property.[13] As my friend jokingly said the night she brought this union literature to the group, "Exhaustion seems to be catching among women!" To this comment we could add, "And so is exploitation!"

What is exploitation? Its definitions are rooted in both the Marxist and "materialist feminist" tradition. Theorists in both traditions do materialist analysis of women's oppression, which focuses on how material goods are produced and circulated in our society and hence how jobs are distributed and money is made.[14] The term "exploitation" describes a specific dynamic related to the distribution of labor and money. Exploitation occurs when the people who produce social goods do not share fully in the accumulated benefits of their labor; they work so that another group gains the profit. In traditional Marxist theory, this unequal distribution occurs primarily in the market—that is, in the privately owned sector of the capitalist economy where wage laborers produce commodities that, when sold, produce a profit for business owners and investors but not for workers. When such exploitation happens in the present "business world," its effects on women are disproportionate, for they are usually on the low-paying end of the production line. Materialist feminists also argue that women are exploited in an area that traditional Marxists never considered—the home, where they seldom share equally in the benefits of the labor they expend for "the family." This double exploitation of women, at work *and* at home, describes the experience of the clerical worker in my Tuesday-night group who worked a sixty-five-hour week on her two "jobs."

To understand the cultural and institutional forces that contribute to this double exploitation of women, look at the cultural messages of our society about how work is divided up and valued. One message is embedded in the "lived imaginative construct" of "the social division of labor." According to this construct, work is divided into two spheres: the *public sphere,* where "men work," and the *private sphere,* where "women keep the hearth warm." In the public sphere, men attend to matters of the state, run the economy, and bring home the paycheck. In the private sphere of the home, women raise children, care for the sick and the elderly, cook for the family, clean and manage the domestic space, and (most important) feed, emotionally nurture, and support the men who go to work in the public sphere. This "feminine sphere" is also where women do work traditionally associated with art, religion, and communal traditions.[15] Although in this extreme form, it fails to describe the complex work and home lives of women today, this imaginative construct has a strong hold on our social practices at a number of levels.

To see how this private/public split functions in present-day North America, let us first look at its history. The modern form of the public/private divide began in Europe with the enormous social changes accompanying the rise of the nation-state, the emergence of a predominantly capitalist economy, the subsequent development of increasingly industrialized forms of production, and the creation of the modern nuclear family as the principal unit of social and economic organization.[16] In the context of these emergent social forms, the world of work was reconfigured to include both the modern "wage-earning" man, who sold his labor on the market in return for compensation, and the "home-caring" woman, who maintained the domestic environment necessary to keep the wage earner healthy and strong while providing "reproductive labor" necessary to reproduce (literally) the next generation of male workers and female caregivers.[17] We also find in the "non-wage-earning sphere" the labor of slaves, children, and indentured servants, who worked both inside and outside the domestic sphere.[18] Because the domestic sphere was associated with "women's work" and could be under- or uncompensated, capitalism profited from this labor, which was necessary to keep the economic machinery humming, but did not have to remunerate the laborers. In other words, women reproduce, raise, and care for the workers that capitalism needs, but the system never pays them for doing this work.[19]

Although these social forms have undergone significant changes over the years, they continue to shape our work lives in both the workplace and the home. Take, for example, the university where I teach (and where the woman in my group went on strike). While it is no longer a place where only men teach and study, it is still divided according to "men's work" and "women's work." At the senior level of the faculty, only 7 percent of the jobs are held by women.[20] The chief executive officer is a man, and the majority of departmental chairs are held by men. The women at the university work, for the most part, in areas associated with the "feminine." They are found predominantly in offices doing clerical work, in dining halls cooking and serving the food, and in janitorial services cleaning dorm rooms, hallways, and offices. Mostly male employees do the so-called hard-labor maintenance work on the buildings, and mostly female employees do the "light work" of cooking and cleaning. The women in clerical jobs are predominantly European American, whereas the women who cook and clean are predominantly Latina and African American, a continuing reflection of the racial divides that marked the public/private division in earlier times.

Looking at situations like this one, feminist theorists have little difficulty arguing that the old public/private dichotomy profoundly affects our lives. As a "lived imaginative construct," it is materially productive in that it produces and reinforces institutional arrangements in which women live and work. For example, according to the old, extreme form of the construct, men were responsible for making rational decisions and women for providing nurture. While no one in the university would say today that this reason/nurture split is true, it still seems to structure the division of labor. Moreover, because the work women do is traditionally defined as "feminine"—a claim undergirded by the argument that the work requires less skill and education—they are paid less. This is true not only for the jobs I described but also for the "helping" professions in general, such as elementary-school teaching, nursing, day care, home health care, social work, and psychotherapy, to name only a few feminized sectors of the job force.

The flip side of this dynamic is the fact that the "two-spheres" construct also functions as a social myth that hides the work women have always done outside the domestic sphere. Examples of this dynamic are evident in North American history. The public/private split emerged in North America at the same time European-immigrant, working-class women were filling factories in the Northeast and enslaved African women were laboring in the fields of the South.[21] In both instances, women were doing traditionally "masculine" gendered work, but because the broader culture only conceptualized "labor" according to the two-spheres model, work done by the women in these areas went unnoticed. Feminist theory, in contrast, allows us to see this labor and the lives of women who have never conformed to the dominant culture's perception of appropriate gender work.

In addition to helping us see the traditional workplace as a site of gender exploitation, feminist theorists argue that exploitation occurs in the home—a point that earlier Marxists failed to consider. But how can housework be exploitative if no pay is involved? The materialist feminist theorist Christine Delphy suggests we look at the power dynamics in a traditional, heterosexual, nuclear family.[22] The nuclear family forms around a marriage contract, which implicitly assumes that the wife will work for the husband in the domestic sphere without pay. This seems natural since women are socialized to want well-ordered domestic space, and men expect a woman to do the work because they are socialized not to care about housekeeping—"they don't see dirt." In light of this socialization, women end up doing the lion's share of household chores because they supposedly "want to," and the underlying gender dynamics are never discussed. Delphy also points out that women do jobs inside the home that would be paid for outside. They thus create and distribute social goods necessary to the economy, but because they do so "in house," no monetary remuneration is offered.[23] Delphy suggests, moreover, that rather than receiving a wage in exchange for this work, women are promised social commodities of "security, status, and financial stability" for themselves and their children. Again, the gender training women and men receive from their earliest year prepares them for such an exchange: women are taught to seek safety and status through relationships with men, and men are taught to provide for and protect women. Given that men earn higher wages and have longer employment records than women, it makes sense that heterosexual women seek financial security through their male partners—the system has been set up that way. Also, because a woman's monetary contribution to family income is typically less than her male partner's, she is expected to make up for the discrepancy by doing more housework and child care—even if she works longer hours than her partner and has no control over the fact that she earns less than he does.[24]

Given all these factors, why is this domestic relationship exploitative? In this gendered system of housework, women are exploited because they produce goods that are unequally distributed. In the typical nuclear family arrangement, women buy and prepare food, offer emotional support, and work to create a home environment where the family can rest and play. But women eat less than men, typically depend not on their husbands but on other women for emotional support, and spend fewer hours than their husbands sleeping and engaging in leisure activities. Women are thus exploited at home in that they expend energy to produce benefits for men without reciprocally sharing in the created "profits." This "private" exploitation plus women's lower wage-earning power adds up to a picture of a woman who, as an unpaid domestic worker (often with a low-paying job as well) is over-worked, exhausted, exploited, and yet expected to perform happily her gen-dered roles. My Tuesday-night group has no problem calling this women's oppression in one of its most blatant forms.

Oppression as Marginalization

> Marginals are the people the system [of labor] . . . cannot or will not use. *Marginalization* is perhaps the most dangerous form of oppression. A whole category of people is expelled from useful participation in social life and thus potentially subjected to severe material deprivation and even extermination.[25]

Not every woman in the Tuesday-night group faces the same form of exploitation that the clerical worker confronted in her office. There are two women who have entered the higher salaried world of "men's work" and can afford to pay for child care and housecleaning, although they still do more domestic work than the men in their lives and face sexism in the workplace. There are also three women who do not "work" at all, in the traditional sense: the retired, widowed woman in declining health, the depressed woman with drug addiction who cannot hold down a job, and the woman whose immi-gration status prevents her from officially entering the labor market. The fact that these "unemployed" women are not part of daily workplace exploitation does not mean, however, that they are not oppressed by the economic system. In their stories, we hear about the financial hardships they face because they do not "work" and about the emotional strain of being "unemployed depen-dents" in a culture that values hard work, self-sufficiency, and independence. Because they do not fit into the dominant system of labor exchange, they often feel their lives do not matter or, perhaps more accurately, that they live outside a system of economic value. According to feminist theorists, these women are feeling "marginalized" and hence are experiencing a form of oppression feminists aptly call "marginalization."[26]

What is meant by "marginalization"? As described above, "marginals are the people the system [of labor] . . . cannot or will not use." In Marxist theory, marginal persons constitute the permanent underclass of the unemployed, those who in advanced capitalist societies depend on state subsidies to sur-vive. In this country, marginalization hits several groups of people. It occurs along racial lines: African Americans, Latinos, and Native Americans are sys-tematically excluded from the workforce and therefore denied the dubious privilege of providing "exploitable labor." Marginalization also threatens elderly persons and persons with disabilities because they are considered physically unemployable. Lesbians who are public about their sexual orientation also risk under- or unemployment because their labor is not considered crucial to the maintenance of the mythic nuclear family. In recent years, single women with children have been forced into the ranks of the marginal as well, not only because their labor as mothers remains uncompensated, but because they cannot afford child care and must depend on a welfare bureaucracy that requires the energy of a full-time job to negotiate.[27]

Feminist theorists include these women in their analysis of economic oppression even though they do not play an obvious role in the production and exchange of market goods in our society. Because the dominant culture has deemed these persons "unusable" and "dependent" and has relegated them to the impoverished edges of the market economy, these women are often denied their "basic rights to privacy, respect and individual choice" through the invasive practices of social service agencies that define their needs and refuse to hear their voices.[28] The ideological rhetoric of "suitable work" in our culture hides the economic and political factors that marginalize persons and makes it appear as if poor, old, or disabled persons and racial and ethnic minorities are "naturally" disinclined to conform to social definitions of productive work. In reality, however, the threat of a fall into marginality, particularly in a city like New Haven where unemployment is high, keeps those who do have jobs wary of job actions that might destroy their tenuous hold on the market economy. As such, maintaining groups of "marginals" serves to keep labor low-paid and passive and hence works to benefit more powerful economic interests.

One of the principal contributions feminist theory has made to the struggle against this dynamic is to reconceive the meaning of both "dependent" and "productive." They suggest that we recognize that "dependence is a basic human condition." For persons to survive and flourish, social interactions and interdependency are inevitable; the modern myth of the self-sufficient individual is illusory in that it implies one can exist in social isolation and carry out one's life plans without help from anyone.[29] Once we debunk the notion that dependence is bad, we can discern the various forms that dependency takes and the kinds of power relation that undergird them. On that basis, one can develop models for social cooperation that value the varying degrees to which persons need one another (for instance, children, elderly persons, and sick persons have basic dependency different from the needs of healthy middle-aged persons). One can also identify structurally coercive forms of dependency (like the dependency of the racially stigmatized who are unemployed) in order to minimize their debilitating consequences and to "denaturalize" the dominant order's account of their origin. In a similar fashion, feminist theorists try to rearticulate the definition of social productivity so that values other than those of the market mark contributions individuals make to the common good.[30]

Oppression as Powerlessness

> *Powerlessness* is the inhibition in the development of one's capacities, lack of decision-making power in one's working life, and exposure to disrespectful treatment because of the status one occupies.[31]

A third face of oppression in the contemporary world of work has less to do with how money is circulated and more to do with how decisions are made and power distributed. It concerns the degree to which women are given control over and power in their work environments. In the language of the Tuesday-night group, it concerns what we call "having a voice." We often share stories of frustration about not being asked to participate in defining the rules that regulate our jobs or in determining how we should organize our time and implement our duties. Someone with more power is always telling us what to do and how to do it, usually without asking for input in return. When this happens, the women in my group therefore feel infantilized, patronized, made invisible, and not respected. This sense of powerlessness also makes us feel trivialized and silenced. We talk, as well, about how this dynamic orders not only our workplaces but organizations like our churches. Mainly men chair the committees, particularly those that control the church's money, and yet it is women who implement the church programs on a weekly basis. This gendered division of decision making is also reflected in the fact that the vast majority of senior ministerial offices in this country are held by men. Women are mostly associate ministers, assistant ministers, choir directors, Christian-education facilitators, or solo pastors in small urban and rural churches.

The feminist theorist Kathy Ferguson has mapped this dynamic of powerlessness in decision-making processes by looking at how the culture uses terms like "professional" and "nonprofessional" to describe the work people do. The modern-day bureaucratized workplace is organized so that "nonprofessional" workers are managed by a "professionalized" cadre of directors and organizers. This organization follows a gendered logic: the managed worker (whether a woman or a man) is imaged as feminine (passive, obedient, less rational, and dependent) and made to follow orders from other more "qualified" persons, who are figured as masculine (assertive, rational, and independent).[32] Ferguson illustrates this with the example of "impression management" in the office. In the typical hierarchical workplace, the feminized worker is constantly required to perform in ways that the more powerful find acceptable—acting dependent and happy to be so, being receptive to criticism, and conveying a sense that it is a privilege just to be noticed. This requires constantly calculating the temperament and moods of the "boss" so as to create an image of responsiveness that will favorably impress—calculations that the "boss" is not reciprocally required to make.[33] Recent studies of the phenomenon referred to as "the glass ceiling" suggest that perceptions about the appropriately "feminine" behavior of subordinate workers prevent women from moving up in organizations where unspoken assumptions about masculine leadership qualities are valued.[34]

How do feminists suggest we address this dimension of women's oppression? One suggestion is that as a nation that supposedly values democracy, we should not limit this form of decision making to politics only but should consider it as the model for structuring decision-making processes in the workplace as well. Bringing democratic sensibilities to bear on economic arrangements, feminists suggest, may open up space for the voices of women in institutions where they have traditionally been silenced and, in doing so, help us reconceive the nature of authority and power in distinctly feminist terms.

Oppression as Cultural Imperialism

> To experience *cultural imperialism* means to experience how the dominant meanings of a society render the particular perspective of one's group invisible at the same time as they stereotype one's group and mark it out as the Other.[35]

At Christmas, our Tuesday-night gatherings are often more tension filled than they are joyful. This is especially true for the woman in our group from Jamaica: during the holidays, she feels a deep longing for her family at home and feels "out of place" in New England. She misses traditional food, and family friends who gather to tell stories at Christmas. Last year, this experience of being out of place was exacerbated by her failed attempts to find a new job with the temporary agency where she works—a failure related to her being a middle-aged, large-sized, African Caribbean woman with a strong Jamaican accent and a quiet demeanor. Nothing about her values, her appearance, her voice, or her sense of humor fit the unstated cultural standards of the employers she met. This was particularly difficult for her because her Jamaican identity is a source of enormous pride and empowerment for her and hence is not a "problem" she wants to overcome. The fact that others saw it as such put her in an untenable position.

Feminist theorists refer to oppression when it takes this form as "cultural imperialism." Cultural imperialism has to do with the way groups develop and apply cultural standards for defining, interpreting, and regulating beliefs, actions, and attitudes.[36] Although being culturally constructed is unavoidable, cultural imperialism occurs when a more powerful group universalizes its standards and imposes them on less powerful persons. Not surprisingly, this imposition usually includes rules and standards about appropriate gender roles and behaviors. In present-day North America, cultural imperialism with respect to gender occurs when an interpretive frame of reference that is male, white, and heterosexual defines a complementary set of rules for behavior that is appropriately female, white, and heterosexual. This ideology of complementary femininity creates a "cult of true womanhood" in which women are to be nurturing, pure, emotional, and saintly in appearance and attitude. The imposition of this standard on women is oppressive because it construes female identity as a supplemental (yet inferior) mirror to the masculine norm, and because women who do not conform to its rules are labeled deviant, sick, bad, or immoral. As my previous discussion of feminist constructivists suggests, this gendered rhetoric of cultural norms cuts deep into the fabric of Western society, shaping its most treasured institutions and philosophies.

When the women in the Tuesday-night group described their experiences at work, the effects of cultural imperialism were clear. When the administrative assistant acted the role of dependent, accepting, nice (but hardworking) womanhood, she was considered a good worker in her office. When she challenged the rules of her workplace by asking for a more democratic decision-making process and by questioning her pay scale, her behavior was labeled as deviant. Her superiors personalized her challenges as paranoid, bitter and hard, overly anxious, and unattractively ambitious rather than directly addressing the issues she raised. Because she had an Italian working-class background, her behavior was further stereotyped as crude and hotheaded. She suffered a "double consciousness" as a result: on the one hand, she knew herself to be deserving of respect, capable of creative expression, full of hope, and hardworking; on the other hand, the dominant culture labeled her aggressive, obstructionist, and unruly. Although she struggled not to internalize these demoralizing stereotypes and to maintain a healthy sense of herself apart from the script handed to her by a more powerful group, she found it emotionally and physically exhausting. This experience also helped her appreciate even more how formidable this challenge must be for women, unlike herself, whose social affiliations are with cultural groups whose language and practices are even more dramatically different from those of the dominant culture.[37]

Feminists in psychology have also identified cultural imperialism in the dominant culture's understanding of the "normal" processes of moral decision making.[38] According to Carol Gilligan, the model for moral development that values disinterested, objective reasoning and uses abstract conceptions of rights and duties is based upon the reflective processes of economically privileged European-descended boys and men. This model has been mistakenly universalized, she argues, and for this reason, the girls and women she studies—who have been socialized to value not objectivity but relationality, not rights and duties but the responsibilities of care—appear "underdeveloped" or deviant. As a form of cultural imperialism, this universal imposition of a distinctly masculine-socialized model devalues and silences cultural difference, the difference of women as relationally oriented decision makers.[39]

Oppression as Violence

> I also include in this category [violence] less severe incidents of harassment, intimidation, or ridicule simply for the purpose of degrading, humiliating, or stigmatizing group members . . . violence is a social practice . . . that approaches legitimacy.[40]

For the last two years, the young incest survivor in our Tuesday-night group has spent her Saturday mornings in the basement of the church attending self-defense classes taught by the New Haven Women's Self-Defense Alliance. Composed of young, middle-aged, and older Asian American, African American, and European American women who are professional, working-class, and poor, this is a rather anomalous group in the city: one rarely finds women from such different backgrounds coming together around a shared concern. This shared concern becomes painfully obvious in the stories told by the students; it is rooted in the fear of being targets of physical violence and sexual abuse by men. The young woman from our group often recalls the violence unleashed on her as a child in the privacy of her home. The lesbian from the group tells of her fear of being sexually assaulted by men threatened by her sexual orientation. Some of the self-defense students tell of seeking refuge in the New Haven battered women's shelter. These stories all resonate well with the statistic that three out of five women have been sexually assaulted, be it by incest, rape, or some form of sexual harassment in the workplace.[41]

Feminist theorists analyze and critique these specifically gendered forms of violence as a systemic and structural component of women's oppression and not merely the product of the pathologically maladjusted behavior of small numbers of individual men. A growing body of empirical data measuring incidents of assault and harassment perpetrated by men against women supports this critique.[42] Between 1983 and 1987, domestic violence shelters recorded a 100-percent increase in the number of women seeking refuge. Between 1976 and 1984, reported sex-related murders in this country dramatically increased; at least one-third of the women killed were murdered by husbands or boyfriends. In a 1990 Virginia Slims poll, 72 percent of women (compared to 49 percent of men) surveyed said they felt "more afraid and uneasy on the streets today" than they did only several years ago.[43] While these statistics may not measure an actual increase in the level of violence but rather an increased awareness and willingness of women to report and document their abuse, the overall picture is far from ambiguous: violence against women is a structural feature of everyday life in the United States.

When feminist theorists refer to this violence as "systemic and structural," they do not mean only that it is widespread; they are also pointing out how various institutions and cultural beliefs and practices create a social climate where violence is not only imaginable but tolerated or accepted as "natural"—part of the human condition. In response to this climate, feminist theory has tried, in recent years, to "denaturalize" violence against women by exposing the mechanisms through which it is socially constructed (and hence not natural). This task, however, is extremely difficult because, even among feminists, there are a number of differing opinions about how the reality of violence might best be theorized. One school of thought, represented by the French theorist Julia Kristeva and her students, analyzes violence through the lens of psychoanalysis and claims that the social desire to brutalize and efface women's bodies is tied to a social unconscious that secures its masculine identity by wounding or destroying the metaphoric "body of the mother/feminine."[44] Jacquelyn Rose discusses violence as an unconscious, structural feature of the drive to win identity through negation.[45] Drawing on the work of the cultural anthropologist René Girard, a closely related school of thought analyzes how social groups achieve definition and coherence through ritually enacted "sacrifices" of victims who embody the group's collective fears and whose deaths appease disruptive forces within the community.[46] Feminists using the work of Girard argue that communities create a feminine victim whose body becomes an acceptable and accessible site for this definitive act of sacrifice. Feminists in cultural anthropology have also criticized traditional understandings of the incest taboo by arguing that, instead of working to stop incest, moral codes against incest have imposed a silence about it—a silence, they argue, that protects the abusers by stifling the voices of those who are abused.

In her work on pornography and sexual harassment, U.S. legal theorist Catharine MacKinnon offers yet another way to understand the systemic nature of violence against women. MacKinnon argues that pornography—both its economic structure and its cultural images—expresses a power relation in which women are depicted as submissive objects that men desire to dominate. This power relation, she points out, is not limited to the individual pornographer but draws upon (and helps to construct) real and pervasive power relations between men and women in our culture at large. This basic relation of dominance and submission/subordination runs so deep in our public conscious and social institutions that, according to MacKinnon, it is impossible for heterosexual interactions to escape it: in this constructed script, sexual pleasure becomes synonymous with men's raping women. It is a script that is sanctioned by the dominant culture: the state publicly protects the first amendment rights of pornographers, while even the most mundane forms of social intercourse between men and women enact it.[47]

One of the principal questions feminists ask is whether one conceptual scheme can grasp the complex forms of sexual and physical violence experienced by women. The conceptual schemes offered by Kristeva, Rose, Girard, and MacKinnon each seek to describe violence's fundamental origin—in the individual unconscious, in the dynamics of group configurations, or in the masochistic economy of exchange produced by relations of domination and subordination. They also make violence against women appear universal in scope by constructing analytically sophisticated accounts of how the social construction of "women" produces acceptable victims, and the social construction of "men" makes them abusers. Such conceptual schemes have the rhetorical power to expose interconnections among the various forms of violence perpetrated against women and to resist theories that absorb the gendered specificity of such violence into broader, nongendered accounts of oppression. The disadvantages of these approaches, however, should not be overlooked: universal claims about the inevitability of violence might stifle the constructive work of imagining a world where women are not assaulted, terrorized, and forced to bear the pain of both physical and psychic domination, and might thereby stifle resistance.[48]

In this regard, feminist theorists have learned from conversations in settings like the self-defense course in New Haven new ways of theorizing beyond violence. In battered women's groups, incest survivors' support networks, and rape crisis centers across the country, the voices of women are forming a chorus of insights into the complex process of healing from and moving beyond abuse. In this chorus, one hears the need for an analysis that takes seriously the role of institutions, such as the legal system, the medical community, and social service agencies, in perpetuating systemic violence against women. One also hears the need for analysis of the subtle and not-so-subtle ways in which the dominant culture creates a context for such violence by the media portrayal of women as objects of a dominating, masculine sexual desire. Using these feminist analyses, women have made great strides in bringing violence against women into the realm of public discussion. But much work remains to be done, and the depth of public backlash against those who speak out about violence should not be underestimated. Such backlash is presently emerging in groups organizing around the claims that feminist therapists are creating "false childhood memories" of sexual abuse and that "date rape" is the fabrication of an overzealous victim consciousness among feminists. The theories that support such claims often draw on the insights of feminist theory into human nature and language, but they do so to increase feminist losses rather than gains.

This analysis of violence has focused primarily on physical and sexual violence against women. As this section's opening quotation suggests, however, violence also takes more subtle forms, as in the case of degrading joke telling or in a quick look or gesture that demeans or dismisses—both of which feminists analyze. Feminists also focus on the ways institutional realities such as racism and ageism perpetrate real and sustained physical and emotional harms. Once we broaden the definition of violence to include these dimensions, the scope of the feminist theories on this topic expands significantly. In fact, one could label each of oppression's five faces as "violence," because in each we find social forces unleashed that inflict enormous bodily and emotional pain on women. I hope my discussion of the four other forms of oppression has captured some of this complexity by making it clear that although I have focused on sexual violence the conversation about violence and women is more complex and unfortunately much broader in its scope than my comments in this section might suggest.

In the previous section, I examined many aspects of feminist discussions of oppression. I moved through a range of disciplines and perspectives, from empirical psychology and sociology to the more ethereal world of French poststructuralism and linguistic philosophy. Recall, however, that the preceding account by no means claims to be comprehensive. Readers will no doubt have experienced oppressions that fall outside these areas. Indeed, the character and shape of women's oppression in North America is changing as I write—taking new institutional and personal forms that have yet to enter feminist theory's field of vision. For this reason, it is important to remember that feminist theories of oppression are "theories on the move"—agile, adaptive, pragmatic, and open.

The women of the Tuesday-night group recognize this "agility" quite well. Over the past five years, our understanding of the hardship and harms we suffer has shifted and evolved. When we first began to meet, we often felt nervous and uneasy about the young woman's stories of sexual abuse, and we often met them with silence. Today, however, thanks to her courage and to feminists across the country whose writings about sexual abuse have educated us, we listen more openly and have words of understanding and hope to offer. When the woman who works in the university union first joined the group three years ago, she spoke only about her oppression at work in terms of pay. This year, however, we have all become aware that the bigger threat to her is "casualization"—the threat that she will be replaced by two part-time, no-benefits workers. Thanks to feminists working on labor and gender, her union is devising new theories and strategies to address this form of oppression.

In the midst of all these shifts in our understanding of women's oppression, several things remain constant, however. Perhaps the most significant constant is our belief, as a Christian women's group, that the brokenness we experience is not right, that there must be another way for us to live, a way that enables the flourishing of women and of all people. We often speak eschatologically of "God's coming realm," of the world as it "might be," redeemed and healed by God. Against the backdrop of this vision, our conversations often turn to sin. When we move feminist theory into this new world of theology, our understanding of injustice deepens and our basic assumptions about women and the character of our brokenness are challenged. The following chapter takes up this discussion.

5

Sin: Grace Denied

Be appalled, O heavens, at this, be shocked,
be utterly desolate, says the Lord,
for my people have committed two evils;
they have forsaken me, the fountain of living water,
and dug out cisterns for themselves,
cracked cisterns that can hold no water.

—Jeremiah 2:13

Two years ago during Lent, our Tuesday-night women's group engaged
in an intensive theological study of sin—the theme of the season. Several members were initially and understandably wary of "sin-talk." Christian
views of sin had taught them they were "bad," that they should be ashamed
of their bodies and sexuality. While not everybody shared these negative
experiences, we all could well imagine the destructive ways Christian views
of sin have been used to oppress our sisters, not only in our group but in
communities around the world and throughout the ages. It was thus important that our Lenten study honor the particular stories of our members and
proceed cautiously. This meant allowing our experiences of oppression to
guide us as we turned to the study of Christian themes such as the Fall, original sin, total depravity, and guilt for our Reformed tradition.

Interesting conversations occurred in the group as our understandings of
women's oppression guided our reflections on sin. The hours we spent listening to and analyzing one another's stories of oppression dramatically
shifted the way we looked at sin. When we turned to scripture, creeds, classical theology, and liturgy for Christian views of sin, we brought with us our
stories of incest and addiction, of racism and heterosexism, of strikes, unemployment, and depression. To use again the metaphor of mapping, our

Lenten study took us into the familiar territory of sin, but to our surprise, the territory mapped differently. We were moving across well-known theological terrain but with a new map shaped by feminist theory's insights. Although this map did not create the doctrine of sin we studied, its lines allowed us to journey through the landscape of "sin" in a new way; the sights we beheld were both surprising and powerful.

The least surprising part was the study's confirmation of our worst fears about oppressive views of women and sin, as in classical accounts of Eve's role as temptress in the Garden of Eden. We were surprised, however, by sin's pertinence to our present-day situation. We found that when remapped, concepts like original sin offered a comforting account of God's presence in the midst of our brokenness. We also found views of sin that directly contradicted those that had damaged our self-image. We discovered praise for the glory of God's creation and descriptions of God's grief for the harms done to the human body. In the context of our deepening grasp of women's sufferings, the tradition opened and expanded to a new breadth of insight, beauty, and faithful truth telling. By attending to women's oppression, we moved the doctrine of sin in directions it had not moved before; we tilled new soil in the variegated landscape of our tradition; and again, both surprise and beauty met us there.

In this chapter, I use chapter 4's summary of feminist theories of oppression to remap a conventional account of sin. As with all themes in Christian theology, numerous views of sin have developed over the centuries. The view of Eastern Christianity is distinct from the Western Augustinian tradition; within the West, different communities of faith give this doctrine different nuances. While any of these views could fruitfully converse with feminist theory, I focus on only the traditional Reformation rendition. I again limit my reflections to themes that emerge when sin is considered in relation to the doctrines of sanctification and justification. By linking these discussions, I demonstrate one way that the insights of feminist theory have systematic implications for theology. My decision to link reflections on sin to sanctification and justification is not common in contemporary feminist theology.[1] For the most part, feminists link sin systematically to the doctrine of creation and the *imago dei*. They describe sinful humanity principally in terms of its lost "original integrity" or "original harmony." Such discussions of sin also reflect extensively on theodicy, focusing on the relationship between our responsibility for sin and the larger reality of evil in the world. While this creation-centered approach is legitimate, the systematic issues and images that surface within it differ significantly from those in this chapter: approaching sin from the perspective of justification and sanctification means seeing sin from the eschatological perspective of the woman who knows herself as sanctified and justified in faith, both now and in the promise of things to come.

If doctrines are imaginative landscapes that persons inhabit and wherein identities are formed as beliefs, attitudes, emotions, and actions take shape, approaching sin as a theological doctrine means that, as in chapter 2, I ask the question, What kind of person is shaped in its space? Answering this question means asking, from a feminist perspective: How does sin-talk construct *her* subjectivity? Who does this doctrine call *her* to become? What kinds of action might it dispose *her* to take? Related to these questions are doctrinal ones concerning larger social structures, such as: What kind of community might emerge from a particular view of sin? What kind of social relations and institutions might sin-talk produce? Even more specific: What economy of gender relations might be established in the context of the doctrine of sin? Although it is an exercise in imaginative speculation, making judgments about how doctrines craft persons and institutions is necessary if one is concerned, as a feminist of faith, about the power of Christian doctrines to both tear down and build up. This is especially so with notions of sin.

Because of this, feminist theological reflections on sin have to negotiate a difficult tension. On the one hand, feminist theories of oppression make one highly sensitive to the ways sin-talk has been used historically against women. The cultural mechanisms that drive oppressions, such as marginalization, violence, and cultural imperialism, require that social groups be cast in the role of the despised or defiled Other. Anyone familiar with current North American culture recognizes the role that sin-talk continues to play in rhetorics of otherness.[2] This history accounts in large part for the strongly negative reaction that secular feminist theorists often have to the notion of sin; for many, it represents the most damaging legacy of Christianity. This antipathy between feminism and sin-talk makes a constructive feminist rereading of sin more difficult and potentially volatile than rereading such less culturally salient ideas as justification and sanctification.

On the other hand, this antipathy is balanced by the fact that no single topic in Christian theology has more resonance with feminist theory than the much disdained topic of sin. As I mentioned in the introduction, feminist theory is based on the belief that oppression of women is profoundly *wrong*, that the world is not as it should be, and that the brokenness we experience cuts deep into our social fabric and has done so for a long time.[3] This recognition of the pervasive, insidious, and historically persistent forces of destruction at work in the world sits at the heart of the feminist movement. Additionally, feminists contend that women are not only victims of these destructive forces but perpetrators as well. Feminists also assert that these forces of destruction are structural and hence larger than individual intentions or actions, and yet they still insist that individuals be held responsible for harms done and goods left undone, for oppressive forces unleashed and then left unchallenged. In other words, when analyzing forces of women's oppression, both persons and structures must be held culpable.

Anyone familiar with the history of Christian theology hears in these assertions echoes of theological voices like Jeremiah's. In such descriptions of sin, we encounter a faith that proclaims that the world is not as it should be, that we have forsaken living water and built cisterns that are cracked and dry, and that these cracks run deep into the core of our society and have long done so. At the heart of the Christian story lies this insistence that human sin is pervasive in scope, debilitating in force, and stubbornly persistent. One also hears in feminism strong echoes of the Christian claim that sin takes on historical momentum larger and more powerful than any single human will, and yet it is the individual who must finally be held accountable for the destruction wrought by these forces. The tradition further asserts that the term "sin" not only describes the harms we do but the harms done to us. In sin-talk, perpetrators and victims as well as historical forces and individual wills are included in the picture of our brokenness. The similarities between feminist theory and theology are once again easy to identify.

A Reformation Map of Sin

Let me begin remapping the doctrine of sin by moving out of the Tuesday-night gathering and into that seemingly quite distant theological world of John Calvin's sixteenth-century text *Institutes of the Christian Religion.*[4] I take us into this world to survey a few key concepts that constitute a traditional theological account of sin before I turn to the task of feminist reconstruction.[5] This shift will be a bit disorienting because Calvin's language and imagery are quite different from those of contemporary North America. Moving into this landscape, however, allows us to get our bearings on classical Reformed themes in the doctrine of sin before we undertake the task of using feminist theories of oppression to reconceive this doctrine from a liberationist perspective.

Calvin begins his account of sin by asking a question that never occurred to the women in the Tuesday-night group: How do we come to know ourselves as sinners? The question never arose for us because, as Christians, we take for granted that we are sinners; this is part of the faith landscape we occupy. While we might not be certain *what* this means, *that* we are sinners is never doubted. Such doubts would arise, however, were I to talk about my fellow feminist theorists gathered for a Women and Gender Studies Council meeting as sinners. Not only would I get strange looks, but I would be queried: Serene, why do you describe us that way? What is the source of this peculiar claim? In struggling to answer, I would no doubt become acutely aware of what a distinctly Christian concept "sin" is. In asking, How do we know we are sinners? Calvin pushes precisely this point. He asks us to remember what a strange concept it is and to situate our knowledge of it.

In responding to this question, Calvin sets the course for the remainder of his discussion, one that I will later argue is a useful course for feminist theology to follow. He answers, in short, that we only know ourselves to be fallen when we recognize in faith the "noble gifts with which we were originally endowed"—gifts lost in the Fall but offered again to us "in Christ."[6] We can see ourselves "in sin" only if we measure our condition against a vision of how God calls us to live "in Christ." The doctrine of sin, therefore, depends on a prior doctrine of grace: fallen humanity comes into view only when redeemed humanity is displayed in its full splendor. In the colloquial language of Calvinism, only the cure can reveal the disease and only in the mirror of Christ's glory can we see the spots on our face. Knowledge of sin lies in knowledge of humanity apart from sin, a knowledge that is given in faith alone.

Several significant consequences follow from this. First, "sin" is identified as a theological concept: it makes sense only within a theological framework where God's positive purposes for humanity are a normative model for what sin deforms. "Sin" is therefore not an all-purpose word describing everything "bad" or "wrong" as measured by our own personal standards or general social codes. To use the term "sin" properly, one must have a theological measure—grounded in scripture and authenticated by the Spirit—that tells us what goes against God's will for humanity.

Second, sin is a distinctly dogmatic concept: one can know the divine purposes that measure sin only if one has been blessed with the gift of true piety. According to Calvin, the Fall has wiped out humanity's capacity for general knowledge of God.[7] Left to our own devices (our natural knowledge), we are unable to know God, much less know ourselves as creatures who have fallen away from God's will. To use Calvin's image, in the Fall we have been "blinded by sin" and thus to our own condition as sinners. The epistemic hold of sin on us is complete; we can see the wretchedness of our situation only if God reveals it to us by opening our eyes in faith.

A third consequence follows from Calvin's decision to make knowledge of sin a function of faith. By virtue of the faith through which we see, we should know that our wretchedness is already overcome in Christ. As a grace-dependent concept, sin can never be understood apart from a simultaneous affirmation of the promised grace that contradicts it. This means the horror of sin in the world and "on our faces" should not lead us to despair but to thanksgiving: in faith, we know God holds out the balm that heals, a balm that is cause for great rejoicing. Calvin hereby rejects any view of sin that debilitates and breaks us without returning us to God. The absence of grace reveals such views of sin to be lies.

This brings me to a fourth point concerning sin: its *rhetorical function*. Because knowledge of sin is grace-dependent, Calvin believed that all sin-talk should have the practical aim of nurturing our awareness of God's grace. Knowledge of sin should teach us how to strengthen our faith; it should instruct us in love of God, prompting us to seek God with greater zeal. In this regard, sin-talk is a tool of faith's pedagogy.

Having looked at Calvin's epistemological comments on sin, let us now turn to the substance of his acount of the Fall. Calvin has a multifaceted vision of "redeemed humanity," which serves as the contrasting measure of our "fallen humanity." He borrows scriptural and doctrinal images that, at times, hearken back to humanity "before the Fall," recalling an "original righteousness" in which humanity lived according to an "original justice." At other times, christological images depict Jesus Christ not only as the means of our redemption but also as the model of perfected humanity. At still other times, more general phrases drawn from the prophets and the psalmists speak of humanity as loved, forgiven, and embraced, as "obedient to God's purposes for our lives," and as adorned in the "fullness of glory" and the "splendor of righteousness and justice."

These varied images of redemption coalesce for Calvin in a key concept: faithfulness (*fidelitas*) or piety (*pietas*)—when we are faithful, we put on Christ, and in his redemption, we are restored to our original righteousness.[8] Faithfulness is formally defined as "a firm and certain knowledge of God's benevolence towards us, founded upon the truth of the freely given promise in Christ, both revealed to our minds and sealed upon our hearts through the Holy Spirit."[9] In my previous discussion of the Christian life, I laid out Calvin's understanding of the two principal parts of this faith: sanctification and justification. Revealing our sin is thus the vision of the faithful person who, as sanctified, is clothed in the glory of God, and who, as justified, is forgiven, set free, and promised life eternal. In both ways, this image of faithfulness describes a humanity living according to God's purposes by accepting God's grace. It thus describes a humanity marked by gratitude and freedom— graced humanity.[10] As noted earlier, the vision thus entails both individual faithfulness and broader, social faithfulness, a collective state of righteousness and glory in which the gifts of God flourish and bear fruit in community.

Against the backdrop of this image of a "graced" humanity that flourishes in the lavish gifts of faith, sin is defined as the opposite of faithfulness, as "unfaithfulness" or "disbelief."[11] To illustrate unfaithfulness, Calvin uses images of a humanity bereft of the gifts of true piety. In sin, we "shake off reverence," "spurn God's great bounty lavished upon us," and are thus "stripped of the spiritual gifts (of faith)." In this fallen state, our "worship is not perfect" and "God's majesty does not dwell among us."[12] Compared with the fullness of graced existence, unfaithfulness is "to be laid bare," "to be without adornment," to be "empty" of grace. In the words of Jeremiah 2:13, sinful humanity is "a cracked, dry cistern that can hold no water." Although many natural gifts—such as reason, common morality, and a sense of beauty—remain once these spiritual gifts are forfeited, even these natural gifts are severely damaged by the loss of the gift of faith.

According to Calvin, whole hosts of actions, attitudes, and dispositions display in varying ways the depths to which we have fallen. Referred to as the "fruits of sin," they range from concrete actions (such as theft, murder, and "carousing") to more dispositional states (such as selfishness, concupiscence, envy, and ill will). Calvin's lengthy list of the fruits of sin also covers attitudes that pertain to the worship of God, such as idolatry and ungratefulness, and actions directed against one's neighbor, such as lying and adultery. Calvin defends the breadth and imprecision of his discussion here by explaining that sin is not a stable or static state but more a furnace burning with ever new flames or a spring unceasingly bubbling up from the earth.[13] Sin is always changing, assuming ever-new forms and traveling into ever new terrain of human experience. In our day-to-day activities, sin takes shapes particular to each individual and each community. Sin therefore never wears a universal face but instead takes contextual form as it travels. As such, "sin is peculiar to each" and, because of its many guises, cannot be analyzed exhaustively.

In describing sin's many fruits, however, Calvin himself singles out one particular form of sin—the sin of pride—which captures for him an important dimension of humanity's unfaithfulness. Following Augustine's lead in this matter, he characterizes pride as a willful act of disobedience in which human beings turn away from God and "into the self" (*in curvetus su*). By "curving into the self," human beings replace love of God with an idolatrous love of their own power; "puffed up with ambition," they greedily seek the pleasures of this world.[14] In doing so, they become vain and arrogant, and they spawn injustice.

Original Sin

Having given a broad definition of sin as "unfaithfulness," Calvin then turns to another well-known topic in traditional theological discussions of the Fall: original sin. His treatment of original sin addresses three questions about the nature of humanity's unfaithfulness. First, how is sin "passed on" from generation to generation? Second, how extensive is our unfaithfulness? How pervasive is sin's scope? And third, who is responsible for it? Who bears the guilt for rupturing our positive relationship with God by spurning God's grace?

In his concise definition of original sin, all three questions are answered. Original sin, he states, is "an hereditary depravity and corruption of our nature, diffused into all parts of the soul, which first makes us liable to God's wrath, then also brings forth in us works of the flesh."[15] To the first question, he answers that sin is "inherited"—it is passed on to us at birth. To the second, he answers that the scope of sin is vast—it moves into "all parts of the soul." We are, to use Calvin's well-known phrase, "totally depraved." To the third question, concerning responsibility for the Fall, he responds that although we cannot choose *not* to sin, we alone are liable for this breech and its consequences. Echoing once again the words of Jeremiah where he tells us that the cracks in our dry cisterns run deep, Calvin affirms that our corruption is total, and that we alone are responsible for it—the guilt is all ours.

Let us look more closely at each of Calvin's responses, beginning with his answer to the question, How is sin passed on? Calvin rejects two well-known descriptions of how we "inherit" sin. First, we are not, as Augustine thought, born into sin by virtue of a genetic or biological defect that our parents pass on to us in a lineage traced back to Adam. Calvin rejects this model for two reasons. First, it implies there is something inherently corrupt about the human body, and this implication, he argues, denigrates the goodness of humanity's original integrity before the Fall. Second, he argues that, by placing the blame for the Fall in biology or genetics, Augustine excuses human beings in each new generation from taking active, intentional responsibility for the original sin they inherit. The second model of inheritance he rejects is that of Pelagius, who argued that we inherit sin as each new generation decides, by force of will, to "imitate" the disobedience of Adam. This model suggests that certain human beings could choose to not imitate Adam's fall and thus escape the taint of original sin. When this possibility is left open, he explains, we turn sin into an imitative option and thereby eclipse the original aspect of its character.

As a counter to these two models, Calvin suggests that sin is "imputed" to us. Recall that, for Calvin, "imputation" is a process whereby an individual "is given a verdict alien to him or her" and thereby wears a judgment that is not his or hers by nature but by divine decision. In justification, this involves faithful persons putting on or being clothed in Christ's righteousness, which is theirs by grace alone. What does it mean to impute sin? While it is difficult to decipher, Calvin seems to suggest that the sin human beings "inherit" is not theirs "by nature" (hence, his rejection of the genetic metaphor); it is something they wear by virtue of a judgment or decision. Because human beings and not God are responsible for the Fall, the judgment in this case originates within the mystery of humanity's freedom—sin is an imputed judgment that *we* are responsible for imposing upon our otherwise good natures. We impute it to ourselves. Further, it is a judgment we cannot escape, for each passing generation imposes this judgment upon the next and each new generation willingly but inescapably puts it on. Alien righteousness, which the faithful wear by virtue of a divine decision, is hereby contrasted with alien sin, which all humanity wears by virtue of its self-imputed decision to be unfaithful to God. *Simul iustus et peccator* is therefore a statement about the two imputed identities that humanity wears. "Imputed" sin thus allows Calvin to say that sin is "inborn" but not "inherent," and "inescapable" but not "irredeemable."

Calvin uses two additional sets of metaphors to answer the questions of sin's scope and responsibility. With respect to sin's scope, organic and structural images of decay and contagion portray the pervasive and ever-spreading reach of humanity's wretchedness and hence total depravity. In response to the question of blame or fault, he turns to jurisprudence and uses the forensic language of judgment and guilt to announce our culpability before God and the willful nature of our unbelief. Using these two sets of images, he divides the discussion of original sin along the same lines as his discussion of sanctification's organic character and justification's juridical form. This is, of course, no accident: recall that descriptions of fallen humanity find their opposites in respective descriptions of humanity redeemed by faith. Of what does faith consist, if not the gifts of sanctification and justification? If so, then what is sin, if not the opposite of these gifts—decay instead of growth, unrelenting guilt instead of forgiveness? Let us explore these two sets of images further.

The scathing and often disturbing language Calvin uses to describe his notion of humanity's "total depravity" and "corruption" remains vivid in our imaginations even today. Here we meet the Calvin who finds in the human condition nothing but "shivering nakedness," "putrid decay," "filth," and "incurable disease."[16] While evoking haunting images from our own day, these words present a clear picture of humanity's dire need for God. Because discussions of sin should move us to God, presenting our "dire need" was for Calvin a task of salvific proportions.

Calvin depicts the scope of this dire need at two different levels. First, by claiming that humanity is "totally depraved," Calvin drives home that no part of our bodies, intellect, or soul is untouched by sin; there is no pure essence within our being that escapes the need for grace—sin goes "all the way down," and not even our reason can save us. The reach of grace into our lives is therefore just as total.[17] No part of us is untouched by its healing force. Second, by asserting that sin has spread through Adam to all generations, Calvin claims no one eludes its taint. For Calvin, as for Luther, sin includes not only the obvious sinners but also the pious saints. All of us stand in urgent need of God's grace, and hence the scope of grace is just as far reaching.

The significance of Calvin's use of organic metaphors to portray the pervasive reach of sin becomes apparent when we recall what happens to sinners sanctified by grace. In sanctifying grace, one's life receives new form as one is *con*formed to God's will; one is placed within the structure of the law and the gospel, and this structure gives one's life shape, edge, and definition. Calvin describes this reconstruction as both an organic process where healing occurs and a journey where new life unfolds and is nurtured. Against these images of reconstruction, healing, and journey, Calvin's description of total depravity becomes more striking. The opposite of sanctifying grace, depravity and corruption are processes that "undo" humanity, robbing it of its true form by removing it from the structures of law and gospel that give it definition. In this way, sin destroys the borders of grace that delineate the character of faithful personhood and community.

Calvin uses many different metaphors to describe this organic process through which the structures defining humanity in its positive form are destroyed by sin. The term that best captures the process is "despoilment."[18] "Despoil" derives from the Latin *despoliare,* which means both "to undo" and "to plunder or ravage." Undoing is most aptly depicted by the image of stripping away the sheath that holds a thing together. To despoil is to remove the skin that maintains the internal integrity of a being, the skin without which the being falls apart as its insides spill out. When such stripping occurs, no part of the now despoiled being remains unaffected. The scope of despoilment's damage is therefore total. With the loss of skin, the borders that distinguish outside from inside disappear, and disorder and death soon follow. The notion of "plunder" bespeaks the violence of this undoing. According to the Latin, despoilment consists not of a gentle dissolving but of a brutal ravaging. Undoing forcibly violates the integrity of an entity by taking away all that defines it, offers it structure, and maintains its internal coherence.

To illustrate this disintegration as a state of sin, Calvin uses three powerful images: humanity stripped of clothes, humanity polluted, and humanity plagued by contagion. Building on the notion of losing one's skin, Calvin describes humanity in terms of the clothes it wears first in Christ and then in sin: "In place of the wisdom, virtue, holiness, truth and justice, with which adornments he had been clad, there came forth [from humanity] the most filthy plagues, blindness, impotence, impurity, vanity and injustice."[19] In similar terms, he depicts sinners as naked, and in their nakedness, destitute, with nothing to cover or protect them.[20] He also returns repeatedly to images of defilement. He favors the image of pollution to describe the process wherein that which is pure and clean is stained by that which is impure and dirty—again, an image of transgression of the boundaries or skin that define original integrity and purity.[21]

In the case of disease, the organic depiction of contagion is even stronger. As Calvin states, "All of us . . . are born infected with the contagion of sin. In fact, before we saw the light of this life, we were soiled and spotted in God's sight."[22] This metaphor of a spreading contagion captures for Calvin something that the defilement and clothing images lack. It conveys his relational understanding of sin as a corruption that circulates among people, touching one who touches another until no one remains untouched. In Calvin's day, this would have been a powerful image as his readers recalled the devastating plagues that had swept through Europe only decades earlier, which spread through the daily commerce of human life, touching all, for everyone was susceptible, regardless of faith or righteousness of action. In the grip of a disease that had no regard for social status, intellect, or will, simply to be born human was to be born vulnerable. So it was for Calvin with sin, although in the case of sin the diagnosis was even worse: chance protects no one; everyone falls ill.

The despoilment of humanity by sin makes an additional point about Calvin's understanding of total depravity. For Calvin, despite the ravaging of humanity by sin, the natural gifts with which God endowed humanity remain, gifts such as reason, will, emotion, and moral sense. They remain, however, in a corrupted condition; once stripped of the spiritual gifts that orient us to God in faith, disorder goes "all the way down."[23] To make this point, Reformers compare sin to a drop of green ink in water: while not ceasing to be water, no part of the water remains untouched by the ink.

Despoilment imparts a similar idea but with more emphasis on the violence and disorder of sin. Just as water does not cease to be water when ink is added, losing skin does not make one's entrails disappear; they remain what they are, although without integrity or function. Likewise, one is still embodied without clothes, but in a cold Genevan winter, the body must find warmth to function. Similarly, wearing the clothes of royalty, one moves through the world differently than one would in the rags of the poor. In sickness, one does not stop being the person one was before the illness struck, although one may well feel the illness in all parts of one's being.[24] These varied images suggest that while sin may be total (it goes all the way down, and no one escapes it), human life is never totally sin. Sin touches all of who we are, but it is not everything we are.

Having described the "total" hold that sin has upon us (its all-encompassing despoilment), Calvin shifts to a discussion of the role that human agency plays in this despoiling process. For the topic of agency, however, he finds the organic imagery of despoilment ill suited and turns instead to juridical imagery. This switch signals a marked shift in Calvin's view of sinful humanity. He now looks at human persons not primarily as organisms but as actors whose intentions and deeds incur God's judgment and wrath. To do so, he uses images designed to calibrate the character of willful human action in terms of guilt or innocence. With this shift from the organic to the juridical, his discussion moves from humanity as the *site* of sin to a discussion of humanity as the *agent* of sin—humanity is now assessed not as a "place" that sin attacks but as an agent that "enacts" sin.

Calvin addresses the topic of human agency under the rubrics of "freedom of the will"—from an unusual angle.[25] Instead of beginning with a straightforward answer to the question of who is responsible for the Fall, Calvin recalls the rhetorical function of sin-talk. He reminds us that the preeminent function of the doctrine of sin is to impress upon us our dire need for God's grace and in doing so cause us to sing more gratefully God's praises for having bestowed such grace upon us. A similar challenge of rhetoric arises in the case of free will—it must serve to increase our faith, which presents an interesting challenge. If human beings have too much free will in choosing to sin, we might overestimate our abilities to choose God and underappreciate the unmerited gifts of God's grace. If, however, human corruption affords us absolutely *no* ability to pursue righteousness, then we might become overly complacent, perhaps even despairing about our sinful condition. In order to increase our piety, Calvin thus tries to steer his discussion of free will to avoid these twin perils of "brazen overconfidence" and "miserable passivity."[26]

Calvin therefore develops a doctrine of free will with two distinct rhetorical parts. To counter the tendency toward overconfidence, he offers the Reformation doctrine of "the bondage of the will." To address the problem of complacency and to stir the faithful to action, he offers an account of humanity's singular responsibility and "guilt" for sin and, hence, our responsibility to resist it. Rather than reconciling the seeming contradictions between the two claims—that we have no free will with regard to the Fall and that we sin willingly—Calvin simply allows them to stand as a paradox worthy of a faith that respects the hidden mysteries of God's will.[27]

Let us look briefly at how he develops these two themes, "bondage of the will" and "guilt." "Bondage of the will" receives far more attention than guilt, which suggests that for Calvin the threat of brazen over-confidence (a correlate of the sin of pride he discusses extensively in his definition of sin) looms larger than the threat of complacency or despair. Explaining how we are "deprived of freedom of choice and bound over to miserable servitude,"[28] he draws heavily on the work of both Luther and Augustine. In the Fall, our natural gifts of reason and will are so damaged that we are incapable of choosing not to sin. Our reason is so blinded by unfaith that it can no longer know God or see how to follow the rule of God's love. Its power to distinguish good and evil with regard to the divine will has been extinguished, although in mundane matters it may continue to function quite well.[29] Similarly, through the Fall, our will has lost its capacity to desire God and to choose to follow God. It has been "bound by wicked desires so that it cannot choose right," although again in the world of mundane concerns it may continue to exercise its natural powers.[30]

What happens to humanity when both our reason and will are so severely disabled? We find ourselves caught in a prison of sin. Using the imagery of punishment and imprisonment, Calvin depicts humanity as convicted of the crime of unfaithfulness and handed over to the jail of "wretchedness," from which there is no escape. He makes the same point with imagery of the bondage of slavery. Sin "owns" us, and we are thus "enslaved to it" by miserable necessity. In contradistinction to "despoilment," these images of bondage suggest that sin creates boundaries that confine and constrict our natural flourishing. As images of being "closed in" suggest, Calvin emphasizes that we have no free will when choosing to sin and, even more strongly, that once bound over to sin, there is no escape. No exertion of will or flash of reason can release us. Incapable of knowing God and unable to desire the gifts of faith, we cannot extricate ourselves from the Fall. God alone holds the key to our cell, and only God offers us freedom in faith. Such a promise comes as good news to the ears of the arrogant once their overactive senses of agency have been humbled by this depiction of utter servitude to sin.[31]

Alongside these images of imprisonment is a second set emphasizing our complete responsibility for the sin we do. Continuing with juridical metaphors, Calvin describes our guilt in several ways. First, "guilty" is God's verdict passed upon us in response to our unfaithfulness; it is not an inherent, internal state of feeling guilty or ashamed (although that may well be what we experience when, in faith, we recognize God's pronouncement on our sin). "Guilty" thus refers to our status before God. Second, despite our lack of free will, we have earned this judgment of "guilty" because even in our imprisoned state we continually choose to sin; we do so voluntarily, not because of some external compulsion. We also deserve the verdict "guilty" because our sinning is not just the result of our inability to do good, our lack of a will to be faithful, or our passivity in the face of God's call to righteousness. We are intentionally active in our sin—it has power and energy and is hence ever productive.[32] In this way, Calvin argues that although sin may corrupt the will, it does not finally destroy it; in sinning, we keep willing our disbelief and its fruits as we walk down a path of destruction from which we cannot turn.

Finally, Calvin uses this juridical scenario to stress that, because we have been found guilty of sinning actively and voluntarily against God, we deserve to be punished. We stand justly accused and the judgment of God's wrath rightly awaits us. However, Calvin also reminds us that with the eyes of faith, which allow us to see the extent of our guilt, we can see as well God's mercy instead of wrath, life instead of death. Calvin's whole discussion of guilt is rhetorically designed to encourage those who feel complacent or despairing about the bondage of the will. They are forgiven. Calvin's discourse of guilt, therefore, is crafted to enable rather than diminish human agency.

Let us now briefly review Calvin's account as a whole to get a sense for its sweep and flow. Defining sin as unfaithfulness, Calvin pictures humanity's wretchedness in images of bereavement. To be unfaithful is to be bereft of the benefits of faith; it is to be without both the sanctifying structure of God's love and the ever renewing forgiveness of justification. In this state of radical loss, humanity produces multiple fruits of sin, which constantly travel and change as the conditions of our individual and collective lives shift historically. To understand the complexity of our life bereft of God's good gifts, Calvin uses two families of metaphors. First, he depicts humanity as an organism whose original integrity is despoiled by sin. Despoilment consists of a loss of skin or, to use the language of sanctification, the loss of the enveloping grace that holds us together and gives our lives direction and purpose. The self deteriorates in the absence of its constitutive boundaries, and society is plundered of the justice that gives it integrity. Despoilment also spreads among us as a collective process of corruption into which we are born. Although some of our natural gifts remain, corruption is total. We cannot escape it, because it touches us all, and in each of us, it brings a thorough breakdown of our original integrity.

Calvin also depicts humanity's condition according to juridical metaphors that highlight the role that free will plays in original sin. First, our agency must be tempered by an assertion of our miserable servitude to the sin that binds us. Second, we must take responsibility for the sin we commit by becoming aware of God's righteousness. Thus, on the one hand, Calvin highlights the fact that our will alone cannot extricate us from sin, while on the other hand, he affirms the continued work of the will by focusing on our culpability as sinners before God. Having affirmed humanity's total depravity, denied our free will, and convicted us of sin, Calvin reminds us once again that the purpose of sin-talk is to edify. Does he accomplish this task? To find an answer to this question in our present-day context, let us begin the process of remapping sin from a feminist perspective.

A Feminist Remapping of Sin

Having wandered through the landscape of a sixteenth-century view of sin, we now step back into the more familiar world of the Tuesday-night group. Vestiges of the older Reformation language about sin remain here, but dramatically different issues regarding women and their oppression set the scene. This return from the past to a modern context might be disorienting, since the two contexts seem so dissimilar. But as the Tuesday-night women discovered in our Lenten study, there are notable points of shared insight. The women's group, of course, also uncovered issues the Reformers never imagined. To explore them, we needed new cartographical lines within the doctrine of sin. As with the remapping of sanctification and justification, we asked: What does it mean for women to occupy the space of this doctrine? How might this doctrine shape their becoming? Answering these questions required revisiting, with a new map, a number of old sites and familiar scenes in the traditional landscape of sin.

Let me begin where Calvin did, with the question, How do we know sin? From a feminist theological perspective, the question might be more pertinently put: How do we come to call women's oppression "sin"? Or, Why does a feminist theorist see "oppression" where a feminist of faith sees "sin"? The short answer is that the two are viewing the world through different "lived imaginative constructs"—different interpretive lenses. A more expansive answer unfolds, however, if we look at the distinctive features of the latter lens of faith.

To better understand how this lens works from a feminist theological perspective, look at several features of the Tuesday-night group's way of "seeing." Central to this way is the faith claim seldom articulated but nonetheless present in every theological affirmation made: God wills the flourishing of all persons, including women. This theological affirmation of God's will and divine purpose opens, as I have said, into an eschatological vision of women's flourishing—an already/not-yet vision of the world, in which women no longer suffer oppression but enjoy the full benefits of just community. Although implicit in the Tuesday-night group's discussions, this vision—drawn from scripture, the tradition, and our own faith experiences—functions as the model of "redeemed humanity." It is the measure by which we judge our brokenness as "sin." Ours is a distinct knowledge-in-faith that shows sin first and foremost to be living against God. For us, then, women's oppression is no longer simply a social phenomenon (as feminist theorists see it) but that which defies the will of God.

Several features of this faith-knowing are worthy of note and echo themes raised by Calvin. The women in my church often have difficulties naming their experiences of sin because this theological vision of flourishing easily slips away. A vision of a time when women's lives and all creation unfold according to God's good purposes is hard to hold onto because it is not supported by the everyday world. It often drifts before us like a distant dream, one we must strain hard to see, given the powerfully destructive ways in which oppression structures our thinking and makes even the most profound forms of brokenness seem normal. For example, the incest survivor in our group sometimes finds it impossible to imagine her body as a site of graced light, space, and joy—the damage of sexual abuse has cut deep into her psyche. The Caribbean woman's imaginative power cannot stretch to see her without muscles tensed each day to repel racism. She can name her oppression, but to call it "sin" and tie it to a vision of God's redemption is a different matter. For the woman on strike, envisioning an empowering work environment seems equally far-fetched. "Such environments don't exist anywhere," she sometimes tells us. For the lesbian, walking down the street with her arm around her partner and receiving friendly glances from passersby seems a similar fantasy. For many of us, it is sometimes easier to pretend our brokenness does not exist, to say that we exaggerate our suffering and everything is really "just fine." In this regard, oppression works like a blinder preventing us from seeing that our "cisterns are cracked" and our lives dry. Or, stated in a slightly different way: caught in sin, we cannot see it. Its hold is total.[33]

The Tuesday-night women recognize that, given sin's hold upon us and our consequent inability to see, the theological vision of redeemed humanity has to come from outside the frame of what the world teaches us to expect about what women should be and do. As Christians, it comes to us as a gift of faith. As God's gift, it is a vision that has the power to transform our knowledge of harms and injustices into a knowledge of sin. This gifted knowing is a feminist version of the dogmatic/theological knowledge of sin discussed earlier. Related to this knowing is another distinctive feature: the inherent hopefulness of feminist knowledge of sin. Anyone who knows the many faces of women's oppression knows well the feelings of despair and hopelessness that set in as one realizes the pervasiveness and seeming intransigence of the structures that harm women. It is difficult not to be overwhelmed by oppression's magnitude and not to feel as if all one can do is stand helplessly in its shadow. For the woman who views these oppressions as sin, however, the grip of despair does not linger long; in faith, she affirms the reality of redemption, the future of women's flourishing. In this way, when feminists of faith speak of oppression as "sin," they shift its meaning by invoking a powerful sense of hope. When one sees women's brokenness as sin, one is already proclaiming that all is not lost, that the eventual flourishing of women will come as God promises.[34]

When will it come? The Tuesday-night group continually returns to the notion of the "already/not-yet" of women's liberation. They simultaneously affirm a present-day experience of transformation and a future horizon of flourishing. This makes clear the anticipatory optimism of sin-talk in feminist perspective. This anticipatory optimism covers the exhaustion and burnout that constantly threatens feminist movements. It also challenges women's despair about their lives and the possibility of change. The incest survivor in our group was taught growing up that she was so dirty, bad, and "sin-filled" that nothing could save her. In the context of abuse, to know oneself as sinful meant losing one's voice, retreating into silence and seeing oneself as deserving only punishment from God. The secretary on strike explained how her former belief in sin's pervasiveness made her suspicious of collective organizing. She saw such actions as naively utopian, because, for her, to know the depth of sin was to know all such actions were futile. In both cases, sin-talk occasioned hopelessness and despair. From the perspective of a hopeful feminist doctrine of sin, such positions are lies betraying an absence of grace and hope.

The final feature of feminist knowledge of sin is its rhetorical character. As Calvin knew, the purpose of sin-talk is to edify the faithful, to be a tool of piety's pedagogy. Knowledge of sin should strengthen the faithful by kindling in them a desire to seek God and live according to God's purposes. This rhetorical aim obliges careful consideration of the audience to whom one preaches sin. When remapped in a feminist context, Calvin's insight means we need a doctrine of sin that kindles the faith of an audience of women. We need to ask then: How would a given view of sin affect a particular community of women? Would it encourage them to more fully embrace God's good purposes for women's lives? How might sin-talk be crafted to lead women back to grace? To analyze sin-talk in these terms is to ask, as I have repeatedly: How might woman occupy the space of doctrine in a manner that promotes her liberation and challenges her oppression? In this case, how might a feminist theology of sin be a tool of faith's pedagogy?

Since Valerie Saiving's groundbreaking work on women's experience in theology in the early sixties, feminist studies of sin have made rhetoric their starting point.[35] Their analysis begins with the varied forms of brokenness that women experience by asking the question, When women are considered the audience of sin-talk, what do they need to hear? They then craft models of sin that respond directly to those harms. These models include naming sin as "triviality," "hiding," and "self-loss" as well as "violence" and "abuse of the vulnerable."[36] Along with naming these descriptions, feminists criticize traditional models of sin that assume an audience of men socialized to value autonomy and having social power. When this is the type of audience, feminists argue, the traditional doctrine of sin is structured to counter aspects of male socialization by curbing arrogance, tempering pride, and teaching humility. Such lessons, they point out, are not obviously applicable to women (or to certain men) who have little social power and suffer not from an abundance but a lack of self-esteem.[37]

In light of these criticisms, it has been clear to many feminists that Calvin's map of sin needs significant revision. Calvin's focus on pride is too limited. Similarly, his extended orations to the overconfident on the "bondage of the will" need to be tempered when speaking to persons whose sense of agency is far from brazen. Calvin's diatribes against the "miserable passivity" of persons who harm others and then refuse responsibility also needs reconfiguring when spoken to an audience of women struggling to name the ways they have been harmed. His defilement imagery for describing total depravity also needs refashioning. Such images can be damaging to women struggling against cultural stereotypes that exploit and shame the female body. Finally, on Calvin's map of sin, it is difficult to identify the role that social structures play in perpetrating the harms of sin—a role feminist theory has taught us to take quite seriously in understanding the complex ways women are oppressed and oppress.

To see how these reconfigurings might be done, let us take the first step of remapping sin: let us redefine "sin." How might feminist theories of oppression help us do this in a manner that takes into account the complexities of women's lives? How might we describe sin so that it speaks to stories of brokenness shared by the Tuesday-night group over the years? How can we include in our account incest, addiction, unemployment, racism, workplace powerlessness, and social marginalization?"

One answer our Tuesday night-group gave to this last question was to expand the Reformation map of sins to name women's oppression explicitly—adding incest and gender exploitation, for example, to adultery, thievery, and lying. The advantage of this approach is that it leaves the basic structure of Reformed sin-talk in place while making women's lives present within it. Several group members thought, however, this additive approach to sin was insufficient; deeper changes were needed in the rhetoric of sin-talk as a whole. They suggested that rather than adjusting the list of sins, we should dramatically rethink such pivotal concepts as "original sin," "total depravity," and "guilt."

Several members of the group thought we should avoid a definition of sin altogether. Given the diversity of women's lives and oppressions, it seemed reductive to search for a single metaphor, an umbrella image to cover them all. To embrace our differences, shouldn't we let our understanding of sin travel—as definitions of oppression travel—unencumbered by a root metaphor across varied women's lives? If sin-talk traveled, they argued, it might be more rhetorically sensitive to the varied situations of its many audiences. The women agreed, nonetheless, that we needed a definition or root metaphor for sin to hold these differences loosely together. The reasons were practical (strategic). Echoing the concerns of eschatological essentialism, the women desired a strong, normative definition of sin they could "live into," a metaphor that could bring coherence to the diffuse stories of their oppressions, a coherence finding its unity in the claim that, as sin, such oppressions contradict the will of God.

In light of this, we tried on different root metaphors and finally settled on a version of the traditional term used by Calvin—"unfaithfulness."[38] Unlike many of the root metaphors used in the Christian tradition (terms such as "pride," "violence," "falsehood," and "disobedience"), "unfaithfulness" seemed sufficiently open to admit our diversity while providing a normative definition. It could also be easily reinterpreted to include our experiences as women. Remapping unfaithfulness in terms of these experiences made the whole structure of sin-talk shift, and notions like "total depravity," "original sin," and "guilt" took on new forms. What emerged, in short, was a new rhetoric of sin-talk.

To explore the full ramifications of unfaithfulness as our root metaphor, we first discussed sin's opposite—faithfulness. How might one define the term "faithfulness" in feminist perspective? In chapter 3, I built on Reformation understandings of faith's benefits—sanctification and justification—to describe the state of faithfulness from a feminist perspective. In sanctification, woman's dispersed and fragmented identity is pulled together and held in the "envelope of God's grace." To be sanctified is to be a coherent self in the space of divine grace. In justification, by a divine decree of forgiveness, woman is pronounced a newly born agent and is called to live in just relation with others. To be justified means to be a self renewed and enabled for continued life in community. When faithfulness is described in terms of these two benefits of grace, we glimpse what the flourishing of women, and living according to divine purposes, might look like—what it might mean, in faith, to be both enveloped in a grace that defines and invited into relation by a grace that forgives.

As I shall argue in chapter 7, not only individuals but also communities are called to enjoy and be shaped by the benefits of grace. For communities, sanctifying grace provides faithful, just boundaries, and justifying grace provides ever merciful openings toward the world. To share in the double grace of justification and sanctification, a community must be a cultural and institutional context where the integrity of women as coherent selves is honored and where just and merciful relations between persons and groups obtain. We glimpsed parts of this communal vision of grace in the previous chapter's account of oppression.

Much more could be said about this communal understanding of faithfulness (a topic to which I return), but for now, how does it show to us, as in a mirror, the contrasting face of women's oppression as "unfaith"? The broadest definition of unfaithfulness is "living contrary to divine purposes, living against God." In the language of feminist theology, it is a way of living in which women do not flourish but instead experience (and participate in) oppressive forces. With Calvin, one can say that unfaith consists of being bereft of the double gifts of faith justification and sanctification. Applied to individuals, this unfaith means living without the adorning glory of sanctifying grace, which gives one's life definition and integrity. It also means being bereft of God's justifying grace of forgiveness, which gives one courage to seek just relations. Playing off my feminist interpretations of sanctification and justification, to live in a state of unfaithfulness is to be a fragmented self who knows neither the promise of agency nor the hope of just relation. Viewed in opposition to the true identity of faithfulness, this state is one of false identity, in which the unbounded self is exhausted by relations of oppression.

We must also consider how communities and institutions can be bereft of the double gifts of grace and hence live in a manner contrary to divine purposes. What is an unfaithful culture? It is one in which the social and institutional forms structuring identity are marked by relations of domination. It is a context in which the integrity of persons and groups is threatened by either the absence of normative structure or the constraints of structures that undergird "false identities" or "unfaithful identities." The "sin" of unfaithfulness not only refers to persons who harm others or to institutional and cultural forms that perpetrate the systemic deformation of identity but also describes the brokenness of persons who suffer such harm and whose identities are deformed by destructive cultural and institutional forms. As victims of sin, they wear its effects on their bodies and in their psyches. "Unfaithfulness," therefore, covers all aspects of oppression; it includes, in different ways, those who are harmed and their perpetrators as well as the material and cultural relations of power that form the nexus within which such harm occurs.

How do we actually "wear the false identities of sin" in day-to-day social interactions? What is a feminist description of sin's fruit? Recall the typology of oppression's "five faces." Each of these faces, one can argue, constitutes one of the "peculiar fruits" of sin in the lives of women, although sin-talk transforms one's understanding of each oppression in ways just discussed.[39] As just two examples, a feminist account of the sin of exploitation allows us to see the fruit of sin in a particular form, in the structure of a capitalist market economy that depends on women's unpaid domestic labor to maximize profits while using women's sexually exploited bodies to sell commodities. A feminist theological perspective, however, sees this reality as "against the will of God" and asserts with vigorous hopefulness that such harm must be resisted and not accepted as simply "the way it is." Similarly, feminist theory also allows us to see cultural imperialism as another fruit of sin, one emerging from a cultural value system that cannot honor difference. This fruit of sin thrives in a society that devalues the caretaking dimensions of "women's work" and vilifies nonnuclear models of child rearing because they cut against the dominant ideology of a gendered division of labor. When viewed as sin, however, this imperialism is also understood to be "against God," and the dynamics of oppressive "othering" are seen as "unfaith" and hence not inevitable.

More practical, these five faces of oppression also uncover sin at a variety of levels in individual women's lives. The woman in our group who works as a university secretary can name as sin's fruit the exploitative pay scale that undervalues her labor; the trivializing chain of command that infantilizes her; the gender roles that require her to work double time as the primary caregiver for her children and elderly mother; and the cultural images of beauty that leave her with low self-esteem because she is middle-aged and full-figured. She can also see the fruits of sin in her own destructive actions provoked by these conditions—her dismissal of workers on the administrative ladder below her, her tendency to denigrate the many unemployed women who stand waiting for her job should she lose it, and her domineering interactions with the children and mother for whom she cares. Finally, the five faces of oppression allow her to see sin's fruit in the voluntary actions of persons who harm her (such as the manager who sexually harassed her) as well as in the involuntary actions of persons who harm her yet are caught in the system (the administrator who values her work and yet found a replacement worker for her when she went on strike). By naming all this "sin," she experiences all these dynamics as unfolding in the hopeful grasp of God's grace.[40]

Thus a feminist doctrine of sin committed to respecting the differences structuring women's lives must allow the notion of sin to travel widely.

Remember too those sins in women's lives that often remain hidden, even to those who experience them, sins masked in denial, in a memory lost, in a scream covered, in a silence born of years of subtle violence. Feminist theory has made us aware of the oppressions that live in silenced, eclipsed, and effaced places we have been trained to ignore. From this awareness, we learn that we need not always look for the fruits of sin in the grand and the dramatic. In the everyday world, sin's face is mundane: it marks conversations with neighbors in our kitchens, our grocery-shopping trips, and the exhausted evening hour spent in front of the television. It resides in our language and marks our most ordinary habits. It marks our rising in the morning to put on the clothes of gendered performance and our going to sleep at night with the haunting feeling that we performed badly. These mundane aspects of sin's fruit are crucial to the complex lives of women, and feminist theory helps us to see them better.

Irigaray's Mirror

Much more could be said. Sin's faces are forever unfinished, for sin travels as fast as cultures, institutions, and persons change. To understand this, it's helpful to rethink, in feminist perspective, the image of "the mirror" in which the person of faith looks and sees sin. In Calvin's theology, the mirror into which the believer looked was a flat, reflecting surface of shiny glass where a double visage appeared: both the face of glory (which at its most perfect is the face of Christ) and the face of sin (which at its most personal is one's own face) covered in spots and distorted by unbelief. In Calvin's mirror, the face of sin (and the face of Christ) was male—his own face, that of a man with social power, a robust sense of voice—a face wearing the spots of pride.

If a woman looks into the mirror of faithfulness, I have said, the face of glory and the face of unfaithfulness take different forms. Let me further suggest that to capture the complexity of sin as it travels across the varied terrain of women's lives, we need to do more than shift the visages; we need to rebuild the mirror itself. We need to refashion the tool we use to see our fallenness so that indeterminacy and multiplicity are part of the reflection. Luce Irigaray's image of the "concave mirror"—an image central to her strategic essentialist vision of women's becoming—is an exciting place to start to rebuild this mirror.[41]

Contrary to Western understandings of identity as a flat, stable, singular reflection, Irigaray imagines seeing women in "speculumed glass," a concave mirror in which multiple reflections form, moving off in an infinite play of angled differences. This peculiarly shaped piece of glass serves as a metaphor for the dazzling differences one discovers looking into the lives of women. It gives not a single image of a stable woman but an infinite display of multiple visages reflecting the diversity of identities that exist both internally to each woman and among women as a whole. Holding before her Irigaray's concave glass, the woman of faith discovers a double visage that breaks into patterns of seemingly infinite multiplicity. One of these reflected faces is the christologically illuminated face of her flourishing, wrapped in the gifts of grace; the other, a visage of her diminishment, bereft of these gifts, caught in systems and relations of oppression. This second face moves off in directions as diverse as the oppression she suffers and perpetrates. To push further, we could imagine that this second "face of sin" is not one face alongside the other but the same face in a cracked mirror; its weblike lines running through her face reflect distortions of sin.

Such a mirror might be held up before not just a single woman but before women in all their complex diversity. When we see the reflections of this speculum in feminist theological perspective, we behold a double image, not of one face but of many, infinite in number, moving in an endless variety of directions. Imagining the glass as uncracked, we see the faces of women flourishing in the context of faithful community, wrapped in the gifts of faith. Viewed in the glass marked with weblike fissures, we see the fruits of sin, the faces of false identity. In the reflections of this broken mirror, we see now dimly and distortedly what we will one day see face to face: the face of glory.

Original Sin

I have offered so far a feminist reinterpretation of how we know sin, the definition of sin as unfaithfulness, and the character of sin's fruits. I can now address another important topic in traditional accounts of sin: the doctrine of *original sin*. What might it mean to remap this part of sin-talk from a feminist theological perspective? How might feminists reconceive this complex set of claims about sin's inheritance? The first step is to note that the hereditary metaphors have often been interpreted in ways harmful to women. In the Tuesday-night group, the woman recovering from sexual abuse describes hearing, as a child, that her sinful body and sexuality tempted "man's lust." This made her think that something was inherently wrong with her body. Sin was "in her." Even as an adult, she sometimes feels incapacitating shame. Although not all shared her experience, most members of the group agreed that original sin-talk taps into cultural codes that teach shame about our bodies.

Women in the group also described, however, occasions where being "born into sin" made compelling feminist sense, particularly in light of feminist theory's claim that we all are born into social structures and cultural constructs, such as gender, that we do not choose but that shape us nonetheless, sometimes in destructive ways. For example, the woman struggling with addiction recognizes that the seeds of her alcoholism were sown in a previous generation of "addicts" in her family—a family she did not "choose" to be born into. The woman fighting to get higher pay and more respect in her secretarial position recognizes that the forces working against her were in place long before she applied for her university job—forces such as a capitalist economy, which has historically devalued women's work to maximize profit, and an elitist university, which has a history of marginalizing the working-class values of this woman's Irish-immigrant background. The Caribbean woman describes how helpful it has been for her to understand the complex power, of racist structures in our society into which she was born although she did not choose them, and whose damaging legacy she lives with daily. And as the young lesbian woman in our group fights to get health coverage for her partner, worries about showing her affection in public, and feels the alienating effect of people's assumption that she is straight, she explains to us that, although she clearly chose her present lifestyle, she did not choose to be born into a heterosexist culture that punishes her for the decision. In this sense, she inherited not her sexual orientation but the sins of heterosexism and homophobia, which haunt her daily.

My own understanding of what it means to be "born into sin" was deepened by a small incident that occurred in the delivery room following the birth of my child. Before she was placed in my arms, the hospital staff followed their usual procedures and placed a warming cap on her head after clearing her throat. When I looked down to meet the face of this new human being, to my surprise what I first encountered was a little head covered by a bright pink hat printed with the words, "It's a girl." All doubts about the pervasive and constitutive pressure exerted by gender codes in our culture were banished in that moment as I held a little human being already marked by cultural inscriptions of "pinkness" and "girl" and all the potentially restrictive, sexist assumptions that go with them. In the first ten seconds of her life, my daughter had been placed in a web of social meanings that shaped expectations about her. My daughter's being "born into sin" took the form of a pink cap, a set of hospital rules, and the complex web of social interactions they initiated.

Thus, the notion of inheriting sin is not automatically antithetical to feminist theory's concerns. Being "born into sin" makes sense of how oppression functions in women's lives. The notion of sin as "original" grasps well the reality that we are shaped by oppressive dynamics that predate us and that we do not choose to be determined by. Inheriting sin also captures the fact that while we are not inherently sinful, no privileged area in our lives escapes it—sin touches even a newly born child in her mother's arms. These stories further demonstrate that although sin does not originate in our bodies, the sin into which we are born leaves its marks deep in our flesh, in the crafting of a baby into a "girl" as well as in the diseased liver of the recovering alcoholic and the stooped walk of the overburdened secretary. In all these ways, our stories of oppression reflect vividly the dynamic claim that sin is inborn but not inherent, inescapable but not irredeemable.

Returning to the question of how feminist theory helps to reconceptualize sin's inherited character, again recall the feminist theories of women's oppression discussed in chapter 4. As we have seen, the oppressive social nexus of constitutive relations works to diminish and constrain women's flourishing, what feminist theology calls sin in its many faces and fruits.[42] Given that oppressive forces build our very identities, they cannot be escaped by force of will. The most intransigent of these systems—for example, the oppressive binaries of gender, which construct and privilege what is "masculine" while simultaneously downgrading what is "feminine"—are so endemic to our language and our culture that even when we know they are oppressive, we nonetheless remain determined by them. Similar claims can be made about the nexus of capitalist relations that structure the major exchange patterns of the world economy. While the women in the Tuesday-night group may certainly identify and protest against the unjust features of this system, they also recognize that it is impossible to live in present-day North America and not be implicated in capitalism. Likewise, the material and cultural structures of racism that run through the social fabric of North America are so deeply embedded that no one escapes their destructive force, although each of us, depending on our relation to white privilege, experiences them differently.[43]

If these systems are as inescapable as original sin, how do we imagine the possibility of social change? How are we to construct a just nexus of social relations if these systems are as intransigent as original sin? A feminist theological perspective offers two answers. First, that women are born into a nexus of unjust social relations does not imply that these particular forms will always exist. As history teaches and hope reminds us, these systems will be transformed in the years ahead. Both feminist theory and Christian theology warn us that emerging modes of social relations will carry marks of the past within them and harbor novel forms of oppression and domination, and that eradicating all forms of social sin is impossible. With these acknowledgments, feminist theology is anchored in a pragmatic eschatological vision and not a naively utopian millennialism.

The second answer is that we are offered the possibility of living *faithfully* within such structures. This faithful living no doubt takes forms peculiar to each, such as the healing that occurs when one's life is pulled together in the envelope of sanctifying grace and one's agency is authorized by justifying grace. This faithful living thus resists powers of oppression in the world because it inhabits a vision counter to that of the dominant culture (which constructs women who, among many things, often suffer from fragmentation and a diminished sense of agency). This resistance is constructed according to the eschatological essentialist script of justification and sanctification as an "implicated resistance"—implicated in the sin it contests. And here we return again to the notion of original sin, the sin in which we remain caught even as we live in faith. The institutions, cultural practices, and linguistic forms of the oppressions that perpetrate sin do not simply cease to construct us when we step into faith. Their power remains, though in a form now challenged but not destroyed by the vision of redemption that marks us as *simul iustus et peccator,* "simultaneously sinners and saints."

The image of "imputed sin" effectively captures this feminist perspective on original sin. Recall Luther's and Calvin's claim that in faith we are given an alien righteousness not ours "by nature" but "imputed" to us by divine decree. In my initial feminist reinterpretation of this metaphor, I suggested we think of imputed righteousness as a divinely scripted performance we are called to undertake in the life of faith. As a performance, righteousness becomes a drama we inhabit, a graced character role, which constitutes who we are in the most profound sense. Now, in the context of this chapter, imagine "imputed, original sin" in a similar manner—as the "false performative scripts" into which women are born.

These scripts take many forms and tell us many different stories (the five faces of oppression describe just a few). They are scripts that do not wait for us to act but that, more often than not, "perform us"—as part of the nexus of oppressive relations within which women's subjectivity comes into being. As original sin, they are scripts that we inherit (they are inborn), and yet, as performances, they cannot be said to be intrinsic to our humanity (they are not inherent). Likewise, they are not scripts we could choose to avoid (they are inescapable), and yet, because we are given a counter role to inhabit in faith, they are performances that can be contested (they are not irredeemable). They are roles that I encounter each month in my Tuesday-night group as I listen to the struggles of each woman's life roles that we "put on" in the form of the anxious lines that wrinkle our faces, in harmed silences, in the labor we sell to institutions that leave us powerless and marginalized, and in the oppressions we perpetrate in response. They are, in short, the performative faces we see reflected in the mirror cracked, the speculum shattered—the performance of "unfaith."

Total Depravity and Guilt

Let us now extend this remapping of sin by turning to two more themes in Calvin's account: total depravity and guilt. Using the insights of feminist theory, we can transform "total depravity" and "guilt" into the images of "the unenveloped self" and "the constrained agent." Let us first look at the imagery of total depravity. As Calvin describes total depravity, sin is something that assaults the organically whole self from the outside in and then occupies the self, moving into every part of its host. From a feminist perspective, this description of sin is useful because it allows women to see themselves not only as agents but as casualties of sin. Too often sin as "the bad things we do" overshadows sin as "the damage done to us" and "the social relations that define us." A shift to the latter view of sin is necessary if women are to appreciate how social, institutional, and cultural forces work to oppress us by constructing the social spaces in which we live. Seeing the self as a site "attacked" by sin has the salutary effect of allowing women to be more direct about naming as "sin" the personal harms perpetrated against us, a naming especially important in situations of domestic violence and abuse. When sin is identified as something that "occupies" us, we can also explore how oppressions cut into the very heart of our self-understanding.[44]

Some aspects of Calvin's definition, however, need to be questioned by feminists. Calvin uses metaphors of purity and impurity for the process whereby sin attacks and occupies the self. He describes humanity as defiled by sin; sin pollutes or dirties. For Calvin, sin is also a disease that infects the self and spreads through bodily contact. Yet a third trope is his well-known image of "depravity," a term associated with perverse or immoral sexuality; sin corrupts through a process of sexual degeneration. The representational logic of all these images suggests that the body is the principal site of sin and that its effects are related to our embodied sexuality.[45] In Calvin's day, these images might have been well suited to convey the dynamic process by which sin destroys the self, but they become problematic in present-day women's experience. As noted earlier, women often struggle with a deep sense of their female bodies as "shameful" and their sexuality as "depraved." These feelings reflect age-old binary patterns of thinking that posit women as defiled, impure, and deficient and men as pure, healthy, and sufficient. Given these patterns, a doctrine of sin that casts women as defiled, diseased, or depraved is dangerous because such images valorize identity constructs used to justify women's oppression for centuries.

We can, however, rule out these problematic images of sin defiling the self without rejecting Calvin's central description of humanity as "despoiled" by sin, a violent plundering or ravaging in which the self is "stripped of its skin." Although unfamiliar to contemporary ears, "despoiling" offers feminist theologians a metaphor for women's experience of sin. Drawing on the work of Luce Irigaray, we can transform Calvin's image of humanity "stripped of its skin" into a powerful feminist metaphor. In chapter 3, I laid the groundwork for this by suggesting that Irigaray's "envelope" might be reconceived as an image of God's sanctifying, enveloping grace. Recall Irigaray's claim that "woman needs an envelope to contain her" because she has difficulty establishing the boundaries of her personhood or the bordering edges of her identity and risks dissolving herself into the needs of other persons and institutions. She thus lacks a sense of centeredness and self-possession. She needs a sheath, a skin to hold her together, to "author her new becoming."[46]

When we compare Calvin's notion of despoiled humanity and Irigaray's figure of the unenveloped woman, the similarities are obvious. Both images depict the human person as a site that "falls apart" when its defining border—the metaphorical skin that holds it together—is destroyed or denied. Although the images have profoundly different conceptions of the self contained by these borders—Calvin's sturdy, Aristotelian "man" versus Irigaray's postmodern, fluid, and multiple woman—they both portray the dissolution that occurs as "total" in that no part of the self remains unaffected by this loss of form. And for both, the very existence of the person is threatened when the person is "undone" in this manner. Similarly, for both, grace is depicted as a divinely gifted container, which holds the fragmented self together by wrapping it in redeeming love. In the context of the doctrine of sin, the flip side of this image of sanctification now comes into view when Calvin's "totally corrupted" sinner appears as Irigaray's dissolving woman, dissolved into the projects, plans, and desires of others and thus without a "skin" to define the integrity of her personhood. Bereft of the gifts of a sanctifying structure that confers upon her unique worth and integrity, she finds herself in a fallen world that defines her by her use-value for others. In this way, sin puts her life at risk and defies the God whose grace seeks to hold her together.

Note once again that this sinful process of coming undone is not just the result of internal confusion on the part of women but is tied to concrete relations of power and institutional formations that attack and occupy women (and others), thereby violating the boundaries of their personhood. This unfaithful ravaging of boundaries can be conceived in a number of ways if we recall again oppression's five faces. For example, when sin wears the face of exploitation, the borders of the self are plundered by economic powers that extract the self's labor for another's use and destroy the material basis of women's "self-possession."[47] When sin wears the face of powerlessness, the self is "unsheathed" insofar as it is denied any control over its environment. When sin wears the face of marginality, women who are old, disabled, or unemployed disappear from the register of social meaning—their bounded identities dissolve—because they have no use-value. When sin wears the face of cultural imperialism, women living in cultures outside the dominant value system are forced to engage in cultural practices not their own. To use Irigaray's image, they are clothed in cultural garments fitted to another's taste. Finally, when sin wears the face of sexual violence, it corrupts "totally" as it dominates, violates, and occupies the site of the self, turning insides out and ravaging the fragile envelope of trust holding the self together.

In addition to these broad descriptions, feminist theology must listen to the more personal stories of total undoing in women's lives. In the Tuesday-night group, we hear many such tales—tales of women so insecure and fragmented they constantly question not only their everyday plans and projects but their very right to exist.[48] In halting sentences and with eyes fixed on the floor, one woman tells us how being a victim of date rape in high school ravaged the boundaries of her body and her psychic boundaries and sense of self.[49] She lost parts of her memory, her confidence in negotiating daily tasks, and, perhaps most painful, her capacity to impose order and meaning upon her world. Gripped by a terror at the core of her being, her soul felt vitiated, no part of her untouched. The trauma was total, for the fabric of meaning that held her together had unraveled.[50] Her struggle today is to accept the radical notion that in God's sanctifying grace she is pulled together again, given boundaries, limits, and integrity—in short, the identity of faith.

The women in my church group sometimes respond to this woman's struggles with rich silences; at other times, we pray or affirm our commitment to listen to her story yet again if she wishes. This commitment reflects a collective recognition that parts of our own stories resonate with hers. The elderly woman who feels she is "disappearing" as she slowly loses the things that have defined her life—her husband, her job, her health—is experiencing this coming undone in her own unique way. Similarly, the Caribbean woman tells us how she is being constantly clothed in racist identity constructions not of her own choosing, constructions that we all wear in different ways but that the privileges of "whiteness" make to seem "normal." The stories go on, as does the counterdiscourse of a "faith-talk" that constructs us all, again and again, in a theological landscape where women flourish, difference abounds, power is shared, and justice is enacted as we are held together, fluid and multiple, in the envelope of God's grace.

Having looked at how sin attacks the self from the outside in, let me now briefly turn to Calvin's use of guilt imagery to depict our responsibility for sin that moves from the inside out. How can feminists rethink this notion? First of all, Calvin's decision to posit imagery of the self as agent of sin alongside the self as site of sin is a welcome move, from a feminist perspective. As the five faces of oppression make clear, women can perpetrate harm as well as suffer from it.[51] To assert women's responsibility for sin is, paradoxically, crucial to women's empowerment at several levels. Taking responsibility for how we deal with the injustices done to us is a crucial part of breaking the cycles of oppression. An emphasis on women's agency is also critical to the feminist project because part of women's oppression has been a denial of women's role as leading actors on the stage of history.

How one describes this agency from a feminist theological perspective, however, is complicated. Here, Calvin's description is both useful and problematic; aspects of his account of guilt are troubling when viewed from the perspective of women's lives. For instance, Calvin's humbling image of the "bondage of the will" (directed against those with brazen self-confidence) is not appropriate to use in addressing women who suffer from a lack of self-confidence and from an intense underestimation of their agentic potential. Telling the women in my Tuesday-night gathering who are struggling to claim their voices and to resist oppression that they have no "freedom," and yet sin nonetheless, reinforces the very dynamics of oppression that have silenced them. The ironic flip side of this is that women are also constructed to be the world's caretakers and, as such, they tend to also assume an exaggerated sense of their responsibility for sin. With that burden of caring for all comes an unrelenting guilt for the inevitable failure of such care to rid the world of its problems. An unexamined rhetoric of guilt can once again recapitulate this pattern of thinking that oppresses women.

Once we have critiqued Calvin's use of these terms—"bondage of the will" and "guilt"—we are left with his central insight about responsibility: the claim that theological discussions of agency need to be "rhetorically scaled" to meet the needs and situations of differing audiences. This insight holds great promise for a feminist theology of sin because it allows us to consider the concrete particularities of a given situation of oppression before we begin ascribing responsibility or agency in overly general terms.

Developing a feminist model for "scaling agency," I want to recuperate one aspect of Calvin's discussion of bondage of the will. In arguing that the will is "imprisoned," Calvin asserts that original sin is not of our own choosing (although it is always our responsibility) and that we are not able to escape it. This assertion is linked to feminist theory's claim that we are born into a nexus of oppressive social relations—institutional practices, cultural patterns, and habits of language—we can never completely escape. This nexus of relations is like a theater in which we, as women agents, perform the scripts of our lives. It is often hard to tell when we are being performed by imputed social codes and when we perform roles of our own making. So too in the case of sin, it is difficult to distinguish between an exercise of our creative agency and playing a scripted role.

Making these theological distinctions and hence appropriately "scaling our agency" within this theater of sin is a difficult, complex process, one that benefits from both feminist theory and the finely honed local wisdom of women's lives. Laying out these insights has been the task of this chapter. Most important from a feminist theological perspective, however, is to affirm that the scaling of guilt is continuously renewed by the eschatological discourse of justification that pulls our agency into God's future. For feminists of faith, justification comes as the promise of a continued forgiveness that revitalizes our actions daily. This divine promise allows us to criticize our failings because we are continuously invited to start over again. Justifying grace also reminds us that in starting again, we are invited by God to embrace our neighbor in just relation. Thus guilt's converse image of justification stands as a vision that constructs us in hope, thereby authoring the theological space of our becoming.

Sin Awaiting Redemption

Much remains to be said about feminist theological remappings of sin; this chapter serves only as an introduction. In its incompleteness, however, this treatment demonstrates the richness that feminist theory brings to discussions of sin. Feminist theology also makes contributions to feminist discussions of oppression, contributions that grow out of the differences (and not just the similarities) between theology's sin-talk and theory's oppression-talk. These contributions increasingly come into focus in chapter 7's discussion of the nature of Christian community, but I can also sketch them now.

The contributions rest in feminist theology's demand that sin be understood in an economy of grace. For feminist theologians, sin is a concept embedded in the language of an ecclesial community that confesses redemption from sin already made present (yet still awaiting full consummation) in God's sanctifying and justifying grace. This perspective permits feminist theologians to have a broader understanding of oppression than do feminist theorists. It allows them to be both less and more optimistic about the brokenness of our world, particularly with respect to women. The confession that sin is "original" forces us to remember that the fractures running through creation are deeper and more intransigent than sexist oppression, and that liberation from them involves more than simply banishing gender binaries. It involves being freed to celebrate the giftedness of creation and to praise the God who gives. Feminist conceptions of sin also provide hope for women's liberation against what often seem daunting odds; in faith, grace accompanies us in the struggle, and we know that the victory has already been won and is assured in the future. Even though we may not currently have created perfected social structures and personal relationships that manifest the enveloping and freeing character of God's grace, grace continues to define God's undaunted love for humanity nonetheless. The graced character of sin-talk creates the security and sense of belovedness that enables us to honestly confront our own sinfulness—our daily shortcomings as well as gross wrongdoings. We can never be content with simply dividing the world into evil perpetrators and innocent victims because we recognize that sin implicates us all, just as grace embraces and opens us all. Knowing sin and living in the bounded openness of grace thus become a cause for rejoicing as much as a call to work for a future in which women (and all people) flourish.

6

Community

Without community there is no liberation, only the most
vulnerable and temporary armistice between an individual
and her oppression.

—Audre Lorde, *Sister Outsider: Essays and Speeches*

If by community one implies . . . a harmonious group,
consensus, and fundamental agreement beneath the
phenomena of discord or war, then I don't believe in it
very much and I sense in it as much threat as promise.

—Jacques Derrida, *Points de suspension: Interviews 1974–1994*

My Tuesday-night church group is an important community for me.
Over the years, we have shared the intimate unfolding of our lives.
There are deep bonds of trust between us and we have patterns of practice,
such as our "check-in time," that provide safety and comfort, moments
treasured in our otherwise chaotic days. We know about one another's
families and workplaces; we even recognize details about one another's
clothing, always noting with glee when someone arrives in a "new outfit."
In-house jokes make us laugh, and we can be brought to tears by simply
looking at the agony on a member's face. For many in the group, this experience of community has been profound and healing. Although we are
hardly perfect—we bicker among ourselves and have been unfriendly to
the stranger in our midst—for some this group comes close to being community as it should be, community at its best. What are the marks of this
community? We are bound by a shared purpose and common practices;
within this bounded space, there is trust, safety, delight, intimate knowledge, and reciprocal accountability. Is this the ideal feminist community?

Perhaps, but as feminist theorists remind us, things are never as simple as they seem.

For example, our precious image of this ideal community is quickly challenged and expanded when we consider other forms of community that have been empowering for us. For the recovering addict, the twelve-step rooms are a community that saved her life. The woman in the labor union recalls the monthly gathering of her local chapter. The retired teacher smiles when she describes her quilting circle or exercise class. The young mother thinks of her small family as the most demanding and fulfilling community in her life, and the Jamaican woman fondly describes getting together with Caribbean friends. Others think of groups as large as the New Haven community, the United States, or even the "national community of gays and lesbians." Still others think of communities as small as their close-knit circle of friends or a long-standing neighborhood block-watch. These diverse reflections reveal that community is more difficult to define than our Tuesday-night "ideal" suggests, particularly when we move beyond our shared experience of community and turn to our multiple engagements both inside and outside different groups.

Our experiences of community are further challenged when we consider other, more mundane or perhaps not-so-wonderful experiences we have had of community. In these reflections, the communities we describe are not necessarily intimate, delightful, and empowering. Some images that come to mind are benign, images of communities that, at least on the surface, seem to neither empower nor harm us: the PTA, the community of Oklahomans in exile in New England, the Democratic Town Party. More vivid than these, however, are images of communities that we experience as destructive. To complicate matters further, what one member experiences as a positive community is cited by another as harmful—a tension revealing just how diverse our experiences of community are.

For example, the image of the nuclear family that brings joy to the new mother elicits terror in the incest survivor sexually abused by her grandfather in her supposedly safe home. For the woman who recently came out as a lesbian to her parents (who then exiled her from family gatherings), images of familial community bring deep sorrow and anger. The image of the quilting circle lifted up by the retired woman seems oppressive to the young mother fighting against pressures to be more domestic and traditionally "motherly." The woman who gathers with her Caribbean friends tells us that these dinners can be painful because she is ashamed of not finding work and feels judged by those closest to her. The clerical worker describes for us, in great detail, the two communities in her office: union members and the "others," and her intense dislike of these "others" is palpable. Although she thinks of her union as a positive community, these "others" likely experience it as exclusionary and hostile. In these different ways, the women recount harms inflicted upon them or by them in the name of community, harms of overt violence and exile as well as the more subtle damage of becoming women in the present world.

I begin with this reflection on the Tuesday-night group because the complexity of the women's accounts of community illuminates feminist studies of community.[1] At the heart of these studies are two basic questions. First, feminists ask: How do we empirically define what "community" is? Feminists are interested in this question because, as with many topics, they believe that traditional ways of measuring and defining community are gender biased. Second, feminists ask: What is an ideal community? While all agree it is one in which women flourish, significant disagreements remain on what flourishing entails and what kind of communal patterns produce and support it.[2] These two questions frame this chapter.

On these questions, there are issues of basic agreement. In the first section of this chapter, I introduce these issues by describing general features of feminist conversations about community, at both the descriptive and normative level. In the second section, I discuss various feminist responses to the debate between liberals and communitarians over the nature of corporate social life, a debate that in some ways parallels the essentialism/constructivism debate treated earlier. I conclude by describing the awkward middle ground that many feminists have opted for in this debate, a middle ground that finds value in universal claims about just community while acknowledging the radically situated character of the communal values we hold. In chapter 7, I then take these insights into community, lay them over the doctrinal landscape of a Reformation view of church, and explore how feminist theory once again provides new perspectives on some traditional Christian ideas about our corporate life together.

General Features of the Feminist Theory of Community

What do feminist theorists say about community as an empirical category? How do they define it? What are they looking at or for when they look at community? As the stories from my Tuesday-night group make clear, the answers to these questions are far from obvious.

One common misperception is that feminists are solely interested in women-only or feminist communities. While both of these types of community are important for showing how women interact without the overt constraints of gender expectations and the power dynamics that figure when women and men are together, feminist studies extend much further. They explore the place of women in a variety of communities, many of which include men and may or may not be feminist in orientation or practice. Reflecting on communities like my local church or the university's labor union, for example, is a valid and necessary task of feminist theory, because it reveals new facets of women's shifting experiences of community.

In addition to looking at women in community, feminists also look at how gender-constructs operate in the formation of communal identities and practices. This means feminists often look at communities where women play a minimal role or no role at all but that nonetheless depend upon a lively "logic of gender." For example, gender binaries functioned in the highly gendered self-understandings and gender-exclusionary practices of all-male monastic communities in medieval France,[3] and studying these practices and beliefs provides fascinating insights into the cultural production of meaning in this period and its relations to our own. As another example, feminists also study such practices as the "gender-twisting" that goes on in the communities supporting gay men dying of AIDS; never having conformed to standards of heterosexual "maleness," these men continue, in their illness and dying, to challenge dominant forms of communal relating. In such contexts, their experiences raise gender issues that interest feminists.

As they look at women's communities, women in community, and the play of gender constructs throughout community, feminists also recognize the significant roles race, class, sexuality, geography, and ethnicity play in forming and maintaining communal practices and identities. Indeed, these factors are as constitutive of community as gender. Just as feminists avoid an additive approach to the relation between, say, race and gender in identity formation, so too do they allow race to complicate their analysis of women and gender in community. Such factors are often more evident in the study of community than in studies of individual identity formation. This is particularly clear, for example, when race or geography characterizes a community's self-understanding. Feminists also recognize that as factors such as race, gender, and geography intermingle in community, the definition of community shifts as its contexts change.[4]

Another feature of feminist studies of community grows out of this desire to remain grounded in diverse contexts. Committed to constant contextualization, feminists are immediately faced with a challenge: What is a community and what isn't? Although the question may seem rather straightforward, feminists complicate this question for two reasons. First, what people mean by "community" changes dramatically over time and across cultures, as each generation and each society develop different root metaphors for what a community looks like. For example, rural Italian peasants in the fifteenth century would likely describe their community using images drawn from feudal models of estates and kinship ties; the same metaphoric economy would also drive their vision of ideal community. A suburban family in 1950s Middle America would probably answer with reference to their local neighborhood—their street or the people who live next door—and their ideals would likely build on similar images. A contemporary group of college students would probably give other answers, referring to such identity constructs as race and gender or common interests such as religion, politics, or even weekend hobbies; their visions of ideal community would probably include corresponding images of "differences and sameness." Given this diversity, feminists avoid strict definitions of community and instead trace its shifts across time and space according to its patterned gendered logic.

Feminists also have another, even stronger reason for not rigidly defining what is community and what isn't. Many traditional academic categories used for analyzing communities do not include women or gender. This invisibility of women and gender is partly a product of the hold that the public/private analytic split has on many academic fields, particularly in the social sciences.[5] In a good deal of literature on society, the masculine public sphere—the world of market commerce, government, and the military—receives the most attention, and little attention is paid to the private sphere and, hence, to women's interactions and feminine-gendered forms of communality. This imbalance means the complex patterns of interaction and association in the so-called private sphere have not been traced and assessed. Such modes include patterns of interaction specific to mothering and caring, forms of relating (or being in community) traditionally practiced by women. To counter this tendency, feminists keep the definition of community open in the hopes that doing so will challenge traditional assumptions, blur traditional boundaries, and shake commonplace "truths." This openness makes feminist studies in this field rather unruly. Such unruliness is necessary, however, for feminists to explore creatively an area long dominated by gender-exclusionary standards.[6]

Having looked at the kinds of questions asked when feminists approach the descriptive task of theorizing community, let us now turn to the normative task of those who study community. As with all facets of feminist studies, feminists study community because of their fundamental interest, on the one hand, in analyzing and critiquing forms of communal life that are harmful to women and, on the other, in designing and implementing forms of community that ensure the flourishing of women and all persons. The latter goal is where hope enters the discussion. Feminists yearn for and struggle to realize a vision of community as it should be; in doing so, they remain committed to naming the harms that prevent this vision from becoming reality.

Feminists who study community, therefore, never do so as disinterested academicians. They admit, up front, that their theorizing of community is shaped by their desire to construct models of social life embodying feminist aspirations.[7] The ideal communities feminists seek are inclusive; they encourage the flourishing of all—because, as these theorists constantly remind us, no one will flourish fully until we all flourish together.

This utopian, normative dimension of feminist theories of community has its own set of challenges and insights. One challenge is that the everyday experiences of women often resist utopian visions of a better future.[8] We experience irrevocable losses that will never be mended—the personal loss of a child or partner or the communal losses of history's cruelty, such as the middle passage, the Holocaust, the devastation of Hiroshima, the trauma of endemic sexual abuse. Irresolvable conflicts leave us unable to imagine the way it should be—for example, communal conflicts in which both sides share the cause of justice and the burden of guilt. We also experience great sufferings that social accounts of oppression cannot exhaustively explain—for example, breast cancer, a disease that has changed the face of women's communal organizing in North America in the last two decades. Feminist theories of community need to incorporate such experiences into their utopian vision.[9]

Moreover, a predilection for the future sometimes leads feminists to underestimate the tragic in history and to overestimate what can be accomplished in the present. The utopian impulse may seem naive about the limits of historical transformation. In response to this challenge, feminists lift up the already/not-yet character of their hope, a hope both exuberant and humble. This hope's exuberance lies in the belief that feminist ideals have the power to change the present by shaping our beliefs, actions, and attitudes and, hence, our institutions and cultural worlds. Just as the identity of woman is determined in the present by an ever shifting vision of the future, so too community is determined by the visions it lives toward. This is also humble hope, however, because it realistically confesses both the impossibility of completely fulfilling the vision in the present and the limits of the vision itself as a social production shifting over time. In this way, the feminist predilection for the future is pragmatic; it pushes against the harsh textures of women's lives while moving toward a vision of flourishing and remaining open to the future.

This pragmatic utopian impulse stands in tension with the descriptive project of feminist theory. Feminists are aware that their openness in defining *empirical* community does not always blend well with their *normative* commitment to designing and enacting modes of sociality conducive to women's flourishing. This incomplete blending exists because descriptive openness does not necessarily give one a purchase on the hard work of discerning norms and values that might encourage the flourishing of women in community. If community can mean almost anything, how does one make judgments about forms of community that are genuinely liberating? In most feminist studies of community, a double vision keeps this tension alive. Feminists focus on normative, ideal community, the community they yearn for and seek, while also attending to the nitty-gritty texture of actual communities in their diversity and fluidity. A pragmatic hermeneutic of suspicion thus combines with the utopian impulse so as to always keep in mind the lived diversity of women's experience and the socially embedded character of all normative claims. Can this complex commitment, this form of strategic essentialism or pragmatic utopianism, be held together in theorizing community?

One way that feminists do so is by adopting a disciplinary division of labor. In the current literature, two distinct but interrelated types of analysis focus on community: empirical studies analyze particular communities and their practices, and theoretical studies focus on relations among women, gender, and political organization at a more general and often normative level. In the first group, one finds scholars in such fields as sociology, social psychology, and anthropology;[10] in the second group, in such fields as political philosophy, political theory, ethics, and critical legal studies. As I have already noted, however, the most interesting scholarship in each stands on the edge between both.[11]

To see this focus, look at examples of research by feminists in traditionally empirical fields and how it has generated new theoretical, normative insights into women, gender, and community. One example comes from anthropological studies of women in non-Western communities whose patterns of gender relation are patriarchal in the classic sense of the term.[12] Two such communities are harems in North Africa and women workers in early twentieth-century China.[13] These traditionally gendered communities are rigidly patriarchal in their social ordering and oppressive to women. Yet, feminists have argued through their empirical studies that, even in such contexts, women have developed the means to support and encourage one another, in some instances even creating institutions they control and that protect and enhance their flourishing. These relationships and institutions operate both as a personal support network and as the basis for social change and collective cultural resistance by women. These studies have thus uncovered models of communal flourishing that surprise and test typical Western understanding of the liberation of women. Furthermore, such cross-cultural studies provide new categories for defining community, as evidenced by the absence, prior to feminist scholarship, of reflection on North African harems or Chinese factories. In such ways, empirical perceptions of flourishing and community influence more theoretical, normative work on ideal community.

Another area of empirical research with exciting implications for feminist theory concerns "New Social Movements (NSM)."[14] The common issue, interest, preference, or group identity that draws people together in these "New Social Movements" ranges from a shared ethnicity or sexual orientation to a shared political agenda or activist project. These movements play an increasingly significant role in the lives of many persons in North America, Europe, and beyond. They do not, however, fit the usual sociological classifications of community, where pride of place is given to family, neighborhood, church, and nation.[15] In addition, face-to-face interactions and geographic proximity are traditionally considered necessary for a group to be considered a community. According to such classifications, however, groups united by, for example, their common interest in keeping abortion legal or their shared allergy to peanuts would not constitute a community, and hence they drop out of political analysis.[16] The growing NSM literature, in contrast, takes these emergent forms of affiliation seriously.

This empirical material is important for feminists who do theory because of its relevance to the politics of identity.[17] As discussed in chapter 2, feminists are interested in the ways specific identities mediate our communal self-understandings, many of which spring from one's self-identified social group—such as race or gender—and not one's neighborhood, geographic region, or family unit, the traditional markers of community. NSM literature shows how central these emergent forms of community are to modern persons. It also makes clear, however, that the borders between such communal identities are fluid, that most people stand in multiple communities at the same time, and that people identify what it means to be, for example, "Latina" or "gay" or "leftist" in different ways.

For example, one may need to be self-identified as a lesbian to be part of a local lesbian reading group, but for marching down the streets of New York on Gay Pride Day, the definition shifts.[18] "Lesbian" thus appears to be a fluid term, and hence the community it defines has fluid borders. The ambiguity becomes more evident when one asks: Could a bisexual participate in the reading group? What about a transsexual? A cross-dresser? Or, even more challenging, what about a man-to-woman transsexual with a female partner? Who, moreover, is authorized to make these determinations? At the heart of such questions is an issue critical to feminist studies of community: Do the politics of identity establish the normative borders of community, or are normative commitments more important? Is it more important to be a "lesbian" (an unstable term in itself) or to be committed to the flourishing (whatever that may mean) of lesbians? Answering such a question is not easy. The pragmatic, concrete, and material conditions of daily living (in this case, the lived experience of being lesbian) cannot be pushed aside when considering prescriptive values, yet feminists recognize that these material identities are, at some level, as constructed as the normative commitments with which they are associated.[19]

This example raises three issues that feminists have struggled with in their reflections on the normative dimensions of community life. The first issue concerns the source of feminist normative claims and ideals. Where do feminist communal values come from? As stated earlier, normative reflections emerge in conversation with women's lived experiences. But is this occurrence enough for making normative judgments? Feminists answer no but are divided about what more is needed. Are our ideals rationally generated, self-evident truths upon which we should all agree? Or, does our vision of ideal community originate in the historically particular languages and practices of the communities that shape us? Moreover, how far should our ideals be applied? Should all communities abide by them? Or, is the scope of their application more limited? Should ideals hold only for the communities that generate them? Questions like these reach far beyond the specialized scope of feminist theory, but, in the context of feminist struggles, they take particular form.[20] Reflect on the feminist claim that sexual violence against women is never justified. While all feminists would agree with the claim that such violence is wrong, there are very different feminist accounts of how one generates and thus defends this position. Some describe it as a universal, self-evident truth, while others refer to the tradition-specific value systems that gave rise to it. Likewise, some feminists argue for the universal scope of a principled rejection of sexual violence, while others suggest that what one means by sexual violence varies culturally and, for this reason, universal application may be extremely difficult and politically problematic. Note that this set of issues echoes themes developed in the essentialist/constructivist debate on women's identity, although now in a distinctly communal register.

The second issue concerns the place of sameness and difference in community. Communities inevitably coalesce around some point of commonality, be it a shared belief or a street address, and such points of sameness create boundaries around communities that determine who is "in" or "out." What do feminists make of such borders? On the one hand, feminists are suspicious of such boundaries (my discussion of oppression outlined multiple ways in which such exclusions have historically disadvantaged women). On the other hand, feminist theorists recognize the value of sameness and the positive aspects of boundaries. In fact, they often celebrate such boundaries when they are drawn around communities in a manner that is empowering and politically emancipatory, as in the Tuesday-night group.

Feminists further recognize that in healthy communities some forms of behavior will be appropriately excluded—for example, when a community gathers around the bed of a dying gay man and decides to exclude those who feel AIDS is divine punishment for homosexuality. But how does one manage such borders and exclusions? How are inside and outside to be negotiated so as to allow for critique and the possibility of new, emergent values? Feminists struggling with these issues opt for a form of what I call "bounded openness," a form not unlike the opening envelope described in previous chapters. In bounded openness, the need for communal integrity is affirmed at the same time as is the need for communal fluidity. Again, the ways in which feminists actually flesh out this notion of bounded openness varies.

The third issue concerns the substance of the values feminists embrace in their quest for ideal community. In this chapter's opening description of my Tuesday-night group, I listed several of our values: safety, trust, delight, mutual regard, and reciprocal accountability. Are there other ideals? Yes, but the list is far from static, and questions abound. For example, how should these principles be applied? How does one, for instance, instantiate safety? Will it vary cross-culturally? Similarly, what happens when values conflict? For instance, how does a community establish rules for safety and yet continue to struggle with uncomfortable issues of otherness, particularly "others" who are considered "unsafe"? To further reflect on such questions, let us now turn to an arena in which feminist theories of community have made important interventions.

Feminist Perspectives on the Liberal/Communitarian Debate

In the field of political philosophy, the liberal/communitarian debate asks questions similar to the three just mentioned: Where do communal values come from? Where do ideals for community as it should be originate? Are they universal truths? Or, are they generated in the rich cultural traditions of specific communities? How should they be applied? How do we manage conflicting values? In this section, I explore this debate and the various responses feminists make to both sides.[21] By looking at these responses, readers will get a sense for both the differences among feminists on community and normativeness and their shared critiques of a debate that has long held center stage in the academy without making gender a significant social category.[22] This discussion should also recall central themes in the constructivist/essentialist debate and thus bring us back to the beginnings of our exploration of feminist theory four chapters ago.

Liberalism

The model of political community with which most people in North America are familiar, if not in theory then at least in practice, is the liberal model of political life. While a diversity of present-day theoretical positions can be included under this title, there are several key features that characterize this tradition in its classic form.[23]

To explain how to best organize our collective lives, liberal theorists tell the following tale of community formation. It begins with the individual unit that constitutes all social bodies: the human person. Understanding the essential nature of the self or individual, they argue, is crucial to figuring out the form of society most conducive to the flourishing of such persons.[24] Liberalism thus gives primacy to a theory of the self in its definition of ideal community. Liberals' account of the self has four features. First, they believe there is a core or essential structure of personhood (the essential self) that analytically precedes the social development of persons. Second, this presocial self has a proclivity toward self-determination and self-creation (freedom). Third, this presocial self promotes its own perceived interests (self-interestedness), and fourth, this self is appropriately capacitated, prior to its social interactions, for common-sense, rational reflection on how to efficiently determine and pursue these ends (reason).[25]

How do these selves come to be in community, and what kind of community would they ideally form? Liberals answer by extrapolating a vision of community from these four outlined features of the self. They imagine what it would be like for these presocial, free, self-interested, rational creatures to meet one another in an original state of nature. Persons in this original situation, they argue, would see that they need a set of rules to guide their social interactions, to enable them to work together, and to order their competition for resources. This original social order would serve for them as a rational model of a community in which the essential components of their personhood would be honored and protected. Liberal theorists call this original set of rules "the social contract." It is built around the claim that all persons participating in the social contract are equal, in the sense that all are bearers of freedom and correlative rights. The ideal contract thus consists of rules or laws that guarantee procedural fairness (equality) to all. It is a contract designed to insure that, as diverse people gather to form community, all voices will be heard, and basic rights and freedoms will be protected.[26]

According to the tenets of mainstream liberal theory, the social interactions regulated by this social contract are "public"—that is, they concern persons' roles as citizens, taxpayers, voters, and legal benefit claimants. For some liberals, economic transactions are included in the public realm as well.[27] As discussed previously, this definition of the "public" is predicated upon its distinction from the "private" sphere—the family, a domestic space where women care for the young and the old and where religious and moral values are taught and cultural traditions passed on. In this second realm, liberal theory argues, the social contract should seek not to regulate people's interactions but to protect their right to have their own unique form of life, their own values, their own domestic patterns. To do this, liberal theory creates a legal hedge around the private sphere; this hedge marks off a space where personal freedoms are protected by the relative absence of legislation.

This legal hedge around the private sphere is also designed to keep considerations of a private nature out of the public realm. According to liberal theory, the values and traditions that mark social interactions in the domestic realm—a community's vision of "the good life"—emerge out of religious commitments and ethnic traditions that are culturally specific and hence not based on a purely reasoned assessment of individual self-interest. As such, if they were to be brought into the public conversation, they would have to be coercively (not naturally) imposed upon people who do not share them, because they are not grounded in a common (universal) rationality. Therefore, if such values are kept out of the realm of public, political policy, liberal theory argues, the social contract has a greater ability to insure respect for personal freedom and the equality of all persons.

As one can see, liberal theory is driven by the desire to create a rationally ordered social environment in which persons with differing interests and aspirations can peacefully coexist. This coexistence is ensured through procedural structures that prevent restrictive and authoritarian views of what persons should be and do from being imposed upon the general populace in violation of their right to self-determination. Persons must be freed from the weight of particular traditions so that they can create a future of their own making and so that difference might flourish. These structures must also mandate that in exercising their freedom, persons do not harm one another. Classical liberal theory is thus concerned about those vulnerable to violence because their mode of self-creation does not conform to that of the dominant culture. The social contract exists to protect them in their difference.

Feminist Responses to Liberal Contract Theory. The first thing to be noted about feminist responses to liberalism is that feminism, on the whole, has historically affirmed many of liberalism's fundamental claims.[28] This history of affirmation is rooted in the fact that liberal political theory has been a friend to women, and feminists have used its principles to great effect. For example, feminists have used the liberal conception of equality to promote the cause of women. Arguing that women are equal to men and should be treated as such, feminists have increased political voice and legal protection for women. Feminists have also claimed self-determination and freedom as fundamental conditions for women's flourishing. In contemporary politics, when feminists advocate a woman's right to control her own reproductive capacities and freedom to secure an abortion, they usually make a liberal appeal to a person's fundamental right to self-determination and self-ownership—including, in this case, control over one's body. As was discussed previously, feminists seek a social order in which women help determine the conditions under which they live and work. Without appeal to liberal values, such a goal would be hard to achieve.[29]

Feminists also share liberalism's basic commitment to creating a society where differences can flourish, where rules and laws exist to secure the rights of all to be different within limits—a version of bounded openness. In this regard, many feminists agree with the liberal argument that value judgments about "the good life" are best kept out of politics; feminists realize that traditional, patriarchal visions of "the good life" have not been good for women, and thus their forced imposition would be dangerous. Similarly, feminists appreciate the liberal desire for social structures that democratize power, diffuse authority, and constrain violence, for it has traditionally been women who have suffered the abuses of authority and violence.

Feminists question, however, other features of liberal theory. They argue, in short, that liberal social contract theory has problems with issues of women and gender. They argue that these problems are not just theoretical but are directly linked to social practices and public-policy decisions that have had long-term, negative implications for women in liberal democracies. Let us look briefly at the problems they list.

To begin with, in critiquing liberalism, feminists point out that liberal theory's "universal self" is in fact socially constructed to reflect a highly gendered "male" self.[30] Look at the features of personhood that liberalism highlights: self-determination, self-interest, and rationality.[31] Compare these supposedly presocial, universal features to the list of gender binaries in traditional accounts of sexual difference. Masculinity is usually described as the principle of activity (agency) and femininity as the correlative principle of passivity and receptivity (determined). Masculinity is the attribute of the agentic self who seeks to actualize its desired ends (self-interest), whereas femininity primarily serves the masculine in its pursuit of such ends (other-relatedness). Likewise, masculinity is frequently home to the principles of rationality (reason), whereas femininity is the seat of irrationality and emotion (nonreason). Liberal theory thus creates, with some revisions, its presocial self by collecting attributes designated as masculine and pinning them on the self that is supposedly gender free. In doing so, liberalism not only smuggles in a masculine conception of the self under the rubric of nonparticularism, it also eclipses the role that the feminine plays in the construction of this masculine ideal; gender seems to play no role in its construction whatsoever. Values typically associated with the feminine—care, receptivity, self-giving, and emotionality—are thereby undervalued by liberalism without any recognition of its own gender subtext.

This initial mistake "engenders" others. The social contract extrapolated from this masculine self is masculine as well. The social interactions regulated by the contract are the actions of an ideal man. What are these actions? At the time contract theory emerged, these were activities of commerce, military exploit, and government—activities that even today are gendered masculine. Liberal theory takes these masculine activities and designates them the proper context for political reflection. As the public sphere, liberal theory cordons off this arena and makes it the privileged object of its reflections on the nature of just society. With this unreflective link between the masculine subject and the masculine public arena of action, liberal theory inadvertently overlooks or undervalues many other forms of labor, practices, and values (some of them typically feminine). Instead of offering us an integrated picture of social life, liberal theory thereby leaves us with a truncated view of community and its normative possibilities. It leaves us with the public/private divide.[32]

Problems with this divide are reflected in the gendering of two key liberal concepts: reason and self-interest. According to liberal theory, people join in the social contract because of rational self-interest alone. Feminists suggest several problems with this view of social bonding. First, liberal theory accepts the gendered binarism of reason/emotion and subsequently ignores the role of emotion in the making of social bonds. This is a naive account of how persons bond, and it overlooks the positive role that emotion can play in contract-making enterprises. Similarly, the liberal description of self-interested bonding fails to acknowledge the place of more altruistic (typically feminine) bonds, such as between parent and child or between friends. These bonds of care are necessary to the healthy functioning of any political unit, feminists argue, because, for example, they allow us to raise children. Without these relations of care, feminists further point out, liberal theory cannot account for the social production of the adults who enter into social contracts.[33]

Another problem concerns the principle of equality. While feminists have long argued that women are equal to men, they also recognize that to encourage the flourishing of women, they need to secure legal protections for women that are based not on equality but on women's differences from men. Liberal theory, however, has difficulty accommodating the notion of "special rights"—the idea that some people have rights that others do not—

precisely because the principle of equality is so fundamental to its conception of the self and the social contract. The matter of special rights has been raised by feminists on a variety of issues, the most well-known of which is maternity leave.[34] According to the principle of equality, employers are required by law not to differentiate between men and women with respect to sick leave and paid vacation. What this means in practice is that women are not allowed extra leave for pregnancy and delivery (something men cannot experience), a policy with the effect of discriminating against women: they are forced to take extended, unpaid leaves (or lose their jobs) in order to have children. Situations like this, feminists argue, fall outside the liberal framework because "differences" are typically relegated to the realm of the private and left unregulated.

Another closely related problem is liberalism's voluntarist theory of power. According to the liberal story, power is something an individual has and exercises. One has it *naturally* in virtue of one's ontological constitution as a free agent as well as in virtue of the legal rights, such as the power to vote, accorded to one by the contract. Liberal theory also holds that individuals acquire power through acts of self-determination that bring social status or monetary standing. In both instances, however, the view of power is the same. The individual exercises power as a fundamental component of his or her freedom. It is "the power to act." The corollary claim is that power needs to be constrained only when it violates the basic principles of the contract; it should otherwise flourish in unregulated competition.

Feminists argue not that this view of power is wrong, but that it is dramatically limited. When we look at social realities like gender relations, we see that power is not just something individuals exercise. Power is a relational term; it exists in relationship—between two persons, between a person and a group, between or among institutions. In these relationships, power is mediated in myriad ways—economically, politically, socially, and, perhaps most important, culturally. Power is mediated culturally when, through the socialization process, persons acquire social identities (such as gender) that position them in relations of power vis-à-vis other persons, groups, and institutions. I have discussed extensively how these relations of power are culturally mediated in gender formation, supported as much by age-old belief systems and unexamined cultural expectations as by individual action and institutional policies. Because these cultural patterns do not take the form of overt violence against persons or obvious forms of procedural discrimination, liberal theory has difficulty regulating them. Liberal theory also has difficulty with a cultural analysis of power relations because it requires admitting the political force of communal value systems in the public realm; as the reader will recall, the liberal project is determined to prevent questions rooted in personal/traditional value systems ("the good") from arriving at the public table. This issue has been raised forcefully in conversations about affirmative action, a set of regulations designed to address culturally mediated power inequalities.

Yet another point of shared critique by feminists concerns liberal theory's limited definition of political community. According to social contract's ideal community, the communities that matter most politically are the ones free selves choose; they emerge out of the voluntary commitments of persons to a common enterprise. While feminists agree that such communities are an important part of our social interactions, we also participate in (and are shaped by) forms of community that we do not voluntarily choose. These communities "happen to us," they claim us. These include such communities as the family, which a child hardly joins by choice, or the previously discussed NSMs, which persons join because of identities not always described as voluntary. These communities play an enormously important role in how we conceive of community and its ideal functioning. Because liberalism fails to register them, however, it cannot take into account their social force. For example, representative districting in most liberal democracies follows lines of propinquity and political party, not the significant communal categories of race, gender, or ethnicity.[35]

Note that running through each of these criticisms are three common themes, each of which illumines the limits of liberalism's supposedly universalist vision. First, feminists point to gender exclusion: liberal theory's masculine orientation leaves the space of the feminine either undervalued or invisible. Second, feminists claim that liberal theory fails to consider difference and the myriad ways in which forces beyond the individual, such as culture, language, and power, affect the character of our communal interactions. Third, feminists claim that liberal theory's view of the self and the social contract is not as unbiased as its proponents suggest; rather, it is shot through with value judgments and laden with cultural assumptions. This last feminist contention, of course, conflicts with liberal theory's resistance to considering the "good society" in its deliberative model of procedural fairness. Also note that each critique aims not just at liberal theory in the abstract but also at the practices these abstractions engender—particularly public-policy decisions (a few of which have been mentioned) that harm women.

Let us now return to the two very different responses feminists have had to these problems in liberalism. On one side, a number of feminists— referred to as "liberal theory feminists"—believe that, despite these problems, the liberal project remains the most positive political option for women at the end of the twentieth century.[36] What the liberal project needs, they argue, is not wholesale rejection but a rigorous feminist internal critique. If this critique occurs, liberalism can be made to actualize more fully its goal of a social order where diverse individuals are free to flourish under a set of common laws protecting their inherent rights. Further, these feminists affirm liberal theory's universalist agenda. They believe it is possible to tell a universal story about human persons and the contracts they make and to extrapolate from it universal principles to govern our collective lives. What this story needs (and what classical liberal theory failed to deliver), they argue, is a sharper analysis of the role gender plays in the self and its contracts. This is what feminism offers.

This feminist perspective on liberalism is quite well-known in North America. References to feminism in popular culture are almost always to this perspective. Think of such feminist cultural icons as Betty Friedan, Gloria Steinem, *Ms.* magazine, and the National Organization for Women. At the heart of each of their social visions is a grand (universal) tale of humanity and society and, along with it, a celebration of such liberal principles as freedom, equality, self-determination, and the universal rights necessary for the individual flourishing of women. One also finds a strong defense of such liberal principles in feminist organizations, ranging from local pro-choice groups and anti-domestic-violence organizations to more militant lesbian separatist groups.

Other feminist political theorists, however, are less enthusiastic about reforming the liberal vision. Although they often affirm such values as self-determination and equality, they remain deeply troubled by several of liberalism's most fundamental claims about the nature of the self and the character of ideal community, most particularly its universalism/essentialism. This second group of feminist political theorists—whose opinions include those of communitarian feminists as well as some socialist and Marxist feminists, postmodern feminists, and some forms of so-called radical feminism[37]—argue that the flaws in liberal theory are so deep that feminism would be better served by constructing new, alternative models for social organization. This second group takes a more constructivist approach to community, politics, and values.[38]

To see the difference, look at what each group of feminists proposes as correctives to liberalism. First, consider the argument that the liberal self is masculine. Liberal theory feminists suggest in response to the liberal masculine self a more comprehensive account of the presocial self—an account that includes, among other things, the feminine attributes that were devalued or left out before. In this way, liberal theory feminists maintain the liberal attempt to generate a universal account of humanity; they simply hope to make it more genuinely universal. In contrast, stronger feminist opponents of liberalism suggest that simply adding "feminine attributes" to the liberal self will not solve its gender problems. While it may help us see the historically binary dynamics at work in our communities, we are still left with the problem of falsely universalized gender binaries. We need instead a political theory with a more particularized appreciation for the many conceptions of selves in our corporate lives, a theory communitarianism tries to provide.

The two groups have similarly divergent responses to liberal theory's public/private divide and its neglect of social bonding that is not rational or self-interested. Liberal theory feminists argue that the public/private distinction should be blurred because of its sexism but not rejected, because it is an important mainstay in the argument for individuals' right to privacy—a sentiment expressed in the slogan: we don't want the state in our bedrooms. They suggest we should revalue bonds of care (perhaps think of mothering as an image of politics compatible with social contracting) and make a place for emotion in ideal community. In contrast to this position, stronger opponents of liberalism push us to conceive of social life according to other, more complex, integrated, and flexible models of sociality. While these theorists agree that we could certainly benefit from valuing bonds of care and emotion, they argue that these bonds are themselves products of historical traditions and should not be falsely universalized.

The two groups also part ways on the question of the principle of equality's exclusions and rights based on difference. According to liberal theory feminists, liberal theory can accommodate difference in a class called "special rights," which might support policies such as maternity leave for women.[39] Feminist theorists on the other side argue that liberal theory is so tightly wedded to a logic of sameness that true difference cannot be admitted. The two camps diverge in much the same way over liberalism's theory of power and culture. According to strong feminist opponents of liberalism, the universal structure of the liberal view of the self will always trump human differences and hence eclipse the deeply constitutive roles of power and culture in society. Liberal theory feminists respond that a fuller account of power and culture can be integrated into liberalism's conception of the social contract.[40] An example of this divide is the disagreement between the two groups over the effectiveness of the affirmative-action policies liberal theory has developed to address discrimination in the workplace.[41]

Despite these differences, however, both sides share a political vision for the flourishing of women and a social analysis of the gender problems that undergird the oppression and domination of women. They share a suspicion of the gender biases in liberalism's universalism, and yet both realize that some of liberalism's universal principles can promote the well-being of women. They share a recognition that culturally mediated relations of power shape identity and community in ways that traditional political theory over-looks, and yet they want to avoid a relativistic historicism that undercuts emancipatory visions. They share a commitment to differences in commu-nity, having experienced the deadly force of patriarchal communities that exclude and repress, yet both recognize that not all differences are good, and that communities committed to the flourishing of women need broadly applicable policies that concretely embody this commitment, a necessity that inevitably creates borders. In short, they both appreciate the need for bounded openness in ideal community.

In theorizing this vision, however, each group has its strengths and weak-nesses, a point often acknowledged in conversations between them. The strength of those sympathetic to liberalism rests in their ability to defend lib-eralism's universalism and argue rigorously for its principles—principles that feminists affirm, such as self-determination and a respect for basic human rights. Their weakness, on the other hand, is the difficulty in theorizing dif-ference, power, and culture. In other words, liberalism's universalism cannot accommodate the particularizing reflections necessary for understanding the complex character of our social interactions. The strength of those less sym-pathetic to liberalism lies in the agility of the group's social theory and hence its ability to account for the concrete ways oppression functions and identi-ties are formed. Their strength thus lies precisely in their ability to theorize what liberal universalism cannot: difference, power, and culture. But this ability is this group's weakness as well. Because of their constructivist orien-tation, this group of theorists finds it difficult to defend their political vision as universal, yet they admit the need for such commitments. In light of these strengths and weaknesses, recent debates in feminist theory have seen a con-certed effort to negotiate the gaps between the two sides, each to the good of the other.

Communitarianism

Like "liberalism," the term "communitarianism" refers to a wide range of perspectives in contemporary political theory. These perspectives are known under a spectrum of political names, from Radical Marxism on the left to Neo-Conservative Civic Republicanism on the right.[42] What these perspec-tives have in common—what makes them communitarian—is their rejec-tion of liberalism's isolated individualism in favor of a more community-centered understanding of human life. They worry that liberalism has failed to describe the complex nature of our communal life and has left us with a dry, alienated view of politics. In response, communitarian political theory seeks to reinvigorate politics by turning attention away from grand, univer-sal principles of the self and contract and toward the actual communities in which we live and work. In the nitty-gritty texture of these everyday communities, they argue, our visions of ideal community originate; here, politics has its origin and hope.

What do we find when we look to actual communities as the starting point for our reflections on ideal community? According to communitarians, we find that persons are profoundly determined by the specific character of their communities. Instead of a collection of presocial selves with accrued social attachments, communitarians find persons deeply formed by their varied social locations and communal environments. This recognition has led communitarians to assert, using the language of constructivism, that we are intimately interconnected beings (not originally isolated individuals); our personhood emerges out of complex engagements with the persons, places, practices, discourses, and traditions into which we are born and within which we continue to live.

The best way, then, to construct a political theory concerning our corporate lives (and ideal community) is to analyze the complex formation processes of these varied communities. Although these communities are wide ranging in scope, certain ones play a more significant role than others in constructing our identities. The more significant communities are of four basic types: (1) communities based on kinship ties, such as family; (2) communities of shared culture, language, and ethnicity; (3) communities marked by geographic proximity that permits face-to-face interactions, such as a neighborhood or region; and (4) communities that share a religion or a tradition of values. In many cases, formative communities are a combination of these types. What makes them formative is the constitutive role they play in developing a worldview and instilling the values that govern our interactions. This formation of worldviews and values occurs as we learn in community how to reason and make meaning. It happens when we learn a social code for emotions and a communal grammar for interpreting our bodily experiences. We learn these things not only by imbibing the ideas of a community but by participating in the common tasks, practices, rituals, and enduring habits of heart that unfold in daily life. Out of this rich blend of practices, ideas, and habits, persons emerge with fundamental instincts about what makes a good or not-so-good society. This stew is called "tradition," and its vision of the good inspires our differing perspectives on politics.

Rather than ground their reflections on ideal community in a rational account of the abstract, isolated, self-interested "man of reason" and his actions in the public realm of politics, communitarians thus look to our neighborhoods, our churches, our ethnic traditions, and our extended family networks to find a whole clutch of values and views of self that form our view of communality and our sense of a good society. They ask us to give up the illusory project of generating principles on which all rational people must agree. The starting point for political discussion is instead the traditions of the persons engaged in discussion. This means communitarians usually begin the task of theorizing community by doing "thick description" of specific communities and traditions—not with an exploration, via universal reason, of a grand picture of the self and the social contract. The theorist best suited to this task of thick description is, moreover, not the impartial "man of reason" but the admittedly partial theorist who stands in the community and the value system being described. In this position of "inside informer," she or he has access to subtleties of practice and language that might not be apparent to those outside.

Communitarians also hold that it is important to understand communities in their own terms. Their thick descriptions, therefore, usually emerge from carefully listening to what the sanctioned, authoritative voices of a community say about its view of the world, its values, and its vision of the good life—and not what a supposedly "objective" outside observer might report.

Communitarians recognize that we live in a world of enormous diversity, a world where communities offer different visions of flourishing, have different values, and hence, hold radically different views of what a good society is. Like liberal theorists, communitarians affirm that the challenge for political theory in such a pluralistic context is to devise ways for diversity to flourish while also establishing rules to manage effectively our larger corporate lives together. Communitarians suggest, however, that decisions about these public interactions cannot be guided by a singular, precommunal truth we all hold. We must give up appeals to an objective common ground and, instead, articulate to others the communal values we embrace, thereby opening ourselves to intersubjective conversations about collective public goods. While such conversations may be hard to manage, they have the advantage of encouraging a quality of learning that respects differences and honors particularity without placing them under the circumscription of a universal standard. Because communitarians do not have recourse to a grand theory of the self and a social contract, however, they cannot offer a universal template for this conversation or what it will produce. By leaving the question of both process and product open-ended, communitarians permit us to be more creative in our political imaginings and more pragmatic about what might encourage conversation in a given time and space. Further, communitarians do not claim that the conversation itself is the model of ideal society (as it is in the case of liberalism). Given our different and often conflicting visions of ideal community, conversation is simply the best we can hope for at present.[43]

Feminist Responses to Communitarianism. Were one to poll feminist theorists in North America about communitarianism, one would most likely discover a small handful of feminists who enthusiastically applaud the project, a larger handful who categorically reject it, and an even larger majority who are conflicted in their assessment of it. While there are many features of the communitarian project with which feminists agree, parts of the project are antithetical to feminism's basic commitments. For these reasons, those feminists in the middle group (feminists ranging from postmodernists and liberals to socialists and womanists) nod yes to several of communitarianism's treasured tenets, in particular its emphasis on community, while shaking their heads no to some of its conservative positions on social policy. To get a sense for this conflicted middle ground, let us begin with those points of the communitarian project that many feminists (even some liberal theory feminists) heartily embrace.

The strongest similarity between feminist theorists and communitarians is their shared constructivism. In an earlier chapter, we heard this position, in its feminist version, defended in de Beauvoir's famous quote: "One is not born, but rather becomes, a woman." We hear it echoed now in the communitarian argument that communities precede persons. As such, feminists often experience the communitarian claim that values are communally anchored as a breath of fresh air in an otherwise stale tradition of political theories wedded to universals and essentials that exclude women. Constructivism alone, however, is not a guarantee of emancipatory politics.[44]

Feminists and communitarians also agree that the self liberalism gives us—the isolated, rational, freedom-loving self—is not as unbiased and universal as it purports to be; and both groups enjoy revealing the biases hidden in liberalism's account of this presocial person. Both feminists and communitarians advocate a view of personhood that is more relational, socially interactive, and communally oriented.[45] They share as well a critique of the social contract that these mythic, liberal individuals supposedly form. Both point out that the liberal social contract presupposes the bifurcation of society into the public and private realms—a division that fails to account for the complexity of social interactions. Both suggest that political theorists need a more integrated model of communality where, for instance, one can appreciate the interconnections between the work done by the woman who cleans house and feeds children and the work done in the high halls of Congress on matters of military preparedness. Both suggest as well that political theory can benefit from an open-ended definition of political community. Such open-endedness, they argue, frees us to consider important forms of sociality that the liberal model overlooks in confining the world to the two spheres of public and private.

They also both reject liberalism's claim that social bonds in political community are solely ones of self-interest. Feminists and communitarians suggest that some important bonds are not selfish in nature. For instance, because of religious commitments, people often do unselfish things such as offer alms to the poor and give unrecognized and unremunerated time and energy to community service.[46] Out of commitment to ethnic traditions, people are also willing to die for values (such as honor or friendship) with little basis in reasoned reflection. Out of love for children, numerous adults undergo enormous self-sacrifice. Each of these forms of sociality is not superficial or secondary to our social bonding but constitutive of community life and its politics.

Feminists and communitarians also agree in rejecting the liberal claim that ideal social relations should be mediated solely by rational, universal principles and not by emotional, particularistic sentiments. They point out that forms of bonding such as parenting, friendship, or even professional collegiality are guided not by abstract, universal principles but by a whole series of highly specific and localized considerations. For instance, we seldom ask about those with whom we interact on a daily basis, How might I best pursue my self-interest with this person as an abstract, general subject? We make decisions about our interactions with others based on our understanding of their particularity, their social location, and their needs and desires, as well as on our assessments of our own history with them and the traditions that form the space of our meeting; in this space, feeling as much as logic or reason determines the character of our interactions. In this way, particularized reflections and not universal reasoning (liberalism) give shape to our daily ethical engagements.[47]

Both feminists and communitarians believe, further, that liberalism fails to take seriously the role of conceptions of the good life in our daily lives and political interactions. They argue that communal flourishing involves much more than procedural justice and strict equality. While justice and equality may be important (depending on one's communal tradition), other dimensions of life contribute to communal and personal well-being, such as the need for beauty in one's surroundings and spiritual nurture, the desire to celebrate life passages through the rituals and traditions of one's heritage, the need to be affirmed in one's belonging, and the desire to see those whom one loves flourish. Both communitarians and feminists recognize that these things affect how we imagine our future as community and hence affect how we live in the present; if this imagining is to embrace the complexity of our political lives, it must take into account dimensions of flourishing that the liberal paradigm leaves out, dimensions of life traditionally represented by visions of "the good society."

Yet another point of agreement between feminists and communitarians is the belief that political theorists need to give thick descriptions of local communities in which persons are crafted, political values formed, and visions of the good life nurtured. Both groups of theorists therefore turn to fields such as cultural studies to learn how to "read" communities. Subsequently, both groups have become accomplished critics of culture, an accomplishment liberal theorists rarely claim. This facility for localized cultural analysis is directly linked to a further point of agreement: an appreciation for the localized nature of political change. For social transformation to occur, both argue, one must organize and act locally, for that is where values are created and normative commitments to particular actions are formed. While feminists and communitarians do not believe that the state should never intervene and set policies affecting local communities, they value the particular and local as the principal locus of social change.

Given these points of agreement between many feminists and communitarians—their shared constructivism (both weak and strong), their shared critique of liberal foundationalism, their shared appreciation for the political value of visions of the good life, and their shared insistence that social change most effectively occurs at the local level where values are generated and political actors are formed—it might seem that the only differences between them are ones of emphasis. For a small number of feminist theorists who simply call themselves "communitarian feminists," this is indeed the case.[48] Beyond this group, however, feminist political theorists (from liberal to Marxist to postmodernist) agree that most mainstream communitarians have significant problems with women and gender. For this reason, even feminists with strong constructivist interests (and similarly strong critiques of liberalism) have drawn back from a wholesale embrace of the communitarian project. Their reasons are multiple.

At the heart of their critique is the claim that communitarianism, as a whole, fails to account for the role that gendered relations of power play in the formation of communal values and practices. Given communitarianism's constructivist orientation, this failure is particularly puzzling. When giving a thick description of communal formations, communitarians have no problem adverting to such things as the ethnic background, geographic location, or religion of a given group; they consider these features important to understanding the practices and traditions within a community.[49] One would therefore expect them to do the same for gender (and race, and sexuality, and so on), but they don't. Feminists thus argue that by excluding gender from their analysis of tradition, communitarians fail to carry through on their avowed constructivism.

Feminist political theorists consider how different communitarian themes might look if gender were included. The communitarian critique of the liberal self, for example, could benefit from the insight that it is historically predicated upon a gender binarism that privileges the masculine and devalues the feminine. Without the benefit of a gender analysis of the liberal self, communitarians fall into a sexist critique of the social contract theory. In critiquing the liberal public/private divide, communitarians often call for a retrieval of the lost virtues and traditions of the private realm. Because feminists are aware of the gendered power relations undergirding the public/private division and its view of social bonding, their critique of the contract, unlike that of the communitarians, seldom involves an uncritical call to revalue the private realm. Feminists agree that we should stop devaluing the work women do in the private sphere. But, they suggest, a naive valorization of the private and its bonds of care and emotionality can easily become an oppressive celebration of traditional gender roles. Because communitarians fail to see the role of gender in the construction of the public/private binarism, they fail to be concerned about the gender oppressions implicit in a communitarian call for a return to traditional values.

Feminists also argue that communitarians are strangely silent about the potential negatives of communities. Communitarians often offer an overly simplistic and highly romanticized account of community life. They conceive communities as harmonious groups of persons bonded by common values specific to themselves.[50] The community is "the place where traditional values flourish" and where the good life abounds. They thus tend to focus on the stability and unity of communities and traditions over time. When they listen to people describe communal values, they also tend to listen to the voices of the mainstream leaders in a community. Feminists, in contrast, think that communities harbor as much potential for harm as for hope, and they usually begin their assessment of a community by looking at its fractures and its potential for violence. Feminists are likewise as interested in a community's instability as its stability and, consequently, they focus on aspects of a tradition eclipsed by the dominant voices in the community, particularly those that concern women and gender relations.

In all these ways, feminists have a different image of what a community is. Although they are not opposed to looking at such communities as families and neighborhoods, they push us to consider different forms of community such as the NSMs, which clearly do not meet romanticized communitarian standards. Furthermore, when feminists look at the family or a religious group, they see institutions whose surface stability often hides practices of violence and exclusion. For this reason, feminists are never interested, as communitarians are, in listening only to what the (usually male) leaders of a tradition say. They want to hear as well what others (particularly women) have to say; by listening to a diversity of voices, feminists argue, one better appreciates the ongoing conflicts that mark living traditions and communities. Feminists also point out that because communitarians so strongly desire to trace the continuities of communal life and its values, they fail to develop theories of how resistance and change happen in community. Feminists, in contrast, never separate their theories of community from their theories of resistance. They study community to figure out how to change it.[51]

Tied to this consideration is another feminist critique. Feminists charge that communitarians fail at the level of normative reflection because they tend to promote uncritically social values that, at best, merely reflect the status quo and, at worst, hearken back to patriarchal cultural values.[52] As to why communitarians embrace such values, feminists make the following rather straightforward observation. Given the communitarian view of community as a stable unit whose values are best represented by the dominant, tradition-bearing and tradition-treasuring (male) voices in that community, the values communitarians lift up represent the sentiments of the more conservative, traditional elements of community. Although such voices might occasionally be feminist, in most of the social groups communitarians deem community, the mainstream, tradition-bearing voices are far from feminist.

This problem, feminists add, results from the trouble communitarians have distinguishing the descriptive task of political theory from its prescriptive, normative task.[53] Communitarians fall into defending communal values simply because they are communal and traditional in nature. Hence, they have difficulty mustering principles of self-criticism within communities. They are also unwilling to generate critical principles from outside. To avoid this trap, feminists adopt the double vision discussed earlier. Communitarians, however, shy away from such a posture because it means stepping outside thick description and the normative claims possible within it.

Feminists also worry that communitarians have an overly deterministic understanding of the relationship between persons and communities. In making the point that communities precede persons, communitarians often underestimate the role of individual creativity and innovation in community. Communitarians become so enamored of the power of community to construct identity that they eliminate persons as agents with the capacity to make authentic choices that cut against the grain of the accepted wisdom of their communities. Feminists argue that such theories reinforce patterns of socialization that downplay the moral importance of women's agency and hence paralyze liberating practice.[54]

A Third Way

Echoing the need for a middle ground between essentialism and constructivism—the strategic essentialism of chapter 3—and for a middle ground between strong and weak feminist opponents of liberalism, feminists are beginning to clear a third path between liberal theory and communitarianism, a path that values the liberative potential of both normative rigor and historical openness. Such a path is being blazed by Seyla Benhabib's effort to rejuvenate liberal theory by making a place within it for particularized reflections on community.[55] We see this path as well in Iris Young's and Lani Guinier's efforts to redesign liberal understandings of political representation to reflect social bonds other than those of family, neighborhood, and political party. This middle path appears as well in the work of theorists such as Jane Mansbridge and Virginia Held, who include both rights and care in their assessment of healthy community. Although quite different, they share a sense that for communities to flourish, they need to embody bounded openness. Communities need both normative principles to bind them and a healthy suspicion of norms so as to be open to self-critique and change. Communities need to appreciate the formative power of the structures and traditions within which they exist while appreciating their limits and potential dangers.

In the liberal/communitarian debate, both sides have their versions of bounded openness. Liberal social contract theory gives us boundedness in the form of its universal principles and its robust understanding of rights. It also instantiates openness in its desire to create procedural structures that allow all voices to be heard. As feminists point out, however, liberalism's universals are gender biased and its procedures may not facilitate the openness they seek. Communitarianism gives us boundedness in its insistence on the thick cultural and institutional particularities of communal life. Communities inherently bind us. They offer openness, as well, in their criticism of liberalism's false universalism and their celebration of particular and local communal values. As feminists argue, however, communities' boundedness can become an uncritical celebration of patriarchal values, and without a gender analysis, their openness may be more confining than liberating.

As these tensions suggest, bounded openness is a difficult path to follow; little consensus exists among feminists about its specific shape. Feminists do agree, however, on the destination: a community in which women flourish. Feminist theologians join the chorus, and the path they follow is considered in the next chapter.

7

Church: Graced Community

At Center Church in New Haven, we have a unique way of performing the Christmas story. Someone reads the account of Jesus' birth, and the whole congregation enacts it using the sanctuary as a stage. The Tuesday-night group runs the show, a task we all look forward to. The women in the group agree that, time and again, the pageant provides an occasion to experience our church at its chaotic, grace-filled best. Christmas 1998 was no exception; three surprising events showed why.

One event occurred among the angels. Asked to play an angel, Joyce, who struggles with mental illness and low self-esteem, initially protested. But, through the encouragement of others, she reluctantly agreed. As the heavenly host appeared to the shepherds in the fields, Joyce participated fully in singing "Joy to the World" from the balcony. At the song's end, Joyce turned to the woman next to her, tears in her eyes. Connie smiled at Joyce as they stood there together wearing pipe-cleaner halos and frayed white choir robes. She was accustomed to seeing in Joyce's face signs of her struggle with interior voices of hate and self-loathing. But today was different. "I never knew I could be an angel," Joyce whispered. Her raiment shone.

Another surprise unfolded around the innkeeper, played by Reggie, a homeless man. Reggie was to stand in the center aisle and say no to the pregnant Mary and tired Joseph when they asked him for a place to spend the night. Reggie, however, grinning slightly, said, "Come in," instead. This confused Mary and Joseph, and they decided to ask again. Again, he repeated his quiet welcome to the couple. At first, people were nervous. What will we do if he doesn't give the right response? Then, looks of recognition appeared across the congregation. Reggie was not confused about his role; he understood his part very well. Through his response, he had reminded us of the harsh reality that this was a story of homelessness—and of the surprising "yes" that breaks through in its midst.

At the end of the play, a third event added a further surprise. The sound of loud whispering came from the front of the sanctuary. "Pastor Patricia, I still have something to say"; Lilly was tugging at her pastor's skirt. Although Patricia had just begun the benediction, it was obvious that Lilly, the seven-year-old playing King Herod, was not yet finished. Surprised and a bit curious, the pastor stopped praying and stepped aside, handing the microphone to this very serious-looking child. In a loud, dramatic voice, Lilly spoke to the startled congregation: "I am King Herod, and I have been watching you. I am going to kill all your babies. I hate you." Across the congregation, smiles vanished. Lilly had reminded us that Jesus' birth was met by the slaughter of the innocents, a story we wanted to forget. The service thus ended on an uncomfortably somber note.

For the women in the Tuesday-night group, these events of the Christmas pageant were the source of good conversations about what it means to be a community of faith. In the previous chapter, I discussed what feminist theorists say about community at descriptive and normative levels. The pageant offered our Tuesday-night group a chance to reflect on the same issues in our local church: What kind of community is the church? We had no interest in answering as distanced academics might after observing our community from afar. We asked from the inside, as persons of faith seeking to understand, theologically, what we were doing singing in white robes and listening to feisty seven-year-olds. Approaching the topic of church via our Christmas pageant also kept our reflections grounded in the nitty-gritty, present-day life of a real congregation, not in an abstract image of what some nonexistent church might ideally be. While we certainly did not oppose ideals (along with liberals) nor think that our play was the only form church takes in our lives, we focused on this community and its practices because it kept us anchored in the church as it actually lives in history (along with communitarians).

Although the Tuesday-night women did not name it as such, this conversation brought us squarely into a field of theological reflection traditionally known as "ecclesiology," or the doctrine of the church. Like the other doctrines treated in this book (faith and sin), the church has a long and complex history in the Christian tradition and continues to be a topic of much debate in both church and academy. In the pages ahead, I continue this conversation by developing a feminist ecclesiology that stands in conversation with feminist theory. In the first part of this chapter, I take our local church pageant as the starting point for a general description of Christian *ekklesia* (Greek for "a gathering"). It is a description that pulls together, from previous chapters, many of the feminist themes I developed in relation to doctrine and performance, and it shows the relevance these themes have for a feminist conception of "church." Against the backdrop of these general comments, the second part focuses on two historically significant images of the church—Luther's image of church as a community of saints and Calvin's portrayal of church as mother.[1] I then undertake in the third part a feminist remapping of these images and offer a reconstructed vision of the church as forgiven/forgiving community and the adorned/adorning people. This is the corporate version of the individual identities described in chapter 3 as "justified" and "sanctified." This vision of *ekklesia,* I argue further, is not unlike the feminist ideal of bounded openness described in the previous chapter on community—an eschatological essentialist vision of the church.

Distinctive Features of Church as Community

Eight interrelated aspects of the church surfaced when the Tuesday-night women asked what is distinctive about the church. These eight features were not original to our group's discussion, but they were approached afresh from a local-church, feminist perspective.

The first feature was straightforward: the church is a community in which the Scripture is regularly recounted and listened to. One could clearly see this in the pageant, which centered on telling and listening to the biblical narrative of the birth of Jesus. What is the story told and heard in church? In its broadest strokes, it is the story of a gracious God who out of love calls the world into being and seeks covenantal relation with it. It is the story of a God who seeks this relation for the good of these creatures, that they might flourish, loving God and one another and living together in relations of justice, peace, and beauty—relations in which difference is celebrated and the full humanity of all persons is affirmed. It is the story of a people who reject God's desire for loving relation and, in doing so, fall into sin, but whom God promises to seek out and love nonetheless. It is the story of the people of Israel, who struggle with this covenant, sometimes responding in joy and praise, sometimes turning away. It is the story of God coming to the world in the person of Jesus Christ to reestablish that relationship. It is the story of his life, death, and resurrection and of the faith community formed in response to him, a community awaiting the eschatological breaking in of God's realm yet again. And finally, it is a story that is not itself the final object of our speaking and listening. The story reaches beyond itself to witness to the reality of the God who, through the power of the Spirit, gives the story its life.[2]

The women in the group noted a second obvious feature of the church community: within the scriptural story, the theme of community is sounded repeatedly. For example, the story provides a portrait of a God who is profoundly communal in character. God is depicted communally both as a trinity of persons existing eternally in loving relations of mutual indwelling and as the one who, out of this trinitarian love, creates the world to be in community with it. The story also makes clear that human beings are essentially communal creatures. We are called to be in relation to both God and our neighbors as well as to the world around us. We have the possibility of actualizing this communality in negative or positive ways. We can live toward the normative vision of community in which humanity flourishes as it praises God and abides in relations of justice, peace, and beauty. Or, we can live in community in ways that distort God's will for our flourishing— the ways of sin and evil. Scripture also offers an account of communities that have struggled to live in right relation to God and neighbor: the people Israel, the disciples of Jesus, and the New Testament "church," each of which tries to embody God's will and yet repeatedly fails. Finally, the story suggests that having a personal faith and being part of a faith community belong together. In all these ways, Scripture is not only a story communally read but a story about community: it is the story of a communal God who comes to a communal people who corporately sin and collectively seek to dwell in loving community with God and one another.[3]

In light of the broad sweep of this narrative framework, the women in the Tuesday-night group immediately lifted up a third dimension of church life: *in places like our local church, the story is recounted in many different ways.* In the pageant, the story was read directly from Scripture (albeit in translation). During the worship service, it was also told in hymns, prayers, and the actions of our bodies. On most Sunday mornings, the story is told through a sermon as well. It is also visually displayed throughout our sanctuary—in the scattered stained-glass windows and the children's banners in the narthex. It is enacted in the sacraments. The Christmas pageant further suggests that the story can be told in inadequate ways. As Lilly reminded us that morning, sometimes parts of the story get left out or become distorted in their telling. Even when every part is included, different interpretations of the story abound—a point that feminists repeatedly make. The pageant also indicates how the story can be miscommunicated and yet still be understood, as in Reggie's rewriting of the innkeeper's response. In all these ways, the church can be defined as a community that speaks and listens to the story of God's liberating history with us and the eschatological promise held therein.

A fourth feature of the church also emerged. As the pageant makes clear, people in the church have a rather peculiar relationship to this story. It is not merely an interesting story. In the church, we inhabit this story as the definitive story of our lives. The story serves a normative function in the life of the church. People in the church are encouraged to live into it. Its drama makes sense of our personal lives and of history as well. As the pageant exemplifies, hearing the story requires assuming the role of participant in the narrative world, where God is actively creating and redeeming a fallen people. Upon normatively entering God's story "with us," a community of persons encounters a living Jesus and a future promise that dramatically shapes the church's current living. In my terms, the church is that community where Scripture serves as a collective and normative lived imaginative construct. In traditional language, Scripture and doctrine are the rule of faith (from the Latin, *regula fidei*), the measure by which reality is gauged.

When the Tuesday-night women discussed this feature of church life in light of the pageant, two additional images surfaced—church as the community that imitates and performs the story.[4] The church imitates when it follows the story, aligning the actions, emotions, attitudes, and beliefs of its members with the multivalent patterns of action, emotion, attitude, and belief that structure the narrative. In doing so, the church engages in a profoundly dependent and derivative practice; it depends on a prior, originative reality, which it seeks to mimic but with which it is never identical. This mimetic dimension of church existence also calls attention to the interpretive dimension of church life; as it imitates, it reenacts the story in the context of the lived experience of its present-day performers.

The image of *performance* clarifies the way the church inhabits Scripture.[5] It captures even better than imitation the theatrical dimensions of the church's life in the narrative. To see this, return to the Christmas play. As we entered the sanctuary, we stepped into a Christmas story framed by the larger one of God's creative, redemptive relation to the world. In this story, we encountered subject positions (not all of them positive) that we were invited to imitate by following the directions of the narrative. Stepping into one (or perhaps many) of these positions, we acknowledged both our dependence on a prior script and the inevitable improvisations we undertook to interpret it in the context of our multifaceted lived experience. Thus, Joyce and Reggie occupied the space of the identities of angel and innkeeper in a manner that allowed them to be radically reshaped by the story-event of incarnation. Joyce moved into a performative role in which God's grace met her and thereby contradicted the script she normally followed. Reggie's understanding of God's love for him as a homeless person allowed him to recast the role of innkeeper in a manner that aligned it with God's intention for the world. In both situations, they experienced their performative roles as definitive for their self-understanding as creatures of God.

This brings me to a sixth characteristic of church: people describe themselves as "called" into this community by God. They have been claimed by the divine or chosen by God to inhabit the story. Unlike many communities that we inhabit, the church is not solely a community of choice or voluntary association. The community describes itself as brought into being by an act of divine initiative. The church thus experiences its existence as a gift. This means that the church doesn't just choose to inhabit the story; it understands itself as being inhabited *by* the story. The story of God's loving creation and redemption is a drama that grasps the church by pulling it into its drama and remaking it in its own image.[6] In other words, the story performs the church. The church does not create itself and then decide to inhabit the story of God's love. To the contrary, God's story, through the power of the Spirit, creates the church, which then seeks to live in the narrative that gave it birth.

A seventh feature of church that surfaced in our Tuesday-night group concerns its relationship with the other communities to which we belong. As mentioned previously, the women in the Tuesday-night group have many communities to which they belong, some of which are chosen, some not. The folks who entered the sanctuary on the Sunday of the pageant brought with them the complex worlds of many different communities—their families, their jobs, their neighborhoods, their political affiliations, and so on. These other communities also shape us and claim us, in varying ways and to varying degrees. This is because each has its own set of lived imaginative constructs lending specificity to the experience of its members. However, the church community, unlike some other communities, requires its members to give privileged status to church life and to the church's lived imaginative constructs. The church requires its members to give the church priority over other communal commitments. The members need not eschew these commitments, although where incompatible with faith, they must be reshaped. This requirement highlights the fact that the church never constructs our world in isolation from our other communal commitments; it normatively shapes us in the midst of them.

At this point in our discussions, the women in the Tuesday-night group began to feel uncomfortable with the vision of church that was emerging. We had spent enough time on the doctrine of sin to see the dangers in granting the church unquestioned authority in our lives and in claiming the church to be chosen by God to normatively determine communal practices. For many of us, the church had been a source of oppression and suffering. We knew from history that the church's view of itself as chosen had justified horrendous acts of injustice against women and many others as well. We knew as well that our own church was a long way from the life of communal sharing described in the New Testament. Our church allows one of its members to remain homeless, falters in addressing our racism and heterosexism, and avoids thinking about the slaughter of the innocents; it is a community gripped by and implicated in structures of oppression.

In response to these realities, the women's group lifted up an eighth feature of the church: its identity as a sinful community. The church is dependent upon the story of God's will for creation and should therefore never be viewed as synonymous with that divine reality. In this sense, the church is not the object of faith; it is the community of those who *have* faith. We also recalled that in Scripture, the church is depicted as relentlessly implicated in sin. It is the community that creates the golden calf, that oppresses the poor, that allows women to be raped and murdered in the name of righteousness, and that deserts Jesus as he walks toward the cross. When the church inhabits these parts of the story, it is fallen. To use the language of performance, the church simultaneously performs the roles of the righteous and the unrighteous—of both saints and sinners. The Protestant tradition therefore describes the church as *ekklesia reformata semper reformanda* ("the church reformed, always in need of being reformed"). This description reminds us that the church needs to be engaged in a continual process of internal critique—a process of continued reformation—lest its faith pronouncements and practices become destructive idols of its own creation.

Feminist Perspectives on Church

This is a difficult position for the church to be in: charged to live faithfully and finding itself in brokenness. It is hard to have hope for—much less value—this church when one feels the full force of its fallenness. Here, the women's group found helpful the classical distinction between the *empirical* and the *normative* church.[7] The normative church is the community we are called to be—church as it should be. The empirical church is the one in which we actually live, the church we presently see, touch, and taste, the church of our Christmas play in all its righteousness and sin. These two churches stand in eschatological tension with each other. In light of its obvious brokenness, the empirical church is clearly not the normative church; the empirical church constantly fails to live up to its ideals and the normative church stands as its judge. The normative church does not exist, however, only as a mere dream, because to be church is to be embodied and empirical. To use an eschatological image employed frequently in this book, the normative church is already/not yet embodied in the empirical church.

Feminist theologians have constructed a variety of models for this present-day/future church. Some have envisioned the church as a roundtable where all are welcome; others have described it as "Woman-church," where the gifts of women throughout the centuries are celebrated.[8] It has been depicted as well as the "perfectly open sign," where women find the power to speak, and as a "discipleship of equals" that reflects the inclusive aspirations of early Christian communities.[9] Some feminist theologians have imagined this church as a spiral dance and a jubilee feast; still others have seen it as a community of emancipatory risk and a garden filled with many flowers.[10]

In discussing this claim that the church is both sinful and yet eschatologically graced, our Tuesday-night women's group had interesting things to say about the history of feminism's complex relation to the church. Several women recalled the attitude that they held toward our church in the early days of their feminism. In the sixties, seventies, and even early eighties, these women's struggle to come to voice in the church was met with resistance and often rejection, a reaction that continues in many churches today. In light of this reaction, they experienced the local church as primarily performing the role of sinner—the violence-bound Herod and the uninterested innkeeper. Rejection by the church thus prompted these women, and others like them, to look outside it for sustenance.

Several women in the Tuesday-night group recalled how liberating it was to step beyond the bounds of the traditional church into spaces where they were encouraged to creatively reimagine a church more diligent about its normative end.[11] Several of the Tuesday-night women also developed a strongly anti-institutional and antiauthoritarian attitude toward the church. The church, they believed, was a harmful community, a prison from which they needed to be freed so that they might truly perform and be performed by God's grace.

The Tuesday-night women then went on to describe how their attitudes had shifted during the last decade. They described the tremendous difference it made when our church hired a woman pastor, adopted an inclusive language policy, officially welcomed lesbians and gays, and supported the creation of groups like ours. These actions brought new energy and life into the church, making it a safer space for them to inhabit as women. They also said that it was more difficult than they anticipated to find alternative communities outside the church, particularly in a society growing in isolated individualism. While some of them initially found New Age and self-help versions of women's spirituality empowering, these practices also embodied this individualizing tendency of the broader culture by insisting on the journey of faith as an interior, individual one.

They had also missed the people in the church—even those they did not like. They missed having to sit next to a World War II veteran every Sunday morning and hear his response to the sermon. They missed having to eat regular potluck dinners with a homeless man. They missed being surprised by a seven-year-old's rendition of Scripture. While they hoped for these kinds of relationships outside the church, they rarely found them. As feminists of faith, their major struggle was thus no longer to escape the prison of an oppressive community; instead, their challenge had become to find community in an otherwise atomized and isolated culture of individuals. In the context of this challenge, our local church, for all its shortcomings and harms, began to look like the truly radical alternative.

My own approach to the church is closer to the second description of the church than to the first. While I am aware of the church's ongoing sinfulness, I experience it as a place where I can respond to the Christian and feminist call to live in and struggle with communities of diversity seeking justice. I find myself unable to worship God and love my neighbor in isolation from the Christian community; the very tissue of my faith resides there. As a feminist, I am deeply committed to creating communities in which women, in all their diversity, can be safe and flourish, and I realize that the church is not currently such a place. But I have also come to see, along with many other feminists, that opportunities to live in intentional and diverse communities are few and far between. The church remains one such place.

Church as Community of Saints and Sinners and as Mother

In chapter 3, I began my feminist theological remapping of identity by looking at what Luther and Calvin had to say about the faith identities of "justified" and "sanctified." In this section of our discussion of church, let me now ask, similarly: How might Luther and Calvin have interpreted my church's Sunday-morning pageant? Given their views of the church, would they have appreciated or disapproved of it? To answer such questions, let us turn to their doctrines of the church. As with the Reformation doctrines of justification, sanctification, and sin, this consideration will be the basis for my feminist remapping of similar themes.

Luther's Community of Saints

Luther held strong views about the church. He both loved and despised it. He was deeply committed to and yet profoundly alienated from it. It was for him a source of great strength as well as cause for profound despair. His writings bear witness to these tensions yet are unified by a bold ecclesial vision. At the heart of this vision is Luther's depiction of the church as the community of saints.[12]

For Luther, saints are not a special group of individuals who perfectly model the Christian life; a saint is anyone who sincerely confesses faith in Jesus Christ. Therefore, Luther means by "church" a gathering of people who share a common faith—a community of believers.[13] Central to this shared faith is the word of God. Faith occurs when people hear the word of God announced in their midst and respond by believing. This announcement can be made through a sermon or the sacraments, or even through a Christmas pageant. What is crucial about the announcement is not its particular form or substance but that the gospel is conveyed through it.[14] For Luther, the content of that gospel message is straightforward: in Christ, our sins are forgiven and we are promised life eternal. When people hear this announcement—this word of God—and believe, Luther contends, the church happens. It happens when, through the power of the Spirit, people listen to the proclamation of God's love for the world and respond with a faith that gathers them together.[15]

Luther develops a number of accounts of what this gathering involves. One image, although underdeveloped in his thought, captures the complex nature of the community he is trying to describe: the church as *simul iustus et peccator* (simultaneously justified and sinner)—an image that grows directly out of his doctrine of justification.[16] Recall that in Luther's drama of justification, he tells us a story of how each person of faith is devastatingly undone by the law and then graciously and miraculously remade by God's forgiving love. In addition to this story of personal faith, however, Luther's drama bequeaths to us a rather amazing account of how an entire community, a *collective people* and not just a single person, is similarly undone by divine judgment and remade by divine grace. Although Luther tells this second story with less focus and intensity than he does the first, it is nonetheless a story that has profound ramifications for how we understand the church and what it is called to perform in the world.

How does the drama of justification unfold when the church, and not the individual believer, is situated in its first role of defendant? The drama begins with the community caught in sin. This community, like the individual person of faith, is called to covenant relation with God, called to obey God's law, and yet has failed repeatedly and miserably to live up to that standard. The struggle to live up to the law in the church has taken many forms over the years. The community has created lovely sanctuaries, glorious art, powerful rituals, and magnificent orders of ministry, all in an attempt to follow the law and to win God's approval. And yet, in creating such things, it has failed to understand that God's love cannot be won; it must be given. The church has also struggled to merit divine approval by performing certain functions in the world, charitable functions such as caring for the sick and soteriological functions such as saving souls. In doing so, however, the church has failed to realize that such performances will never meet the measure of the law and that it is God and not the church who has the power to save souls.[17]

Standing under the judgment of the law, this church is not only condemned because of its false institutional pride and its arrogant functionalist pretensions; it is so leveled by the law that it can finally claim no special standing, in its own right, before God. In this context, the church under the law remains fully implicated in the sins of the world. It therefore cannot claim superiority over other communities; viewed through the lens of the law, its own brokenness is as profound as others. In all these ways, the church stands before God as sinner—a sinner sometimes unrepentantly boastful while at other times beleaguered and exhausted by its struggle to be perfect. Like the individual sinner, this church awaits its rightful sentence: eternal alienation from God. It is a church undone, a church dissolved.

The story continues, however, with a surprising turn of events. The judge who should rightly condemn the church for its sin makes an unexpected decision. God forgives this church its sins and decides to love and care for it, despite its fallenness. In an unmerited act of divine graciousness, God deems the church justified. Through Jesus Christ, God reconciles this community to Godself. Here is the most important moment in this story about the church, the moment when the church becomes the beloved of God not because of anything it has done but because God has decided to love it. The church as a graced community thus comes into existence not because of its merit but by divine decision. It becomes a forgiven community by virtue of a divine gift. As such, it is a community whose identity comes to it from beyond itself.[18] It receives the name "forgiven."

As in the individual's justification, the church's story does not end with this divine decision. In the third part of the story, the church has the privilege of hearing this verdict of forgiveness publicly proclaimed—through the church itself. In knowing about God's grace, the church is filled with such gratitude and joy that it must turn to the world and announce the good news of God's love. Its principal task becomes this joyous act of bearing witness to God's reconciling the world to Godself in Jesus Christ, a performance that the church undertakes not out of duty but out of thankfulness. It realizes it has not earned the privilege of performing this witness. It remains a society marked by sin and caught in the grip of pride, and it therefore recognizes its need for permanent self-critique.

The church also finds in the freedom of grace permission to stop being obsessed about its own merit and to truly open itself to others.[19] The church finally has nothing to prove or defend. It has only cause to celebrate and joyously serve. It is, therefore, at odds with a world that does not know God's love. As Luther tells us, the church lives in the shadow of the cross. Grace has opened the community up so that it may freely bear the burdens of others, but in doing so, the church stands alone in a world that knows it not.[20] Yet even as it stands in the shadow of the cross bearing such a burden, it knows itself to be fully implicated in the sin the cross reveals. It is thus a church both condemned and freed, both denounced and justified by the cross it proclaims.[21]

Given Luther's view of the church, what would he have thought of our play? Most likely, he would have delighted in the different saints and sinners we became and the radical undoing and remaking that took place as we assumed both familiar and unfamiliar roles—roles not of our own making yet ones we assumed fully. He would have probably seen it as a form of proclamation—that is, in hearing and seeing it performed, we all believed anew.

Near the end of the pageant, another unexpected event transpired that Luther would have particularly appreciated because it so beautifully illustrates his vision of a church joyously witnessing to the Gospel. The event involved Simon, a man from the Congo who had joined the church two years before. Simon felt awkward speaking in church. He was self-conscious speaking English, and no one in the church could understand his native language, Kicongo. On the morning of the pageant, however, things were different.

Simon was assigned to the group of wise-folk (magicians, kings, and queens) who were to present the newborn Jesus with gifts. Simon is very tall, and he towered above the other wise ones. Clad in royal, magical garments, he was clearly in the spotlight, and he seemed to enjoy it. After offering the baby Jesus his present, he turned to the congregation and, to our surprise, burst into song. He sang for us a treasured hymn from his childhood in the Congo. And in our hearing, we knew that although no one in the entire sanctuary knew a single word of Kicongo, the word of God had just been proclaimed and Luther's "community of saints" had come into existence once again.

Calvin's Church as Mother

Let us now turn to the theology of John Calvin and explore his views of Christian community. In many ways, these views parallel Luther's. Like Luther, Calvin had a conflicted relationship with the church of his day. Like Luther, Calvin felt that the church in its truest form is a gathering of believers who have heard the word of God and responded in faith. Calvin also shared Luther's belief that the chief task of this faith community is to witness to the Word.

There are, however, a significant number of differences between Luther's and Calvin's approaches to ecclesiology. First, they differ significantly in their style of writing. Whereas Luther's work is unsystematic and passionate, Calvin's reflections are clearly ordered and presented in a pedagogical form. Another difference has to do with their attitudes toward the practical matters of church life. While Luther loves to reflect on the gritty texture of the daily life of faith, he seldom approaches practical matters, such as the orders of ministry, with great precision or rigor. Calvin, in contrast, devotes many pages of his *Institutes* (to say nothing of his commentaries and treatises) to practical issues such as the ministerial offices, church discipline, and the church's relation to civil authority. At times, in fact, Calvin's writing reads more like a how-to book on church development than a work in church doctrine. Yet another difference lies in their general attitudes toward the institutional features of church life. Although Luther realizes that the earthly church inevitably takes institutional form, his basic disposition toward authority and institutions is largely negative, at least in his early writings. He reminds us often that the church can never be identified with its "brown brick building." Calvin, in contrast, dwells on the institutional features of ecclesial existence; he delights in them, struggles with them, and in his own life tried to shape them. He is even so bold as to include positive references to church buildings in his reflections on church life. [22]

To understand why Calvin found these institutional aspects of ecclesial life so interesting and important, recall his social context. Calvin understood his principal vocation to be a teacher of ministry students. Most of his students were headed for parishes in France, the homeland from which Calvin had been exiled. Life in these churches was difficult and dangerous. In addition to the hard task of building up young communities of faith, these pastors were actively persecuted. They were therefore concerned to foster forms of community resilient enough to resist outside forces seeking to destroy them. In such an environment, clear teaching, precise advice on practices, and careful wisdom about institutional form would have been highly valued. Calvin as an astute teacher no doubt understood these concerns and responded appropriately.[23]

Recall that in chapter 4, I described Calvin's doctrine of sanctification. This particular doctrine, I believe, is one of his responses to the hardships faced by this community. Just as Luther uses the drama of justification as the subtext for his account of the church as a community of saints and sinners, Calvin constructs a doctrine of the church that draws heavily on the process and growth imagery of sanctification. Calvin's doctrine of the church therefore focuses more on the processes by which a faith community is formed and maintained than on the momentary juridical decision central to Luther's account of community. Grace works in community in much the same way it works for the individual. Just as Calvin described the individual believer's life as being pulled together and given definition by sanctifying grace, he describes the church as a communal context in which people are pulled together and given defining practices and institutional form by a sanctifying grace.

To understand the depth to which the logic of sanctification informs Calvin's views, look at his two central metaphors for the church: the church as "God's accommodation" and the church as "Mother." The first image is implied by the title of book 4 of the *Institutes*. Concerning the church, the title reads: "The external means or aims by which God invites us into the society of Christ and holds us therein." This short statement tells us much about the theological underpinnings of Calvin's doctrine of the church. It portrays, in abbreviated form, the central drama of the sanctified life in its corporate dimensions. The portrait looks something like the following.

At the center is God inviting humanity into the society of Christ. This society is where humanity flourishes, where God's creatures live adorned in faith, hope, and love. Here the beloved of God dwell together in peace. Is this society the church we see on Sunday mornings? Perhaps, but Calvin leaves the question open. The society of Christ is the Christian community as it should be; as such, it is both an embodied reality and a future promise. Note that this society is established by divine invitation and sustained by divine nurture. God's grace welcomes us into it and then contains and embraces us once we arrive. The ones invited and embraced, however, are rather "dim witted," according to Calvin. They are not only distracted and childlike but disobedient. Try as they might, most cannot comprehend the splendor of the invitation God has issued. Even those who have heard the invitation and entered the community are depicted as troubled. They resist being "held therein" and are prone to wander off.

Calvin draws yet another portrait of the God who invites us in and promises to hold us in the society of Christ, a marvelous image of God as a creative, enlivening teacher seeking to engage the attention of this unruly, distracted group. Like a good teacher who employs a number of strategies to capture the minds and imaginations of her students, God uses a variety of teaching aids to attract our attention and focus our thoughts and actions on matters divine. These teaching aids are the "external means or aims" that book 4 vividly depicts God using.

The props that God uses are as diverse as our varied forms of knowing. God uses visual aids such as art as well as bread and wine. God uses the richness of sound to attract our attention—instrumental music and hymns as well as the verbal expressions of preaching.[24] God also uses Scripture and its many stories to captivate our imaginations and bring us to new knowledge of God and ourselves. God uses such human activities as healing the sick and caring for the poor as teaching aids that depict for others the tender mercy of God. God uses the ritual action of baptism to illustrate vividly that in Christ our sins are washed away and we are forgiven. God even uses buildings such as church sanctuaries to spatially communicate the breadth of God's glory and our call to worship. As Calvin explains it, these are all ways in which God, the master teacher, accommodates Godself to our "slight capacities" and thereby teaches us what we need to know to enter the society of Christ and to be held there: "God, in his wonderful providence accommodating himself to our capacity, has prescribed [in the church] a way for us, though still far off, to draw near to him."[25]

Note two specific features of this account. First, the "external means and aims" used by God do not have the power in themselves to shape us. Only as they are used by God do they attract and form us.[26] Second, however, when empowered by the Spirit, these means are absolutely integral to church life; they must therefore be treated with respect and theological seriousness. To use one of Calvin's favored metaphors, these practices and institutional forms are the "sinews" that hold us together in the society of Christ. Without them, we would not be held together as church, nor would we be capable, as church, of extending our reach into the world.

A similar understanding of the forming power of Christian community is captured in Calvin's image of the church as mother:[27]

> There is no other way to enter into life unless this mother (the church) conceive us in her womb, give us birth, nourish us at her breast, and lastly, unless she keep us under her care and guidance until, putting off mortal flesh, we become like the angels. Our weakness does not allow us to be dismissed from her school until we have been pupils all our lives. Furthermore, away from her bosom one cannot hope for any forgiveness of sin or any salvation.[28]

As this rich (and potentially problematic) metaphor suggests, Calvin understood the relationship between the church and believers to be like that between mother and child. Just as a child is knit together in her mother's womb, the people of faith are conceived and brought to life in the corporate body of the church. The image of the church as womb emphasizes the material and embodied ways in which the church forms us. We are made from the tissue of her many practices, rituals, institutional forms, and orders as well as from the numerous human relationships she engenders. All of these components work together to form and shape sinners despoiled (skinned, undone) by sin. In the womb of the Christian community, we are pulled together and refashioned in a manner that contradicts the chaos of sin and gives us new patterns of living in Christ's life. Baptism, the rite of Christian initiation, depicts this process well.[29] Just as a child comes into the world through the breaking water of the womb, the Christian is born from the birthing, baptismal water of the church.[30]

Calvin also describes how the maternal church raises and nurtures believers into adulthood. As children, we sit at her knee and learn of life and God.[31] We are disciplined by this mother; she establishes rules and boundaries for our actions and our knowledge of ourselves and the world.[32] This formation takes place not just through the spoken word but through the material practices of the church. We are, in this way, "nursing at the bosom" of the church. The process of raising us is gentle. The mother church teaches softly, comforts, and offers protection.[33] In all these ways, she provides a bounded space—a sanctuary—within which her children, now capable of making their own decisions, mature and thrive.[34] For Calvin, this bounded form of Christian living is not a restrictive prison; for him, the real prison is the fragmenting despoilment of sin. The church is where we are gently gathered together and tended to as children by a mother who desires only our abundant life.[35]

Given this view of the church as accommodating teacher and life-giving mother, what would Calvin have thought of our Christmas pageant?[36] Most likely, he would have appreciated how enacting the birth of Jesus shaped us in particular ways, and he probably would have attended closely to the important forming role of material things like costumes and sanctuary props as well as scripted lines. Joyce's frayed angel robe, Simon's royal garbs, Reggie's inn, all these concrete, ecclesial things opened our minds and bodies to the experience of God's grace, and as such, Calvin would have understood their place in the economy of sanctification.

One scene in particular Calvin would have liked. When my two-year-old daughter Charis and I walked through the door of the sanctuary Sunday morning, we were assigned to the shepherds' group. Charis had been up during the night, and we were both tired. I wondered, with a parent's apprehension, how we would make it through the service. Several women in the shepherds' group decided that Charis would look great in a cow costume (these shepherds were herding cattle), and I helped her get into the outfit, which she loved. I put on my own shepherdlike garb and felt relieved that my daughter seemed to be enjoying herself.

The angels finished singing, and we were cued to begin walking toward the front of the church where we were to gather around Mary, Joseph, and the baby Jesus. It had been decided that Charis the cow would lead the procession. She was, however, suddenly overtaken by shyness and tears. Not wanting to hold up the shepherds' procession, I gathered her up in my arms and walked slowly to the manger. We were quite a sight—a frumpy shepherd with a whimpering cow clinging to her neck—but no one seemed to mind.

"Oh mommy, look," she whispered when she saw the baby cuddled in an old wooden box. I kissed her forehead and smiled. My embracing arms had made it possible for her to see the baby Jesus. Like the church that embraces and contains the faithful, a real, physical, living body had carried her to the place where she could behold the wonder of Christmas.

Adorned in Freedom: The Bounded Openness of Church

My church building is architecturally impressive. Its imposing red-brick and white-pillared structure stands in the center of the New Haven green, bearing witness to our colonial past and our Puritan roots. As the city's founding institution, its history is rich; plaques hang on its walls commemorating famous pastors. Its windows are large, and its stained glass is priceless. Viewed from a distance, it looks like a postcard-perfect New England congregational church.

But looks can be deceiving. This is not the quiet green one imagines surrounding our postcard-perfect church. It is filled with people during an average weekday lunch hour. Walking across it are tired lawyers in suits, distracted students with backpacks, and hurried shoppers pushing baby strollers. Many people are sitting on the grass; some of them are picnicking, while others wear layers of worn-out clothes and have the far-off look of addiction or mental illness. A gathering of young men yell at a police car that drives slowly past them at regular intervals. An old woman digs cans out of a nearby trash bin, and a purple-haired, nose-pierced young couple stroll along hand in hand. Salsa music fills the air. The pounding beat of rap shakes a passing car.

The church too is not quite postcard-perfect. On Sunday mornings, our two hundred members fill only a fraction of its pews. Our faces are more like those on the green than the imagined faces of the church in days past. Like those of our Puritan forebears, our meetings are conflictual, but we argue now about racism, lesbian covenanting services, and what to do with a large endowment in a poor city. During the prayers, we lift up a child with lead poisoning, a member dying of AIDS, a breast cancer survivor, a teenager shot the night before on a nearby street, and the international arts festival happening on the green that afternoon. The sounds and smells of the city pour in through the church's windows and swirl around the space of our worship, disrupting any illusions we might have about the social prestige of our gathering or the cloistered purity of our space. This particular church will never be immortalized in history books or postcards, nor will its members claim fame in centuries ahead. We are a gathering of rather marginal people who belong to a now marginal institution, which, because of its history, sits at the center of the city—and the world whirls around and through it.

How might one portray the peculiar reality of this new millennium *ekklesia* in the language of feminist ecclesiology? What image of church might we generate if we started here, with this downtown church and its green, and not with an image of church nostalgically conjured up from the past? For years, I struggled with this question, trying to come up with an ecclesial metaphor that captured both the empirical character of our congregation as well as the normative, eschatological vision that undergirds and drives it. One Sunday morning, it struck me that the image was right before my eyes: the church itself. The image was of a sturdy structure with open windows and doors, an ever opening structure through which the life of the city circulates. This building and its people embodied well (but far from perfectly) the image of bounded openness that I had been seeking.

In this last section, I explore this image of the church as a space of bounded openness in order to develop a feminist, eschatological ecclesiology. The image draws together our discussion of feminist theories of community as well as Luther's and Calvin's perspectives on church. At the heart of both is the tension between the inevitably rule-bound and yet necessarily open and fluid character of communal life. In secular feminist theory of community, this is the tension between normative agendas and suspicions about false universals. In theology, it is the tension between law and gospel or between the priestly and prophetic dimensions of communal life. In my Tuesday-night group, it is the tension between creating a communal space of safety and creating one open to critique and change. As we saw in chapter 3's discussion of faith, it is the tension between the enveloped, integrated self and the constantly undone, agentic self—the sanctified and justified woman. At the heart of Christian life, all these tensions are captured by an eschatologically essentialist image of church.

Because the image of bounded openness sums up the liberal/communitarian debate over the nature of community, an ecclesiology of bounded openness maps out a space for the church between the two. *Ecclesial boundedness* embraces both the boundedness of liberalism's universal principles and the boundedness of communitarianism's thick community formation. *Ecclesial openness* affirms both the respect for difference crucial to liberalism and the irreducible particularity of tradition important to communitarianism. Because the language of "church" and the language of "community" (in the liberal/communitarian debate) are so different, however, one cannot simply correlate them. Instead, one must tell the ecclesial story in a new way, uncovering dramatic forces similar to those in the story of political community.

To understand the church as the gift of God, one must tell, simultaneously, at least two stories about how God relates to it: the story of a God who creates, forms, envelops, and protects the church and the story of a God who judges and forgives the church. In each story, the economy of grace in the God-church relation is different; both, however, are necessary to apprehend the singular yet complex reality of ecclesial community.

In the first story—the story of God's sanctifying relation to the church— God creates church as the space where God's will for human flourishing might be embodied; in this space, people might know God and be formed by God's love. This church is created by a grace that embraces and contains it; God reaches out in grace and gently holds the world in this space. The economy of relating here is one of touch. Flesh meets flesh. Jesus Christ dwells in it; its materiality is as substantial as his own. This is also an economy of adornment. When God reaches out and touches the world, God places the garments of faith, hope, and love upon her people. These clothes give the people defining edges; they are beautiful garments, different from the sinful clothing worn in the world. They are robes we see in varied aspects of the church's life—in its rituals, its buildings, its rules, its doctrines, its discipline, its everyday order, its multifaceted membership. This God is perhaps best described as "the adorning God."

In the second story—the story of God's justifying relation to the church—God speaks to the church rather than touches it. God's word brings the church into existence as people hear the gospel news and believe. This word breaks in upon the church as a judgment that profoundly undoes it. Grace disarticulates the sins of the community, and God's judgment ruptures its boundaries, exposing the arrogance of its false adornments and undoing its many pretensions. And yet this graced word also redeploys the church as a constantly forgiven community of sinners; it permits the church to forever start again, knowing that God's love embraces it regardless of its feeble mistakes and gross misdeeds. This redeeming forgiveness is not something the Christian community owns "by nature"; it is imputed to it. Forgiveness is a God-given identity that the church lives into, although it continues to be implicated in sin. As such, this grace creates the church as *simul iustus et peccator*—straddling the worlds of brokenness and redemption. This is a community of implicated resisters who know that God's love is finally victorious. The God of this people is perhaps best described as a "forgiving God" because of her act of justifying forgiveness in the midst of sin.

Out of these two economies of divine grace (an economy of adornment and an economy of forgiveness) emerge two different pictures of the same church: the church marked by its boundedness, on the one hand, and by its openness, on the other. *The bounded church is distinguished by the specificity of its adorning practices and disciplines.* A community adorned by God, it performs the activity of adornment in its own space and time. This church is deeply concerned about the formation of its members; it is the nurturing space out of which they grow and mature. The church knits back together and holds tightly and safely those broken by the fragmenting and dominating powers. In this place, women ideally are safe from violence and from the constraints of gender expectations that form them as "the lesser of the two." In church, people receive emancipatory identities; they are authored as beings who know God's abundant grace in the form of sanctification and justification. This church takes its materiality very seriously. It attends to the implications of its language, for it recognizes the forming power of words. It carefully considers its liturgy, for it knows that people are becoming in its space. It is a church aware of how it touches others. It cares about real harm to bodies and real forms of healing. It is, in short, a church that wears the thick texture of its institutionality as a gift and not a burden. In all these ways, this is a church of the law (in its third use).[37] A mother church?[38] Perhaps. An adorned and adorning church? Absolutely.

The church of justification and forgiveness is defined by its openness to the sins of the world as well as to the redeeming grace of the God who forgives these sins. This church recognizes that it lives only insofar as God, speaking to it anew each day, allows it to come into existence. It is constantly posited by the God who is "other" to it. This church's boundaries are continually undone by the word of God that breaks in upon it. This community, therefore, does not possess itself but always receives itself from God. This community does not own the terms by which it is collected, named, and defined; these too it receives. This community's core identity cannot therefore be defined by kinship ties, geographic region, and ethnicity. While perhaps marking its historical reality, the church's self-description has at its core a confession of its radically contingent and thoroughly gifted nature. Thus, at the most fundamental level, this church knows itself to be constituted by its intrinsic openness to God—and, more important, by God's *openness* toward it.

Openness makes this church deeply vulnerable to the sin of the world. As an institution, it is shot through with the contradictions and conflicts of its local contexts. As both a site and an agent of sin, it cannot claim purity. It is a stained church—a church that has harmed women for centuries and continues to do so, and that is judged harshly by God for those harms. This church should therefore not resist the harsh criticism feminist theory brings against it. It has no idealized reputation to protect. Feminist theory should, in fact, be welcomed by the church, for this theory can help the community understand anew its fallenness. In this way, feminist theory assists the law in its first use. And yet, this grace-posited, sinful church is also a church constantly forgiven its sin. It is therefore not a community bound to repeat its past. To the contrary, this open church is constantly remade by a grace that permits it to forever start again. This community, therefore, never rests in the comfort of its guilt. Its harm must be addressed. This healing is done not from duty but out of gratitude and as an expression of its freedom in God. In all these ways, the church is constantly undone by a grace that judges its sin and is constantly remade by an opening grace that forgives it and authorizes its agency ever anew. It is therefore a community whose borders are porous to grace and sin alike. A witnessing church? Perhaps. A community forgiven and forgiving? Yes. An activist church living to praise God and serve the neighbor? Absolutely.

To understand the differences between these two images of community—both of which ideally define the one church—look at the two kinds of emancipatory practices associated with each.[39] For the church adorned/adorning, practices focus on enclosure and formation. These are sanctifying practices that create borders and define edges; in these practices, order takes precedence over improvisation, and formation and growth take precedence over devolution and critique. Many different practices fall under this rubric: practices of birthing, nurturing, comforting, and protecting. Practices abound that attend to and honor the body.[40] Sabbath practices allow people to step away from the hectic pace of daily life and remember the giftedness of time.[41] This church is aware of the kinds of persons and relationships created and nurtured by its own household rules.[42] It thus seeks to create a space in which women can feel safe and embraced. As a church of the law, it seeks an internal environment in which justice reigns. In all these ways, this church gives great attention to the formation and nurture of faithful subjects who know themselves created and redeemed by God.

This church, however, doesn't just attend, to the formation of its own. It seeks practices that honor the bodies of all people. Health-care reform, adequate state aid for children, excellent public child care, livable workplace regulations—the church is an advocate for these in the broader culture as well as in its own midst. It has a positive vision of the kind of space human beings need to flourish. Recognizing the grace that envelops and defines the integrity of all creation, this church contests institutions and practices that fracture and diminish, such as exploitative economic structures, hazardous ecological practices, and degrading cultural representations.[43] The list could go on; with the assistance of feminist theory, it deepens and grows as our understanding of oppression and domination expands.

Interwoven with these practices of envelopment—the bounding practices of church—the Christian community engages in practices that reflect its identity as the justified church of freedom and gratitude. These practices are most aptly described as gestures of opening rather than enveloping. They are practices in which the freedom of the church allows it to reach beyond itself to serve the needs of others. These practices of outpouring mimic the gifted nature of God's forgiving grace. These are practices through which the church is constantly undone by God and by the world around it. Such practices include offering hospitality to the stranger and making a home for the lost. This church also engages in practices in which undoing is harsher, practices of ongoing self-examination and self-critique; this open church is suspicious of rules and borders that close it off from fecund encounters with difference, be it with the divine or with one's neighbor. This is a church in which confession is central to the formation process. This church constructs selves who are radically open to others and who refuse the safety of self-absorption. This open church is also not disposed to defend itself against the world outside. It is never sectarian. It has nothing to protect because it already exists in freedom. And it has nothing to lose because it knows itself to be always/already implicated in the sin it resists. This church has therefore thrown itself into life. It is a messy church.

This justified church engages in social practices that embody hospitality at a broader level as well. This is a church of mercy; it gives to the other out of celebratory wonder and not out of stultified calculations about deservedness. This community realizes it has not "earned" its life and thus resists the urge to estimate the exchange of social goods purely in terms of earnings. This church does not punish, for it knows that God chooses not to punish it. This is a community that forgives. This forgiven/forgiving church cannot support state policies that deal in death; it promotes rehabilitation rather than retribution. It is a community that forgives debts; it resists holding nations hostage because of what they owe. This church seeks communal forms of reconciliation rather than simple justice because it knows that communal healing requires more than a balancing of the scales. As such, it is a naive church, always surprised by injustice. It worries that its institutionality makes it captive to sin, and it always undermines its own projects when they are discovered to exclude. But because the sanctified church (its other side) is institutionally acute, this justified church can be bold in its naiveté.

As these varied practices suggest, these two aspects of church require each other. The sanctified church is skilled in the crafts of creating community; it binds people together by establishing and enforcing shared rules and a common sense of identity. The justified church is forever transgressing those boundaries in order to greet what is different from it. These hospitable actions open the bounded church to God, the source of its life, and to the world, the locus of its celebratory mission. In so doing, these practices make the church's sanctified borders fluid. Similarly, the firm and stable texture of its community-creating, sanctifying practices makes its identity sufficiently resilient and substantive to engage the other. Without its essentially bounded character, it could not be opened. Likewise, this sanctified church teaches its members how to be open, for openness, like the faith from which it flows, must be learned in community. The sanctified church knows that its boundaries exist in order that it might be a community formed for openness. In turn, the justified church knows its openness requires bounded community: how can one greet a stranger if one has no body to open toward the stranger in a gesture of welcome?

These two aspects of church need each other in order to balance their respective problems. On the one side, a community that cherishes its rules can easily become a cloistered or provincial gathering, sealed off from the world to protect itself or arrogantly separated from the world to maintain order. This church also runs the continual risk of creating an envelope that excludes others and resists change. It can forget that its boundaries exist to facilitate openness. These shortcomings describe, in a theological register, the shortcomings feminists have highlighted in the communitarian literature. On the other side, the radically open church can become so anti-institutional that it has a hard time embodying materially specific emancipatory practices.[44] Its resistance to rules can push it toward antinomianism. It can lose itself, much like the dispersed woman described in chapter 4. Just as she needs to be sanctified—wrapped in grace—in order to engage the world as an integrated self, so too the church must have its sanctifying structure—the wrap of grace around it—if it is to be a church that truly meets the world with an offer of real hospitality. Note echoes here of the feminist critique of liberalism's disembodied understanding of selves and power.

This description of bounded openness is rather ephemeral and, at times, even elliptical. I offer it more as a vision of the normative church than as a blueprint for the hard, practical labor of constructing and sustaining Christian community. If these comments were to be developed further, more attention to practical matters would be necessary, to say nothing of attending to the many conceptual complexities only hinted at in this concluding section. Short of this description's limitations, however, what the image of bounded openness offers is a brief glimpse of the principal features of Christian community. In this regard, it is more like a preliminary aesthetic of community. It provides two images of a single community that, when laid upon each other, create a portrait of communal life in which a substantive, walled structure opens itself both to the grace that posits it and the people it is called to serve. This church is where people experience the glory and pride of being adorned by God and the humility and gratitude of being judged and forgiven by God. It is, I believe, a vision of a church that is centered and directed while being radically open and relational, a church therefore capable of creating like subjects. In the traditional terms of theological ecclesiology, this church is both a "sacramental embodiment" of grace and a "witness" to grace.

Throughout these comments, I have alluded to the many ways in which feminist theories of community help the church better understand and live into this vision of bounded openness. What feminist theory cannot provide, however, is the most basic claim undergirding the vision—the claim that ecclesial community is a gift from God and that, as such, its materiality must be treasured and the freedom it affords celebrated. This insight into community is the most profound gift feminist theology has to offer feminist theory as it struggles to balance freedom with destiny, and universals with particulars, in accounts of our corporate lives. Granted, the theological vision of community lifted up in these pages takes as its principal subject the church, a community of faith. For feminist theorists, this subject is but one of many they explore. But like feminist theologians, feminist theorists explore the theme of community in the hopes of envisioning community as it should be. Does this theme function as a kind of church for feminist theory? Perhaps. But church must recognize the gifted economy of grace that creates and sustains it, a claim few feminist theorists affirm.

The radically gifted character of the church's life and its future is hard to grasp. Forgiveness and adornment require one to view community with wonder—not a naive wonder that refuses to see the complex messiness of communal life but a wise wonder that is forever amazed by the gifts of grace before us. This wonder was experienced in many different ways the Sunday morning of our play. We wondered at the adorning grace that calmed Joyce's demons and clothed her in joy. We wondered at the forgiving grace that empowered Reggie to open his door to the holy family. We wondered when we heard the Word proclaimed in Simon's song and saw a child carried forward in her mother's arms. This is wonder our Tuesday-night women's group knows well, although we often forget it and need events like the pageant to remind us.

Most vivid, this wonder cannot help but overwhelm those who gather in spaces of bounded openness like the old church on the green, not just at Christmas but throughout the year. The sounds of the city pour through its windows, and the worries of the world walk through its doors and settle in its pews. In this strange place, it is a wonder that people begin to pray. And then, even more wondrous, they walk back into the city, replenished and ready for the future awaiting us all.

Notes

1. Mapping Feminist Theory and Theology

1. By using these communities as a basis for my reflections, I follow the model of theological authority discussed by Elizabeth Schüssler Fiorenza as the *ekklesia* of women. See *But She Said: Feminist Practices of Biblical Interpretation* (Boston: Beacon, 1992).

2. For general introductions to feminist theory, I recommend Chris Weedon, *Feminist Practice and Poststructuralist Theory* (Oxford: Basil Blackwell, 1987); Josephine Donovan, *Feminist Theory: The Intellectual Traditions of American Feminism* (New York: Continuum, 1985); and Rosemarie Tong, *Feminist Thought: A Comprehensive Analysis* (Boulder, Colo.: Westview, 1989); Patricia Hill Collins, *Black Feminist Thought: Knowledge, Consciousness, and the Politics of Empowerment,* Perspectives on Gender Series, vol. 2. (Boston: Unwin Hyman, 1990). For an earlier text in feminist theory, see Marilyn Frye, *The Politics of Reality: Essays in Feminist Theory* (Freedom, Calif.: Crossing, 1983). For an overview of central texts and figures in contemporary feminism, see Maggie Humm, ed., *Modern Feminisms: Political, Literary, Cultural* (New York: Columbia Univ. Press, 1992). Also see idem, *The Dictionary of Feminist Theory* (Columbus: Ohio State Univ. Press, 1990).

3. It is important to note that the women's movement in North America has a history dating well before the 1960s movement. For a discussion of the varied waves of feminism in the United States, see Nancy F. Cott, *The Grounding of Modern Feminism* (New Haven, Conn.: Yale Univ. Press, 1987). Also see Paula Giddings, *When and Where I Enter: The Impact of Black Women on Race and Sex in America* (New York: Morrow, 1984).

4. As just a few examples, see Audre Lorde, *Sister Outsider: Essays and Speeches* (New York: Crossing, 1984); Adrienne Rich, *The Fact of a Doorframe: Poems Selected and New, 1950–1984* (New York: Norton, 1984); Toni Morrison, *Beloved: A Novel* (New York: Knopf, 1987); Leslie Silko, *Almanac of the Dead* (New York: Simon and Schuster, 1991). On feminist aesthetics, see Isobel Armstrong, ed., *New Feminist Discourses: Critical Essays on Theories and Texts* (New York: Routledge, 1992).

5. A few examples are the works of Judy Chicago, *The Dinner Party: A Symbol of Our Heritage* (Garden City, N.Y.: Anchor/Doubleday, 1979); Eva Hesse, *Sculpture Catalogue* (London: Trustees of the Whitechapel Art Gallery, 1979); and Julie Dash, *Daughters of the Dust: The Making of an African American Woman's Film* (New York: New Press, 1992). Also see the work of artists Jane Campion and Chantal Akerman. Jane Campion, *An Angel at My Table* (New Line Film Corporation, 1992); idem, *The Piano* (Miramax Films, 1994);

Chantal Akerman, *News from Home: un film,* Paradise Films (Los Angeles: World Artists, 1991), *Toute Une Nuit* (Los Angeles: Video World Artists, 1990); Chantal Akerman, Catherine David, and Michael Tarantino, *Bordering on Fiction: Chantal Akerman's D'Est* (Minneapolis: Walker Art Center, 1995).

6. In addition to referring to written materials, the term "texts" describes any cultural expression that an audience "reads," such as a film or a symphony as well as events like a courtroom scene, a protest march, and a university lecture. Like books, these events have distinctive styles, unique purposes, internal languages, and often rather indeterminate meanings.

7. This notion in Latin American liberation theology describes "a preferential option for the poor." See Gustavo Gutiérrez, *A Theology of Liberation: History, Politics and Salvation,* trans. and ed. Sister Caridad Inda and John Eagleson (Maryknoll, N.Y.: Orbis, 1988), xxv–xxviii. In feminist theory, a similar term describes the normative epistemological status of women's experience: "the epistemological privilege of the oppressed." See Alison M. Jaggar, *Feminist Politics and Human Nature* (Totowa, N.J.: Rowman and Allanheld, 1983), 337–89. For a fuller discussion of this analytic category, see Margaret Farley, "Feminism and Universal Morality," in *Prospects for a Common Morality,* ed. Gene Outka and John P. Reede, Jr. (Princeton: Princeton Univ. Press, 1993), 170–90.

8. The work of bell hooks has long advocated a deeper appreciation for the interlocking oppressions that structure women's lives. See *Ain't I a Woman: Black Women and Feminism* (Boston: South End, 1981), 12; and idem, *Feminist Theory from Margin to Center* (Boston: South End, 1984). Also see Cherríe Moraga, Gloria Anzaldúa, eds., *This Bridge Called My Back, Writings by Radical Women of Color* (New York: Kitchen Table Press, 1983) and *All the Women Are White, All the Blacks Are Men, But Some of Us are Brave: Black Women's Studies,* ed. Gloria T. Hull, Patricia Bell Scoot, and Barbara Smith (Old Westbury, N.Y.: Feminist Press, 1982).

9. On feminist theory and narrative, see Lynne Huffer, *Maternal Pasts, Feminist Futures: Nostalgia, Ethics, and the Question of Difference* (Palo Alto, Calif.: Stanford Univ. Press, 1998); Seyla Benhabib, *Situating the Self: Gender, Community, and Postmodernism in Contemporary Ethics* (New York: Routledge, 1992), 124–27, 203–30; Ellen McCracken, *New Latina Narrative: the Feminine Space of Postmodern Ethnicity* (Tucson: Univ. of Arizona Press, 1999); *Telling Women's Lives: Narrative Inquiries in the History of Women's Education,* Kathleen Weiler and Sue Middleton, eds. (Philadelphia: Open Univ. Press, 1999); Lidia Curti, *Female Stories, Female Bodies: Narrative, Identity and Representation* (Basingstoke, England: Macmillan, 1998). Also see Shoshana Felman and Dori Laub, M.D., *Testimony: Crises of Witnessing in Literature, Psychoanalysis, and History* (New York: Routledge, 1992); Martha C. Nussbaum, *Poetic Justice: The Literary Imagination and Public Life* (Boston: Beacon Press, 1995); Saidiya Hartman, *Scenes of Subjection: Terror, Slavery, and Self-Making in Nineteenth-Century America* (New York: Oxford Univ. Press, 1997); Carla Kaplan, *The Erotics of Talk: Women's Writing and Feminist Paradigms* (Oxford: Oxford Univ. Press, 1996).

10. The term "womanist" originates with Alice Walker; it comes from the African American colloquialism "womanish." See Alice Walker, *In Search of Our Mothers' Gardens* (New York: Harcourt Brace Jovanovich, 1983), xi. While seldom found in African American feminist theory, the term is used frequently in the theological reflections of African American women theologians and ethicists. See Emilie M. Townes, "Voices of the Spirit: Womanist Methodologies in Theological Disciplines," *The Womanist I* (summer:1–2); *Womanist Justice, Womanist Hope* (Atlanta: Scholars Press, 1993). See also idem, ed.,

A Troubling in My Soul: Womanist Perspectives on Evil and Suffering (Maryknoll, N.Y.: Orbis, 1993). Also see Patricia Hill Collins, *Black Feminist Thought: Knowledge, Consciousness, and the Politics of Empowerment*, Perspectives on Gender Series, vol. 2. (Boston: Unwin Hyman, 1990).

11. *"Mujerista"* describes the theological reflections of Latina women engaged in liberation theology. See Ada María Isasi-Díaz, *En la Lucha: A Hispanic Women's Liberation Theology* (Minneapolis: Fortress Press, 1993); and idem, *Breaking Boundaries: Latina Writing and Critical Readings* (Amherst: Univ. of Massachusetts Press, 1989). For examples of Latina feminist theory, see Cherry Morga, *Heroes and Saints and Other Plays* (Albuquerque, N.M.: West End, 1994); *Waiting in the Wings: Portrait of a Queer Motherhood* (Ithaca, N.Y.: Firebrand, 1997); Maria C. Lugones and Elizabeth Spelman, "Have We Got a Theory for You!: Feminist Theory, Cultural Imperialism, and the Demand for the "Woman's Voice," in *Hypathia Reborn: Essays in Feminist Philosophy*, ed. Azziah Y. al Hibri and Margaret A. Simons (Bloomington: Indiana Univ. Press, 1990), 18–33.

12. See Paula Gunn Allen, "What Color Is Your . . .: The Red Roots of White Feminism, *"The Sacred Hoop: Recovering the Feminine in American Indian Traditions* (Boston: Beacon Press, 1986), 209–21; Andrea Smith, "For All Those Who Were Indians in a Former Life," in *Ecofeminism and the Sacred*, ed. Carol J. Adams (New York: Continuum, 1993); Kathleen M. Donovan, *Feminist Readings of Native American Literature: Coming to Voice* (Tucson: Univ. of Arizona Press, 1998); Wendy Rose's article in *The State of Native America: Genocide, Colonization, and Resistance*, ed. M. Annette Jaimes (Boston: South End Press, 1992); Inés Talamantez, "The Image of the Feminine in Apache Religious Traditions," in *After Patriarchy*, ed. Paula Cooey, William R. Eakin, Jay B. McDaniel (Maryknoll, N.Y.: Orbis Books, 1991), 131–45.

13. See Gayle Rubin, "The Traffic in Women: The 'Political Economy' of Sex," in *Toward an Anthropology of Women*, ed. Rayna R. Reiter (New York: Monthly Review Press, 1975). I will challenge this simple distinction in chapter 2.

14. For an account of the relationship between French feminist theory and theology, see Rebecca S. Chopp, *The Power to Speak: Feminism, Language, God* (New York: Crossroads, 1989).

15. For an extensive overview of work in each field mentioned, see Shannon Clarkson and Letty Russel, eds., *Feminist Dictionary of Theology* (Louisville, Ky.: Westminster John Knox, 1996).

16. For a fuller discussion of the epistemological issues raised in feminist theory, see Lorraine Code, *What Can She Know: Feminist Theory and the Construction of Knowledge* (Ithaca, N.Y.: Cornell Univ. Press, 1991). Also see Ann Garry and Marilyn Pearsall, eds., *Women, Knowledge, Reality: Explorations in Feminist Philosophy* (Boston: Unwin Hyman, 1989).

17. My critical realism is rooted in a doctrine of creation that asserts both the "factness" of creation and our finite abilities to comprehend it, as well as in a doctrine of sin that holds that our epistemic flaws run deep.

18. Letty R. Russell, *Church in the Round: Feminist Interpretation of the Church* (Louisville, Ky.: Westminster John Knox, 1993).

19. See Cynthia Eller, *Living in the Lap of the Goddess: The Feminist Spirituality Movement in America* (New York: Beacon, 1995).

20. See Maria Riley, *Transforming Feminism* (Kansas City: Sheed and Ward, 1989); Elizabeth Clark and Herbert Richardson, eds., *Women and Religion: The Original Sourcebook of Women in Christian Thought* (San Francisco: Harper San Francisco, 1996); and

Jacqueline Grant, *White Women's Christ and Black Women's Jesus: Feminist Christology and Womanist Responses* (Atlanta: Scholars, 1989).

21. Mary Daly, *Beyond God the Father* (Boston: Beacon, 1973); Carol Christ and Judith Plaskow, eds., *Woman Spirit Rising: A Feminist Reader in Religion* (New York: Harper & Row, 1979).

22. To cover the full scope of contemporary feminist theology, an international focus is required. Some of the most lively feminist conversations take place among theologians in South Africa, Kenya, Chile, Guatemala, India, the Philippines, South Korea, Japan, Germany, and Holland, to name only a few places. I limit my focus in this book to theologians writing in a U.S. context, recognizing that what is lost in scope may perhaps be compensated for in detail.

23. See Christopher Morse, *Not Every Spirit: A Dogmatics of Christian Disbelief* (Valley Forge, Pa.: Trinity Press International, 1994).

24. See George Lindbeck, *The Nature of Doctrine: Religion and Theology in a Postliberal Age* (Philadelphia: Westminster, 1984); and Kathryn Tanner, *Theories of Culture: A New Agenda for Theology*, Guides to Theological Inquiry (Minneapolis: Fortress Press, 1998).

25. Arguing that so-called tightly reasoned and highly logical systems of thought can be used to entrap women, feminist theorists have pointed out that history holds countless examples of "philosophies" and "theologies" that were defended as airtight in their logic and yet harbored deeply misogynist views. Janice Moulton, "A Paradigm of Philosophy: The Adversary Method," *Women, Knowledge, Reality: Explorations in Feminist Philosophy* (Boston: Unwin Hyman, 1989), 5–20.

26. For an extensive discussion of feminism and the theology of the Christian Church (Disciples of Christ), see Rita Nakashima Brock, Claudia Camp, and Serene Jones, eds., *Setting the Table: Women in Theological Conversation* (St. Louis: Chalice, 1995). For a discussion of women in the United Church of Christ, see Alison Stokes, ed., *Women Pastors* (New York: Crossroads, 1995).

2. Women's Nature?

1. For another model of the theoretical options presently available to feminists, see Alison M. Jaggar, *Feminist Politics and Human Nature* (Totowa, N.J.: Rowman and Allanheld, 1983).

2. Hélène Cixous, "The Laugh of the Medusa," in *The Signs Reader: Women, Gender and Scholarship*, ed. Elizabeth Abel and Emily Abel (Chicago: Univ. of Chicago Press, 1983), 279–97. Also see Hélène Cixous and Catherine Clément, *The Newly Born Woman*, Theory and History of Literature Series, vol. 24, trans. Betsy Wing (Minneapolis: Univ. of Minnesota Press, 1986).

3. For more on the relation of the term "morphology" to actual bodies, see Margaret Whitford, "Ethics, Sexuality, and Embodiment," chap. 7 in *Luce Irigaray, Philosophy in the Feminine* (London: Routledge, 1991).

4. Cixous and Clément, 75.

5. The quote continues, " . . . her rising; is not erection. But diffusion. Not the shaft. The vessel." Ibid., 88.

6. Ibid., 93.

7. Within classical philosophy, there were a number of variations on these themes. See Lynne Huffer, "Luce et Veritas: Toward an Ethics of Performance," *Yale French Studies* 87 (1995): 20–41.

8. See Jean Grimshaw, *Philosophy and Feminist Thinking* (Minneapolis: Univ. of Minnesota Press, 1986), 62–63, 36–74. Also see Prudence Allen's *The Concept of Woman: The Aristotelian Revolution 750 BC–AD 1250* (Montreal: Eden, 1985). Also see Natalie Bluestone, *Women and the Ideal Society: Plato's Republic and the Modern Myths of Gender* (Amherst: Univ. of Massachusetts Press, 1987).

9. Elza Vieth, *Hysteria: The History of a Disease* (Chicago: Univ. of Chicago Press, 1965). Also see Michel Foucault, *The History of Sexuality*, vol. 1, *An Introduction*, trans. Robert Hurley (New York: Vintage, 1978), 103–4, 150–59.

10. See Gayle Rubin, "The Traffic in Women: The 'Political Economy' of Sex," in *Toward an Anthropology of Women*, ed. Rayna R. Reiter (New York: Monthly Review Press, 1975); and Judith Butler, "Sexual Traffic," *Differences* 6 (summer 1994): 62. Also see Elaine Graham's discussion of "sex-gender" in idem, *Making the Difference: Gender, Personhood, and Theology* (Minneapolis: Fortress Press, 1995), 19. Also see Graham's shorter article "Gender, Personhood, and Theology," *Scottish Journal of Theology* 48:3 (1995): 341–58. For a more recent discussion, see Moira Gatens, *Imaginary Bodies: Ethics, Power and Corporeality* (London: Routledge, 1996).

11. See Val Plumwood, *Feminism and the Mastery of Nature* (London: Routledge, 1993), 43. For a fuller discussion of these binaries, also see *Sexual Meanings, the Cultural Construction of Gender and Sexuality*, eds. Sherry Ortner and Harriet Whitehead (New York: Cambridge Univ. Press, 1981). Also see Val Plumwood, "Do We Need a 'Sex/Gender' Distinction?" *Radical Philosophy* 51: 2–11; and idem, "Feminism and Ecofeminism: Beyond the Dualistic Assumptions of Women, Men, and Nature," *Ecologist* 22 (January 1992): 8.

12. See Gillian Rose, *Feminism and Geography: The Limits of Geographic Knowing* (Minneapolis: Univ. of Minnesota Press, 1993); Griselda Pollock, *Vision and Difference: Femininity, Feminism, and the Histories of Art* (New York: Routledge, 1988); Teresa de Lauretis, *Technologies of Gender: Essays on Theory, Film, and Fiction* (Indianapolis: Univ. of Indiana Press, 1987); idem, "Through the Looking Glass: Women, Cinema, and Language," chap. 1 in *Alice Doesn't: Feminism, Semiotics, Cinema* (Indianapolis: Univ. of Indiana Press, 1984); idem, *The Practice of Love: Lesbian Sexuality and Perverse Desire* (Indianapolis: Univ. of Indiana Press, 1994); and Tania Modleski, *Feminism Without Women: Culture and Criticism in a "Postfeminist" Age* (New York: Routledge, 1991).

13. One example of this was articulated at the recent Beijing conference on women. For a report, see "Conference Reports," *Signs: A Journal of Women in Culture and Society* 22:1 (fall 1996): 181–226.

14. See Anne Wilson Schaef, *Women's Reality: An Emerging Female System in the White Male Society* (Minneapolis: Winston, 1981), 99–170. Also see Sheila Davaney, "Continuing the Story, but Departing the Text: A Historicist Interpretation of Feminist Norms in Theology," chap. 12 in *Horizons in Feminist Theology: Identity, Tradition, and Norms,* Rebecca S. Chopp and Sheila Greeve Davaney, eds. (Minneapolis: Fortress Press, 1997), 198–214; and Serene Jones, "Women's Experience between a Rock and a Hard Place: Feminist, Womanist, and *Mujerista* Theologies in North America," chap. 3 in *Horizons in Feminist Theology,* 33–53.

15. Mary Daly, *Beyond God the Father: Toward a Philosophy of Women's Liberation* (Boston: Beacon, 1973); idem, *Gyn/ecology: The Metaethics of Radical Feminism* (Boston: Beacon, 1978); idem, *Pure Lust: Elemental Feminist Philosophy* (Boston: Beacon, 1984); idem, *Outercourse: The Bedazzling Voyage* (San Francisco: Harper San Francisco, 1992).

16. This type of feminist theory used to be referred to as "radical feminism" because it claimed to critique the "radical root" of the patriarchal oppression.

17. This argument has also been used to explain the origins of male domination; for example, men are said to be afraid or jealous of women's childbearing capacities and have therefore sought to subjugate women and their reproductive functions. See Mary O'Brien, *The Politics of Reproduction* (Boston: Routledge and Kegan Paul, 1981), 1–64; and Adrienne Rich, *Of Women Born* (New York: Norton, 1979). Also note the presence of quasi-biological universals in the popular work of Sally P. Springer and Georg Deutsch, *Left Brain, Right Brain* (San Francisco: Freeman, 1981), 121–30. (This work is discussed in Rosemary Radford Ruether, *Sexism and God-Talk* [Boston: Beacon, 1983], 90–91.) Some strands of this thinking are expressed in Mary Belenkey's *Women's Ways of Knowing: The Development of Self, Voice, and Mind* (New York: Basic, 1986).

18. See Cynthia Eller, *Living in the Lap of the Goddess: The Feminist Spirituality Movement in America* (Boston: Beacon, 1995).

19. Judith Butler, *Gender Trouble: Feminism and the Subversion of Identity* (New York: Routledge, 1990).

20. Monique Wittig is a well-known constructivist lesbian theorist. See her "The Category of Sex," and "The Site of Action," in *The Straight Mind* (Boston: Beacon, 1992), 1–8 and 90.

21. Feminist constructivism has long been in conversation with other theorists whose questions and analytic methods have been useful to feminist emancipatory projects. See Joan Scott, "Women's History," chap. 1 in *Gender and the Politics of History* (New York: Columbia Univ. Press, 1988); Joan Kelley, *Women, History, and Theory* (Chicago: Univ. of Chicago Press, 1984), 60–61; Caroline Walker Bynum, *Holy Feast and Holy Fast: The Religious Significance of Food to Medieval Women* (Berkeley: Univ. of California Press, 1987): and Caroline Walker Bynum *Fragmentation and Redemption: Essays on Gender and the Human Body in Medieval Religion* (New York: Zone, 1991), 17.

Also see Ruth A. Wallace, ed., *Feminism and Sociological Theory,* Key Issues in Sociological Theory Series (London: Sage, 1989). Look specifically at Dorothy Smith, "Sociological Theory: Methods of Writing Patriarchy," chap. 2; and Jan Acker, "Making Gender Visible," chap. 3.

Also see Linda Nicholson, ed., *Feminism and Post-Modernism* (New York: Routledge, 1990); Chris Weedon, *Feminist Practice and Poststructuralist Theory* (Oxford: Basil Blackwell, 1987), 40–41; and Jane Flax, *Thinking Fragments: Psychoanalysis, Feminism, and Post Modernism in the Contemporary West* (Berkeley: Univ. of California Press, 1990).

For a summary and critique of feminist uses of postmodernism, see Seyla Benhabib, *Situating the Self: Gender, Community, and Postmodernism in Contemporary Ethics* (New York: Routledge, 1992), 203–41. Also see Seyla Benhabib, Judith Butler, Drucilla Cornell, and Nancy Fraser, *Feminist Contentions: A Philosophical Exchange* (New York: Routledge, 1995).

22. See Kathryn Tanner, *Theories of Culture: A New Agenda for Theology,* Guides to Theological Inquiry Series (Minneapolis: Fortress Press, 1997).

23. See Hazel Carby, *Reconstructing Womanhood: The Emergence of the Afro-American Woman Novelist* (New York: Oxford Univ. Press, 1987), 17. See the definition of "doctrine" in chap. 1. When Carby offers this definition, she is as much concerned about the construction of race, class, and nationality as she is about gender. On constructivist positions that try to theorize race and gender together, see Barbara Fields, "Ideology and Race

in American History," in *Region, Race, and Reconstruction: Essays in Honor of C. van Woodward,* ed. J. M. Kousser and James M. McPherson (New York: Oxford Univ. Press, 1982), 143–69. Also see Evelyn Brooks Higginbotham, "African-American Women's History and the Metalanguage of Race," *Signs: Journal of Women in Culture and Society* 17:2 (1992): 251–74.

24. Note that the term "culture" is often used interchangeably with "discourse." "Culture" highlights the material dimension of lived experience in a manner that the term "discourse" sometimes misses. See footnote 6 in chap. 1 on "texts."

25. For a more developed discussion of this de-centering in feminist theory, see Iris Marion Young, *Justice and the Politics of Difference* (Princeton: Princeton Univ. Press, 1990), 125ff. Feminist theorists sometimes use the notion of the "relational self" to describe a similarly de-centered self. Such language is more commonly found in a phenomenological frame, not a poststructuralist one.

26. See Elizabeth Spelman, *Inessential Women: Problems of Exclusion in Feminist Thought* (Boston: Beacon, 1988). Look specifically at "Woman: The One and the Many," chap. 6. Also see Patricia Hill Collins's critique of the "additive view" in her *Black Feminist Thought: Knowledge, Consciousness, and the Politics of Empowerment,* Perspectives on Gender Series, vol. 2. (Boston: Unwin Hyman, 1990), quote on 222: "Black feminist thought fosters a fundamental paradigmatic shift that rejects additive approaches to oppression."

27. Iris Marion Young develops this second model of analysis in her article "Gender as Seriality: Thinking About Women as a Social Collective," *Signs: A Journal of Women in Culture and Society* 19:3 (spring 1994): 713–38.

28. See Mary McClintock Fulkerson, *Changing the Subject: Women's Discourses and Feminist Theology* (Minneapolis: Fortress Press, 1994). Also see Marjorie Garber, *Vested Interests: Cross-dressing and Cultural Anxiety* (New York: Routledge, 1992).

29. See Louis Althusser, *For Marx,* trans. Ben Brewster (Hammondsworth, Eng.: Penguin, 1969); and idem, *Reading Capital,* trans. Ben Brewster (London: Brewster, 1977). See also Clifford Geertz, *Interpretation of Cultures: Selected Essays* (New York: Basic, 1973).

30. Term taken from Jacques Derrida, "Structure, Sign, and Play in the Discourse of the Human Sciences," chap. 10 in *Writing and Difference* (Chicago: Univ. of Chicago Press, 1978).

31. See Collins, 25–28. Also see Young, chap. 5, "The Scaling of Bodies and the Politics of Identity," on Kristeva's abject, 142–48.

32. See bell hooks, *Yearning: Race, Gender, and Cultural Politics* (Boston: South End, 1990).

33. Luce Irigaray, *Speculum of the Other Woman,* trans. Gillian C. Gill (Ithaca, N.Y.: Cornell Univ. Press, 1985). Her interaction with Freud can be found in "The Blind Spot in the Old Game of Symmetry," 11–132; and her treatment of Plato is found in "Plato's *Hystera,*" 243–64.

34. Luce Irigaray, *An Ethics of Sexual Difference,* trans. Carolyn Burke and Gillian C. Gill (Ithaca, N.Y.: Cornell Univ. Press, 1993). See "Wonder: A Reading of Descartes, *The Passions of the Soul,*" 72–83; and "An Ethics of Sexual Difference," 116–32. For additional discussions of Irigaray, see Margaret Whitford, *Luce Irigaray, Philosophy in the Feminine* (London: Routledge, 1991); Carolyn Burke, Naomi Schor, and Margaret Whitford, eds., *Engaging with Irigaray: Feminist Philosophy and Modern European Thought* (New York: Columbia Univ. Press, 1994); and Sandra Lee Bartky and Nancy Fraser,

Revaluing French Feminism: Critical Essays on Difference, Agency, and Culture (Bloomington: Indiana Univ. Press, 1992).

35. Significant works in this area are Diana Fuss, *Essentially Speaking: Feminism, Nature and Difference* (New York: Routledge, 1989); Seyla Benhabib, *Situating the Self,* which uses the term "pragmatic utopianism"; Martha C. Nussbaum, "Human Functioning and Social Justice: In Defense of Aristotelian Essentialism," *Political Theory* 20 (1992): 202–46; and Lynne Huffer, "An Interview with Nicole Brossard," *Another Look, Another Woman,* Yale French Studies 87 (1995): 118. Brossard refers to "a mythic space/mythic essentialism." Also see Patricia J. Huntington, *Ecstatic Subjects, Utopia, and Recognition: Kristeva, Heidegger, and Irigaray* (Albany: SUNY Press, 1998); and Rosi Braidotti, *Patterns of Dissonance* (New York: Routledge, 1991). Also see the volume on essentialism in *Difference: A Journal of Cultural Studies* 1:2.

36. Kathi Weeks, *Constituting Feminist Subjects* (Ithaca, N.Y.: Cornell Univ. Press, 1998).

37. See Martha Minow on "difference arguments" in the law in idem, *Making All the Difference: Inclusion, Exclusion, and American Law* (Ithaca, N.Y.: Cornell Univ. Press, 1990). Also see Kathryn Tanner's argument on similar lines in idem, *Politics of God: Christian Theories and Social Justice* (Minneapolis: Fortress Press, 1992). Also see Drucilla Cornell, "The Maternal and the Feminine: Social Reality, Fantasy and Ethical Relation," chap. 1 in *Beyond Accommodation: Ethical Feminism, Deconstruction, and the Law* (New York: Routledge, 1991).

38. See Efua Dorkenoo, *Cutting the Rose: Female Genital Mutilation* (London: Minority Rights, 1994); Scilla McLean and Stella Efue Graham, eds., *Female Circumcision, Excision and Infibulation* (London: Minority Rights, 1983); Alice Walker and Tratibha Parmer, *Warrior Marks: Female Genital Mutilation and the Sexual Blinding of Women* (New York: Harcourt Brace, 1993); and Alice Walker, *Possessing the Secret of Joy* (San Diego: Harcourt Brace Jovanovich, 1992).

39. Paul Gilroy sums up the role that strategic essentialism plays in progressive politics by pointing to a space "between the absolutism of essences and the agnostic, ephemeral differences of constructivism." See idem, "The Black Atlantic as a Counterculture of Modernity," in *The Black Atlantic: Modernity and Double Consciousness* (Cambridge, Mass.: Harvard Univ. Press, 1993), 1–40.

40. On the pragmatic value of strategic essentialism, see Young, "Gender as Seriality."

41. The Boston Women's Health Collective, *Our Bodies, Ourselves,* 1st ed. (New York: Simon and Schuster, 1973); idem, *The New Our Bodies, Ourselves* (New York: Simon and Schuster, 1984).

42. Carol Pateman, *The Sexual Contract* (Cambridge: Polity, 1998).

43. On the pornography debate, see Catharine MacKinnon, *Feminism Unmodified: Discourses on Life and Law* (Cambridge, Mass.: Harvard Univ. Press, 1987); and David A. J. Richards, "Commercial Sex and the Rights of the Person," in *Sex, Drugs, Death, and the Law: An Essay on Human Rights and Over-criminalization* (New Jersey: Rowman & Littlefield, 1982), 84–153. On defenses of lesbian sadomasochism, see Sue Ellen Case, "Toward a Butch-Femme Aesthetic," in *Making a Spectacle: Feminist Essays on Contemporary Women's Theater,* ed. Lynda Hart (Ann Arbor: Univ. of Michigan Press, 1989), 282–99; Dorothy Allison, *Skin: Talking about Sex, Class and Literature* (Ithaca, N.Y.: Firebrand Books, 1994); and Pat Califia, *Public Sex: The Culture of Radical Sex* (Pittsburgh: Cleis, 1994). Also see *Coming to Power: Writings and Graphics on Lesbian S/M,* 2nd ed., ed. members of Samois (Boston: Alyson, 1982); and Teresa de Lauretis, *The Practice of*

Love: Lesbian Sexuality and Perverse Desire (Indianapolis: Univ. of Indiana Press, 1994), esp. chap. 5, "The Lure of the Mannish Lesbian: The Fantasy of Castration and the Signification of Desire." Also see Susanne Kappeler, *The Pornography of Representation* (Minneapolis: Univ. of Minnesota Press, 1986); Andrea Dworkin, *Intercourse* (New York: Free Press, 1987); idem, *Life and Death: Unapologetic Writings on the Continuing War Against Women* (New York: Free Press, 1997); idem, *Pornography: Men Possessing Women* (London: Women's Press, 1981); and Andrea Dworkin and Catharine MacKinnon, *Pornography and Civil Rights: A Day for Women's Equality* (Minneapolis: Univ. of Minnesota Press, 1988).

44. An interesting example of shifting essences was explained to me by Denise Ackermann, a South African feminist theologian. She was puzzled at a recent women's conference in North America where everyone was talking about "difference" and the importance of attending to one's own "particular" context and not universalizing it. She pointed out that the rhetoric of "difference" and "particularity" was the language of oppression under apartheid. Therefore, the challenge for South African reconstruction is to produce a liberating rhetoric of "sameness" and "unity," a situation that challenges uncritical adulation of postmodern fragmentation and dissolution.

45. For an extensive discussion of many such issues in feminism, see Alison M. Jaggar, ed., *Living with Contradictions: Controversies in Feminist Social Ethics* (Boulder, Colo.: Westview, 1994). Also see Morwenna Griffiths and Margaret Whitford, eds., *Feminist Perspectives in Philosophy* (Bloomington: Indiana Univ. Press, 1988).

3. Sanctification and Justification: Lived Grace

1. Marie Fortune, *Is Nothing Sacred? When Sex Invades the Pastoral Relationship* (San Francisco: Harper & Row, 1989).

2. Feminist theological works on justification include Elsa Tamez, *Amnesty of Grace: Justification by Faith from a Latin American Perspective*, trans. Sharon Ringe (Nashville, Tenn.: Abingdon, 1993); and Kathryn Tanner, "Justification and Justice in a Theology of Grace," *Theology Today*, vol. 55, no. 4 (January 1999): 510–23; and Annelis Van Heijst, *Longing for the Fall*, trans. Henry Jansen (Kampen, Neth.: Kok Pharos, 1995). Feminist works on sanctification include Katie G. Cannon, *Black Womanist Ethics* (Atlanta: Scholars, 1988); Susan Dunfee Nelson, *Beyond Servanthood: Christianity and the Liberation of Women* (Lanham, Md.: Univ. Press of America, 1989); Carter Heyward, *Touching Our Strength: The Erotic as Power and the Love of God* (San Francisco: Harper & Row, 1989); Catherine Keller, *From a Broken Web: Separation, Sexism and the Self* (Boston: Beacon, 1986); and Elsa Tamez, *The Scandalous Message of James: Faith without Works Is Dead*, trans. John Eagleson (New York: Crossroads, 1990).

3. For contemporary feminist theologies of the human person, see Letty Russell, *Becoming Human* (Philadelphia: Westminster, 1982); Elaine Graham, *Making the Difference: Gender, Personhood, and Theology* (Minneapolis: Fortress Press, 1995); Mary McClintock Fulkerson, *Changing the Subject: Women's Discourses and Feminist Theology* (Minneapolis: Fortress Press, 1994); Delores Williams, "A Womanist Perspective on Sin," in *A Troubling in My Soul: Womanist Perspectives on Evil and Suffering*, ed. Emily M. Townes (Maryknoll, N.Y.: Orbis 1993), 130–49; Ann O'Hara Graff, ed., *In the Embrace of God: Feminist Approaches to Theological Anthropology* (Maryknoll: Orbis, 1995); Susan Nelson Dunfee, *Beyond Servanthood: Christianity and the Liberation of Women* (Rochester, N.Y.: Univ. Press of America, 1989); Catherine Keller, *From a Broken Web: Separation,*

Sexism, and the Self (Boston: Beacon, 1986); Mary Aquin O'Neill, "The Mystery of Being Human Together," in *Freeing Theology: The Essentials of Theology in Feminist Perspective*, ed. Catherine Mowry LaCugna (San Francisco: HarperSanFrancisco, 1993); Karen Baker-Fletcher, "Womanism, Afro-centrism and the Reconstruction of Black Womanhood," 183–200, and Michele Jacques, "Testimony as Embodiment: Telling the Truth and Shaming the Devil," 129–45 in *Perspectives on Womanist Theology*, ed. Jacquelyn Grant (Atlanta: ITC Press, 1995); Paula Cooey, *Religious Imagination and the Body: A Feminist Analysis* (New York: Oxford Univ. Press, 1994); Rita Nakashima Brock, "The Character of Being Human and the Making of Human Character," chap. 1 in *Journeys by Heart: A Christology of Erotic Power* (New York: Crossroads, 1988); Rosemary Radford Ruether, *Sexism and God-talk: Toward a Feminist Theology* (Boston: Beacon, 1983); Elisabeth Moltmann-Wendel, *I Am My Body: A Theology of Embodiment* (New York: Continuum, 1995); Dawn DeVries, "Creation, Handicappism, and the Community of Differing Abilities," in *Reconstructing Christian Theology*, ed. Rebecca Chopp and Mark Lewis Taylor (Minneapolis: Fortress Press, 1994), 124–40; Sallie McFague, "Human Beings, Embodiment, and Our Home the Earth," in *Reconstructing*, ed. Chopp and Taylor, 141–69; Sharon Welch, "Human Beings, White Supremacy, and Racial Justice," in *Reconstructing*, ed. Chopp and Taylor, 170–94; Ellen K. Wondra, *Humanity Has Been a Holy Thing: Toward a Contemporary Feminist Christology* (Rochester, N.Y.: Univ. Press of America, 1994); and Lucinda Huffaker, *Creative Dwelling: Empathy and Clarity in God and Self* (Scholars Press, 1998).

4. Rosemary Radford Ruether, *Introducing Redemption in Christian Feminism* (Sheffield, Eng.: Sheffield Academic Press, 1998).

5. For critiques of essentialized womanhood in feminist theology, see Ellen T. Armour, "Questioning 'Woman' in Feminist/Womanist Theology: Irigaray, Ruether, and Daly," chap. 6 in *Transfigurations: Theology and the French Feminists*, ed. C. W. Maggie Kim, Susan M. St. Ville, and Susan M. Simonaitis (Minneapolis: Fortress Press, 1993). Also see Ellen T. Armour, *Deconstruction, Feminist Theology, and the Problem of Difference: Subverting the Race/Gender Divide* (Chicago: Univ. of Chicago Press, 1999); Katie Cannon, *Black Womanist Ethics* (Atlanta: Scholars, 1988); and idem, *Katie's Cannon: Womanism and the Soul of the Black Community* (New York: Continuum, 1995). Also see Joan Martin, "The Notion of Difference for Emerging Womanist Ethics: The Writings of Audre Lorde and bell hooks," *Journal of Feminist Studies in Religion* 9 (spring–fall 1993): 39–51.

6. In recent feminist theology, a constructivist position on gender is almost universally accepted. This does not mean, however, that there are not essentializing moments. See Serene Jones, "Women's Experience between a Rock and a Hard Place: Feminist, Womanist, and *Mujerista* Theologies in North America," chap. 3 in *Horizons in Feminist Theology: Identity, Tradition, and Norms*, ed. Rebecca S. Chopp and Sheila Greeve Davaney (Minneapolis: Fortress Press, 1997), 33–53.

7. Sally McFague, *The Body of God: An Ecological Theology* (Minneapolis: Fortress Press, 1993).

8. Ada María Isasi-Díaz, *En la Lucha: A Hispanic Women's Liberation Theology* (Minneapolis: Fortress Press, 1993) offers a deft example of how localized thick descriptions can be brought to bear on the constructive task of theology. Also see Fulkerson, *Changing the Subject*; and Cooey, *Religious Imagination and the Body*.

9. Delores Williams, "From Harlem to Huairou: A Theological Reflection," *Church and Society* 86 (May–June 1996): 52–61; Renita Weems, *Battered Love: Marriage, Sex, and Violence in the Hebrew Prophets* (Minneapolis: Fortress Press, 1995).

10. See Elisabeth Schüssler Fiorenza and M. Shawn Copeland, eds., *Feminist Theologies in Context,* Concilium, 1996, no. 1 (London: SCM Press, 1996).

11. Lindbeck and so-called Yale School theology seem to miss this point about power/culture altogether. See Amy Plantinga Pauw, "The Word Is Near You: A Feminist Conversation with Lindbeck," *Theology Today* 50 (April 1993): 45–55.

12. See Letty Russell's *The Future of Partnership* (Philadelphia: Westminster, 1979); and idem, *Household of Freedom* (Philadelphia: Westminster, 1987). Russell is clearly the most eschatologically oriented of present-day North American feminist theologians.

13. Nicole Brossard's essentialism is close, in form, to the one I am describing here, although it does not claim to be Christian. See Lynne Huffer, "An Interview with Nicole Brossard," in *Another Look, Another Woman,* Yale French Studies 87 (1995): 20–41.

14. According to Luther, it is the doctrine by which the church stands or falls. See H. George Anderson, T. Austin Murphy, and Joseph A. Burgess, eds., *Justification by Faith* (Minneapolis: Augsburg, 1985).

15. For the scriptural sources of this doctrine, see Rom. 3:28, 2 Cor. 3:6, Gal. 6:15, Eph. 2:1, 5; Col. 2:13, 20; Col. 3:3; and 1 Peter 2:24. See Kevin Mills, *Justifying Language: Paul and Contemporary Literary Theory,* Studies in Literature and Religion Series, ed. David Jasper (New York: St. Martin's, 1995).

16. For Luther, the principal sin is "unfaithfulness," an act of radical disobedience manifested as "pride." See also Heiko Oberman, *Luther: Man between God and the Devil,* trans. Eileen Walliser-Schwarzbart (New Haven, Conn.: Yale Univ. Press, 1989); and Paul Althaus, *The Theology of Martin Luther,* trans. Robert Schultz (Philadelphia: Fortress Press, 1966), 141–60.

17. See Elizabeth Castelli, *Imitating Paul: A Discourse on Power* (Louisville, Ky.: Westminster John Knox, 1991). For a Latin American feminist version of *imitatio,* see Julia Esquivel, *Threatened with Resurrection: Prayers and Poems from an Exiled Guatemalan* (Elgin, Ill.: Brethren, 1982).

18. Luce Irigaray's envelope: see idem, "Divine Women," in *Sexes and Genealogies,* trans. Gillian C. Gill (New York: Columbia Univ. Press, 1993), 55–72.

19. Mary Stewart Van Lewen et al., *After Eden: Facing the Challenge of Gender Reconciliation* (Grand Rapids, Mich.: Eerdmans, 1993). Also see Michael Welker, *God the Spirit,* trans. John F. Hoffmeyer (Minneapolis: Fortress Press, 1994).

20. I am here indebted to Judith Plaskow and her analysis of women and the sin of pride. See idem, *Sex, Sin, and Grace: Women's Experience and the Theologies of Reinhold Niebuhr and Paul Tillich* (Washington, D.C.: Univ. Press of America, 1980).

21. Note that by suggesting that we start with sanctification, I am following the lead of Calvin, who worried about the possible quietism suggested by Luther's strong emphasis on justification alone.

4. Oppression

1. Iris Marion Young, *Justice and the Politics of Difference* (Princeton: Princeton Univ. Press, 1990). These five faces describe, more broadly, the character of oppression in contemporary North American culture.

2. See Michel Foucault, *Power/Knowledge: Selected Interviews and Other Writings,* trans. Colin Gordon (Brighton, Eng.: Harvester, 1980). For a different perspective on power, see Marilyn French, *Beyond Power: On Women, Men, and Morals* (New York: Summit, 1985).

3. See Patricia White, *Beyond Domination: An Essay in the Political Philosophy of Education* (London: Routledge and Kegan Paul, 1983). There can be relations of power in which one term is subordinated in a manner that enhances the flourishing of the person with less power, such as parent-child relations, teacher-student relations, and therapist-client relations. These inequalities can also occasion abuse, however.

4. See Young's discussion of "unintentional oppression," 148–51.

5. Alison M. Jaggar, *Feminist Politics and Human Nature* (Totowa, N.J.: Rowman and Allanhead, 1983), 77–79, 307–17. Also see Patricia Hill Collins's discussion of "standpoint theory" in idem, *Black Feminist Thought: Knowledge, Consciousness, and the Politics of Empowerment*, Perspectives on Gender Series, vol. 2 (Boston: Unwin Hyman, 1990), esp. 3–40.

6. See Gerda Lerner, *The Creation of Patriarchy* (New York: Oxford Univ. Press, 1986), 15–53.

7. For a more developed description of patriarchy in antiquity, see S. Pomeroy, *Goddesses, Whores, Wives, and Slaves: Women in Classical Antiquity* (New York: Schocken, 1975).

8. For an excellent and brief description of patriarchy, see Rosemary Radford Ruether, "Patriarchy," in *The Dictionary of Feminist Theology*, ed. Letty M. Russell and J. Shannon Clarkson (Louisville, Ky.: Westminster John Knox, 1996), 205–6.

9. See David Herlihy, "The Transformations of the Central and Late Middle Ages," chap. 2 in *Medieval Households* (Cambridge, Mass.: Harvard Univ. Press, 1985).

10. For a full discussion of the nuanced meaning of patriarchy in contemporary political theory, see Carol Pateman, *The Sexual Contract* (Cambridge: Polity, 1998), 19–38.

11. For an excellent description of the varied ways patriarchy has functioned in contemporary conversations about women's spirituality and matriarchal religions, see Cynthia Eller, *Living in the Lap of the Goddess* (New York: Beacon, 1995).

12. Young, 53.

13. Delores Hayden, *Redesigning the American Dream: The Future of Housing, Work, and Family Life* (New York: Norton, 1984), 146. For statistics related to women's social and economic status in North America, see Women's Action Coalition, ed., *WAC Stats: The Facts About Women* (New York: New Press, 1993).

14. The term "materialist" highlights these feminists' analytic focus on the material, economic conditions of women's oppression. See Michelle Barrett, *Women's Oppression Today: Problems in Marxist Feminist Analysis* (London: Verso, 1988). Also see her essay "Words and Things: Materialism and Method in Contemporary Feminist Analysis," in *Destabilizing Theory: Contemporary Feminist Debates*, ed. Michelle Barrett and Anne Phillips (Cambridge: Polity, 1992). Also see Donna Landry and Gerald MacLean, *Materialist Feminism* (Cambridge, Mass.: Blackwell, 1993); and Mas'ud Zavarzadeh, Teresa L. Ebert, and Donald Morton, eds., *Post-Ality: Marxism and Postmodernism* (Washington, D.C.: Maisonneuve, 1995). Like Marx, these theorists study the dynamics of oppression by looking at who owns and controls the means of production and by examining the work conditions through which profits are produced and distributed. Unlike Marx, however, materialist feminists argue that an account of women's role in the economy cannot be fully explained in this manner and requires a conceptual framework not provided by classical Marxist theory. On the encounter between feminist materialism and feminist postmodernism, see Teresa Ebert, *Ludic Feminism and After* (Ann Arbor: Univ. of Michigan Press, 1996). Also see Nancy Holmstrom, "A Marxist Theory of Women's Nature," in *Feminism and Political Theory*, ed. Cass R. Sunstein (Chicago: Univ. of Chicago Press, 1990), 69–86.

15. For an excellent discussion of this division of spheres and its economic and social implications, see Susan Moller Okin, *Justice, Gender, and the Family* (New York: Basic Books, 1989).

16. See Pateman, 1–18.

17. Ibid.

18. Ibid., 230–31.

19. See Zillah Eisenstein, *Capitalist Patriarchy and the Case for Socialist Feminism* (New York: Monthly Review, 1979). See chapters by Heidi Hartmann, "Capitalism, Patriarchy, and Job Segregation by Sex," 206–47; Jean Gardiner, "Women's Domestic Labor," 173–89; and Batya Weinbaum and Amy Bridges, "The Other Side of the Paycheck: Monopoly Capital and the Structure of Consumption," 190–205.

Michelle Barrett, *Women's Oppression Today,* 25. On welfare mothers and the production of the worker-citizen, see idem, "Bottomless Pits: Why Single Mothers Fare Worst," in *Glass Ceilings and Bottomless Pits: Women's Work, Women's Poverty,* ed. Randy Albelda and Chris Tilly (Boston: South End, 1997), 65–78; and Dorothy Seavey, "Appendix B: Women and Welfare: Popular Conceptions vs. Facts," in Albeda and Tilly, eds., 189–99. Also see Margaret L. Andersen and Patricia Hill Collins, *Race, Class, and Gender: An Anthology* (Belmont, Calif.: Wadsworth, 1992); Sonya Michel and Seth Coven, *Mothers of a New World: Maternalist Politics and the Origins of Welfare States* (New York: Routledge, 1993).

20. The latest statistics on gender in religion and theology doctorates are quite alarming in this regard. In 1994, in the field of theology, 81 percent of the doctorates were given to men and 19 percent to women. This compares to a gender breakdown in the humanities in general of 52 percent men and 48 percent women. See National Research Council, Summary Report: Doctoral Recipients from United States Universities, 1986–1994, reported in *Religious Studies News* 11, no. 4 (November 1996).

21. Jacqueline Jones, *Labor of Love, Labor of Sorrow: Black Women, Work, and the Family from Slavery to the Present* (New York: Basic, 1985); Paula Giddings, *When and Where I Enter: The Impact of Black Women on Race and Sex in America* (New York: Morrow, 1984).

22. Christine Delphy, *Close to Home: A Materialist Analysis of Women's Oppression,* trans. Diana Leonard (Amherst, Univ. of Massachusetts Press, 1984); Rhona Mahony, *Kidding Ourselves: Breadwinning, Babies, and Bargaining Power* (New York: Basic, 1995); Martha Albertson Fineman, *The Illusion of Equality: The Rhetoric and Reality of Divorce Reform* (Chicago: Univ. of Chicago Press, 1991); idem, *The Neutered Mother, The Sexual Family, and Other Twentieth-Century Tragedies* (New York: Routledge, 1995); Riva Siegel, "The Modernization of Marital Status: Adjudicating Wives' Rights to Earnings, 1860–1930," *Georgetown Law Journal* 82, no. 7 (September 1995): 2127–2212; idem, "Home as Work: The First Woman's Rights Claims Concerning Wives' Household Labor, 1850–1880," *Yale Law Journal* 103, no. 5 (March 1994): 1073–1217; Katharine Silbaugh, *Turning Labor into Love: Law and Housework* (Chicago: Northwestern Univ. Law Review, 1997).

Focusing on gendered spheres in the traditional heterosexual nuclear family does not mean that these models describe *all* family structures. At present, there are more adult women living outside this model than within it: women who are divorced, who never married, who are widowed, who are single mothers, who are in lesbian relationships, and who are in still other situations. Despite the dramatic reconfiguration of contemporary households, however, the nuclear family model continues to structure our work practices—as evidenced by the economic difficulties faced by women who live outside this model.

23. See Nancy Marshall and Rosalind Barnett, *Race and Class in the Intersection of Work and Family Among Women Employed in the Service Sector* (Wellesley, Mass.: Wellesley College Center for Research on Women, 1990); Norma Riccucci, *Women, Minorities, and Unions in the Public Sector* (New York: Greenwood, 1990); Mary Hale and Rita Mae Kelly, eds., *Gender, Bureaucracy, and Democracy: Careers and Equal Opportunity in the Public Sector* (New York: Greenwood, 1989); and Margaret L. Andersen, Patricia Hill Collins, eds. *Race, Class, and Gender: An Anthology* (Belmont, Calif.: Wadsworth, 1992).

24. Rhona Mahony, *Kidding Ourselves: Breadwinning, Babies, and Bargaining Power* (New York: Basic Books, 1995); and Arlie Russell Hochschild, *The Second Shift: Working Parents and the Revolution at Home* (New York: Viking, 1989).

25. Young, 53.

26. See Patricia Williams, *The Alchemy of Race and Rights* (Cambridge, Mass.: Harvard Univ. Press, 1991). On race, women, and marginalization, see Dorothy Roberts, "Punishing Drug Addicts Who Have Babies: Women of Color, Equality, and the Right to Privacy," *Harvard Law Review* 104:7 (May 1991): 1419ff; and idem, "Welfare and the Problem of Black Citizenship," *Yale Law Journal* 105:6 (April 1996): 1563ff. Also see Twila L. Perry, "Alimony: Race, Privilege, and Dependency in the Search for a Theory," Symposium on Divorce and Feminist Legal Theory, *Georgetown Law Journal* 82 (September 1994): 2481 and "Family Values, Race, Feminism and Public Policy," Symposium: Ethics, Public Policy and the Future of the Family, *Santa Clara Law Review* 36 (1996): 345. Also see *Critical Race Theory: The Key Writings that Formed the Movement*, ed. Kimberle Crenshaw (New York: New Press, 1995); Patricia Hill Collins, *Fighting Words: Black Women and the Search for Justice* (Minneapolis: Univ. of Minnesota Press, 1998).

27. See Emily Northrop, *The Diminished Anti-Poverty Impact of Economic Growth, the Shift to Services, and the Feminization of Poverty* (New York: Garland, 1994); Shirley Lord, *Social Welfare and the Feminization of Poverty* (New York: Garland, 1993); and Helda Scott, *Working Your Way to the Bottom: The Feminization of Poverty* (London: Pandora, 1984).

28. Young, 54.

29. Ibid., 55.

30. For an excellent discussion of this situation, see Cathy Cohen, *The Boundaries of Blackness: AIDS and the Breakdown of Black Politics* (Chicago: Univ. of Chicago Press, 1999).

31. Young, 58.

32. Kathy E. Ferguson, *The Feminist Case Against Bureaucracy* (Philadelphia: Temple Univ. Press, 1984), 84. See especially "Femininity as Subordination," 92–98; and "The Manager as Subordinate," 99–110.

33. Ibid., 93–99.

34. Albelda and Tilly, eds.

35. Young, 59.

36. Nancy Fraser, "Social Movements vs. Disciplinary Bureaucracies: The Discourse of Social Needs," CHS Occasional Paper, no. 8, Center for Humanistic Studies, Univ. of Minnesota, 1987. Also see Young, 59.

37. Young, 60.

38. Carol Gilligan, *In a Different Voice* (Cambridge, Mass.: Harvard Univ. Press, 1982).

39. When the clerical and technical workers initially organized, this dynamic appeared in debates about what form the organizing campaign should take. Women workers found that intensive personal interactions with coworkers were much more productive than more general, old-style pressure tactics that appeal to the "rights and duties" of labor and management. They chose to work with the first model of organizing because it was decentralized, democratic, and personalized and proved more effective. This decision did not spring from an abstract decision that women were "naturally" more relational than men. It grew out of a practical awareness that there is not one singularly correct model of organizing but many, and that a truly open "politics of difference" must be flexible enough to embrace the cultural particularities of a wide range of constituencies.

40. Young, 62.

41. For legal discussions of violence against women, see Martha Albertson Fineman and Roxanne Mykitiuk, eds., *The Public Nature of Private Violence* (New York: Routledge, 1994); Kimberly Williams Crenshaw, "The Marginalization of Sexual Violence Against Black Women," The Connecticut Sexual Assault Crisis Services Inc. Newsletter (January 2000); Riva Siegel, "'The Rule of Love': Wife Beating as Prerogative and Privacy," *Yale Law Journal* 105, no. 8 (June 1996): 2217–2308. On sexual harassment, see Louise Fitzgerald and Suzanne Swan, "Why Didn't She Just Report Him? The Psychological and Legal Implications of Women's Responses to Sexual Harassment," *Journal of Social Issues* 51, no. 1 (1995): 117–38.

42. Susan Faludi, *Backlash: The Undeclared War Against American Women* (New York: Crown, 1991).

43. Faludi, xvi–ii.

44. Julia Kristeva, *The Powers of Horror: An Essay on Abjection,* trans. Leon Roudiez (New York: Columbia Univ. Press, 1982).

45. Jacqueline Rose, "Introduction II," in *Feminine Sexuality: Jacques Lacan and the École Freudienne* (New York: Norton, 1982), 27–57. Also, more recent, see idem, *Why War? Psychoanalysis, Politics, and the Return to Melanie Klein* (Cambridge, Mass.: Blackwell, 1993).

46. René Girard, *Things Kept Secret from the Foundation of the World,* trans. Stephen Bann and Michael Metteer (Stanford: Stanford Univ. Press, 1987). For a feminist discussion of Girard, see Martha Reineke, *Sacrificed Lives: Kristeva on Women and Violence* (Bloomington: Indiana Univ. Press, 1997).

47. See MacKinnon's most recent work on violence and sexism in language: *Only Words* (Cambridge, Mass.: Harvard Univ. Press, 1993).

48. On this point, see the work of Peggy Reeves Sanday, *Female Power and Male Domination: On the Origins of Sexual Inequality* (Cambridge: Cambridge Univ. Press, 1981). Also see her cross-cultural analysis of "rape-prone" and "rape-resistant" societies in "The Socio-Cultural Context of Rape: A Cross Cultural Study," *Journal of Social Issues* 37 (April): 5–27.

5. Sin: Grace Denied

1. See David Kelsey, "Whatever Happened to the Doctrine of Sin?" *Theology Today* 50 (July 1993): 169–78.

2. See Susan Sontag on the rhetoric of AIDS, *AIDS and Its Metaphors* (New York: Farrar, Straus, Giroux, 1988). For example, see Alan Davies, *Infected Christianity: A Study of Modern Racism* (Kingston: McGill-Queen's Univ. Press, 1988).

3. Cornelius Plantinga Jr., *Not the Way It's Supposed to Be: A Breviary of Sin* (Grand Rapids, Mich.: Eerdmans, 1995), 10.

4. John Calvin, *Institutes of the Christian Religion,* ed. John McNeill (Philadelphia: Westminster, 1960), bk. 2, chaps. 1–5, 241–340.

5. Calvin's account of "bondage of the will" is not as developed as Luther's. For contemporary assessments of Calvin and sin, see Don Hendrick Compier, *Denouncing Death: John Calvin's Critique of Sin and Contemporary Rhetorical Theology* (unpublished Ph.D. diss.); Mary Potter Engels, *John Calvin's Perspectival Anthropology* (Atlanta: Scholars, 1988); François Wendel, *Calvin: The Origins and Development of His Religious Thought,* trans. Philip Mairet (New York: Harper & Row, 1963), 185–95; and William Bouwsma, *John Calvin: A Sixteenth-Century Portrait* (New York: Oxford Univ. Press, 1988), 32–37, 138–44. Also see Karl Barth's discussion of Calvin on sin in idem, *The Theology of John Calvin,* trans. Geoffrey W. Bromiley (Grand Rapids, Mich.: Eerdmans, 1995).

6. Calvin, *Institutes,* 2.1, 241–42.

7. Ibid., 1.4–7, 47–81. For a fuller definition of "dogmatic," see discussion of "doctrine" in chap. 1, pp. 16–18.

8. Edward Dowey has always suggested that bk. 3, chap. 1, on "faith" be read first when reading the *Institutes.* See Edward Dowey, *The Knowledge of God in Calvin's Theology* (New York: Columbia Univ. Press, 1952).

9. Calvin, *Institutes,* 3.2.7, 551.

10. For more on Calvin's use of the term "freedom," see his section on "Christian Freedom" in *Institutes,* 3.19, 833–49.

11. Ibid., 2.1.4, 245; O.S. vol. 3, 232.

12. Calvin, *Institutes,* 2.1.4. On "Supernatural Gifts Destroyed," 2.2.12, 270.

13. Ibid., 2.1.8, 251.

14. Ibid., 2.1.4, 245.

15. Ibid., 2.1.8, 251.

16. For an extensive nontheological treatment of Calvin's images of total depravity, see Bouwsma, 139ff, and David Kelsey's unpublished paper, "Some Kind Words for Total Depravity," delivered at the Yale Divinity School Faculty Forum (February 15, 2000).

17. Note here the link between this concept and strategic essentialism.

18. Plantinga, 31–32. He borrows the term "despoilment" not only from Calvin but from the Formula of Concord, which reads: "Humanity has been despoiled of its powers by original sin."

19. Calvin, *Institutes,* 2.1.5, 246.

20. Ibid., 2.1.7, 250.

21. See Marilyn Adams's discussion of purity and defilement in *Horrendous Evil and the Goodness of God* (Ithaca, N.Y.: Cornell Univ., 1996), 92–96. See Mary Douglas, *Purity and Danger: An Analysis of Concepts of Pollution and Taboo* (London: Routledge and Kegan Paul, 1966).

22. Calvin, *Institutes,* 2.1.5, 248.

23. Barth makes this point, Church Dogmatics: Vol. 4, The Doctrine of Reconciliation, Part One, ed. G. W. Bromiley and T. F. Torrance (Edinburgh: T & T Clark, 1980). There is no "relic or core or goodness which persists in man in spite of his sin."

24. Particularly telling in this instance is the case of Alzheimer's disease. See David Keck, *Forgetting Whose We Are: Alzheimer's Disease and the Love of God* (Nashville, Tenn.: Abingdon, 1996).

25. Associations with the term "agency" in our modern context are quite different from those of "free will" as used in Calvin's day. I use the two terms interchangeably for heuristic purposes. Calvin defines free will as "a faculty of reason to distinguish good and evil" and "a faculty of the will to choose one or the other." Calvin, *Institutes*, 2.2.4, 261.

26. "When man is denied all uprightness, he immediately takes occasion for complacency from that fact. . . . He should nonetheless be instructed to aspire to a good of which he is empty." Calvin, *Institutes*, 2.2.1, 255.

27. See Wendel, 187.

28. Calvin, *Institutes*, 2.2.1, 255.

29. Ibid., 2.2.12, 270–72, 277.

30. Ibid., 2.2.12, 270–72, 277. Also see 2.2.5, 295: "Simply to will is of man; to will ill, of a corrupt nature; to will well, of grace."

31. He states, "There is no danger in man depriving himself of too much so long as he learns that in God must be recouped what he himself lacks." Ibid., 2.2.10, 267.

32. Ibid., 2.1.8, 251. Note that, for Calvin, sin results not from lack but from active willing. It has energy and power. According to Calvin, "We are fertile with sin."

33. I do not mean that the only way for women to know oppression is for them to have faith. Obviously, this is not the case. Many feminist theorists are able to see women's oppression quite well without the faith framework I describe. I am arguing that while there is a nontheological frame of reference for seeing oppression, "seeing sin" is a distinctly theological concept.

34. Rebecca Chopp, "Anointed to Preach: Speaking of Sin in the Midst of Grace," in *The Portion of the Poor: Good News to the Poor in the Wesleyan Tradition*, ed. M. Douglas Meeks (Nashville, Tenn.: Kingswood Books, 1995). Also see Reta Halteman Finger, "Sin and Grace: A Christian Feminist Perspective," *Daughters of Sarah* 16 (January–February 1990): 3–19.

35. Valerie Saiving, "The Human Situation: A Feminine View," *Journal of Religion* 40 (April 1960): 100–12; Judith Plaskow, *Sex, Sin, and Grace: Women's Experience and the Theologies of Reinhold Niebuhr and Paul Tillich* (Washington, D.C.: Univ. Press of America, 1980).

36. Susan Dunfee Nelson, "The Sin of Hiding: A Feminist Critique of Reinhold Niebuhr's Account of the Sin of Pride," *Soundings* 65:3 (fall 1982): 316–27; Marjorie Suchocki, *The Fall to Violence: Original Sin in Relational Theology* (New York: Continuum, 1994); Mary Potter Engel, "Evil, Sin, and Violation of the Vulnerable," chap. 11 in *Lift Every Voice: Constructing Christian Theologies from the Underside* (San Francisco: Harper & Row, 1990), 152–64. Also see Delores Williams, *Sisters in the Wilderness: The Challenge of Womanist God-Talk* (Maryknoll, N.Y.: Orbis, 1993); idem, "Sin, Nature, and Black Women's Bodies," in *Ecofeminism and the Sacred*, ed. Carol Adams (New York: Continuum, 1993); and idem, "A Womanist Perspective on Sin," in *A Troubling in My Soul: Womanist Perspectives on Evil and Suffering*, ed. Emilie M. Townes (Maryknoll, N.Y.: Orbis, 1993). Also see Kathleen Sands, "Escape from Paradise: Responses to Evil in Religious Feminism," chap. 3 in *Escape from Paradise: Evil and Tragedy in Feminist Theology* (Minneapolis: Fortress Press, 1994). Rosemary Radford Ruether also has an excellent discussion of sin in "The Consciousness of Evil: The Journeys of Conversion," chap. 7 in *Sexism and God-talk: Toward a Feminist Theology* (Boston: Beacon, 1983), 159–92. Also see Sally Ann McReynolds and Ann O'Hara Graff, "Sin: When Women Are the Context," in *In the Embrace of God: Feminist Approaches to Theological Anthropology*, ed. Ann O'Hara Graff (Maryknoll, N.Y.: Orbis, 1995), 161–72; Wanda Barry, "Images of Sin

and Salvation in Feminist Theology," *ATR* 60 (1978): 25–54; and Kathryn Greene-McCreight, "Gender, Sin and Grace: Feminist Theologies Meet Karl Barth's Hamartiology." *Scottish Journal of Theology* 50: 4 (1997), 415–32.

37. Men may also lack self-esteem, but when one considered their access to social power and their training to exercise their freedom in relations of domination, one gets a model closer to Barth's image of "sloth."

38. Scripture offers us no single account of sin.

39. We need not translate every detail of these theories into a distinctly theological vocabulary in order for them to be theologically meaningful. Given that sin as "unfaithfulness" opposes God's good purposes for the flourishing of women, it is enough to let the theories stand as they are, as descriptions of the varied ways in which personal and social forces work to constrain this flourishing. Allowing these theories to enter feminist theological discourse in a manner that respects their analytic integrity allows theologians to profit from these theories in their particularity. Although sin is a theological category, one need not be a theologian to analyze the actual institutional or cultural mechanisms through which sin works.

40. Robert Merrihew Adams, "Involuntary Sins," *Philosophical Review* 94 (January 1985): 3–31.

41. Her mirror is a speculum that collapses two kinds of mirror into one: the speculum used in gynecological exams and a concave mirror, which reflects back on itself (like in a kaleidoscope).

42. Mary Grey, "Falling into Freedom: Searching for New Interpretations of Sin in Secular Society," *Scottish Journal of Theology* 47:2 (1994): 223–43; J. Phelps, "Joy Came in the Morning Risking Death for Resurrection: Confronting the Evil of Social Sin and Socially Sinful Structures," in Townes, ed.

43. Mary McClintock Fulkerson, "Sexism as Original Sin: Developing a Theacentric Discourse" *Journal of the American Academy of Religion* 59 (winter 1991): 653–75.

44. In defining sin in this manner, I am decisively parting ways with discussions of sin that typify the "unprideful" as suffering from "sloth" (Barth) or "concupiscence" (Tillich and Niebuhr) because each of these terms blames the victim. See Plaskow. Also see William Cahoy, "One Species or Two? Kierkegaard's Anthropology and the Feminist Critique of the Concept of Sin," *Modern Theology* 11:4 (October 1995): 429–54. Cahoy convincingly argues that Kierkegaard does not fall into the same trap and develops an understanding of "despair" similar to the notion of "self-loss" developed by feminists. See also Susan L. Lichtman, "The Concept of Sin in the Theology of Paul Tillich: A Break from Patriarchy?" *Journal of Women and Religion* 8 (winter 1989): 49–55.

45. Calvin explicitly rejects Augustine's position on sin's inheritance as genetic or biological because Calvin does not want to blame the body or sexuality. See Margaret Miles, "Theology, Anthropology, and the Human Body in Calvin's *Institutes of the Christian Religion*," *Harvard Theological Review* 74 (July 1981): 303–23.

46. In calling for women to have "containers," Irigaray is not reinventing the Enlightenment subject. Because women are historically and socially other-defined, they need to be strategically imaged as persons with borders, albeit permeable ones, which hold them together as selves who are internally fluid and multiple.

47. Jacquelyn Grant, "The Sin of Servanthood and the Deliverance of Discipleship," in Townes, ed.

48. Dorothy A. Lee, "Sin, Self-Rejection, and Gender: A Feminist Reading of John's

Gospel," *Colloquium* 27 (May 1995): 51–63.

49. See Judith Hermann, *Trauma and Recovery* (New York: Basic, 1992). For feminist theoretical perspectives on trauma, see Cathy Caruth, *Unclaimed Experience: Trauma, Narrative and History* (Baltimore: Johns Hopkins Univ. Press, 1996); Shoshanna Felman and Dori Laub, M.D., *Testimony: The Crisis of Witnessing in Literature, Psychoanalysis and History* (New York: Routledge, and Chapman and Hall, 1992).

50. Irigaray never offers this explicit an account of how women's boundaries are ravaged. Leaving it to her reader to decipher the subtext of terror in her works, she seldom mentions the systemic roots of women's undoing I have lifted up here.

51. Christine E. Gudorf, "Admonishing the Sinner: Owning Structural Sin," in *Rethinking the Spiritual Works of Mercy*, ed. Francis Eigo (Villanova, Pa.: Villanova Univ. Press, 1993), 1–31.

6. Community

1. Some critics of feminism see it as hostile to community, and more particularly to family. See the debate between Jean Elshtain and Barbara Ehrenreich: Jean Bethke Elshtain, "Feminism, Family, and Community." *Dissent* 29 (fall 1982): 442–49; and the response from Barbara Ehrenreich, "On Feminism, Family and Community," *Dissent* (winter 1983): 103–6. The debate can also be found in Penny Weiss and Marilyn Friedman, eds., *Feminism and Community* (Philadelphia: Temple Univ. Press, 1995), 259–71.

2. Weiss and Friedman, This collection illumines my contention that feminist theorists adopt a "double-vision" perspective on community.

3. For an interesting discussion of gender in medieval theology, see Amy Hollywood, *The Soul as Virgin: Mechthild of Magdeburg, Marguerite Porete, and Meister Eckhart* (Notre Dame, Ind.: Univ. of Notre Dame Press, 1995). Also see Sarah Coakley's discussion of gender in patristic thought in "Creaturehood before God: Male and Female," *Theology* 93, no. 755 (September/October 1990).

4. Angelika Bammer, "Mother Tongue and Other Strangers: Writing Family Across Cultural Divides," *Displacements: Cultural Identities in Question* (Bloomington: Indiana Univ. Press, 1994).

5. See chapter 4, pages 81–83.

6. *Women's Life-Writing: Finding Voice, Building Community*, ed. Linda Coleman (Bowling Green, Ohio: Popular, 1997). Also see Anndee Hochman, *Everyday Acts and Small Subversions* (Portland, Ore.: Eighth Mountain, 1994); and *A Tradition That Has No Name: Nurturing the Development of People, Families, and Communities*, ed. Mary Field Belenky, Lynne A. Bond, and Jacqueline Weinstock (New York: Basic Books, 1997).

7. There are some feminist separatist exceptions to this.

8. See Emilie M. Townes, ed., *A Troubling in My Soul: Womanist Perspectives on Evil and Suffering* (Maryknoll, N.Y.: Orbis, 1993); Christine Smith, *Preaching as Weeping, Confession, and Resistance: Radical Responses to Radical Evil* (Louisville, Ky.: Westminster John Knox, 1992); Nel Noddings, *Women and Evil* (Berkeley: Univ. of California Press, 1990); Kathleen Sands, *Escape from Paradise: Evil and Tragedy in Feminist Theology* (Minneapolis: Fortress Press, 1994); Wendy Farley, *Tragic Vision and Divine Compassion: A Contemporary Theodicy* (Louisville: Westminster John Knox, 1990); and Marilyn Adams, *Horrendous Evil and the Goodness of God* (Ithaca, N.Y.: Cornell Univ. Press, 1996).

9. Angelika Bammer, *Partial Visions: Feminism and Utopianism in the 1970s* (New York: Routledge, 1991). Also see Seyla Benhabib, *Critique, Norm, and Utopia: A Study of the Foundations of Critical Theory* (New York: Columbia Univ. Press, 1986).

10. For texts from the social science perspective see *Feminism and Sociological Theory*, ed. Ruth A. Wallace (Newbury Park, Calif.: Sage Publications, 1989); Debra Minkoff, *Organizing for Equality: The Evolution of Women's and Racial-Ethnic Organizations in America, 1955–1985* (New Brunswick, N.J.: Rutgers Univ. Press, 1995; and Cathy Cohen, *The Boundaries of Blackness: AIDS and the Breakdown of Black Politics* (Chicago: Univ. of Chicago Press, 1999) and *Women Transforming Politics: An Alternative Reader*, ed. Cathy J. Cohen, Kathleen B. Jones, and Joan C. Tronto (New York: New York Univ. Press, 1997). For discussions of feminism and science, see Evelyn Fox Keller, *Reflections on Gender and Science* (New Haven: Yale Univ. Press, 1985); Sandra Harding, *The Science Question in Feminism* (Ithaca, N.Y.: Cornell Univ. Press, 1986) and *Whose Science, Whose Knowledge: Thinking from Women's Lives* (Ithaca, N.Y.: Cornell Univ. Press, 1990).

11. This is very evident in critical legal theory. See *At the Boundaries of Law: Feminism and Legal Theory*, ed. Martha Albertson Fineman and Nancy Sweet Thomadsen (New York: Routledge, 1991); Deborah Rhode, *Justice and Gender: Sex Discrimination and the Law* (Cambridge, Mass.: Harvard Univ. Press, 1989); and Angela Harris, "Race and Essentialism in Feminist Legal Theory," *Stanford Law Review* 42:3 (February 1990): 581ff.

12. They are also often referred to as "traditional communities." See *Feminism and Community*, ed. Weiss and Friedman, 7–11.

13. See the works of Lila Abu-Lughod, Emily Honig, and Anna Lowenhaupt Tsing. Lila Abu-Lughod, *Writing Women's Worlds: Bedouin Stories* (Berkeley: Univ. of California Press, 1993); idem, *Veiled Sentiments: Honor and Poetry in Bedouin Society* (Berkeley: Univ. of California Press, 1986); and idem, "A Community of Secrets: The Separate World of Bedouin Women," *Signs* 10 (summer 1985): 637–57. Emily Honig, *Creating Chinese Ethnicity: Subei People in Shanghai, 1850–1980* (New Haven, Conn.: Yale Univ. Press, 1992); idem, "Burning Incense, Pledging Sisterhood: Communities of Women Workers in the Shanghai Cotton Mills, 1919–1949," *Signs* 10 (summer 1985): 700–14; and Emily Honig and Gail Hershatter, eds., *Personal Voices: Chinese Women in the 1980's* (New Haven: Yale Univ. Press, 1988). Anna Lowenhaupt Tsing, *In the Realm of the Diamond Queen: Marginality In an Out of the Way Place* (Princeton: Princeton Univ. Press, 1993); and idem, *Uncertain Terms: Negotiating Gender in American Culture*, ed. Anna Lowenhaupt Tsing and Gaye Ginsburg (Boston: Beacon, 1990).

14. On the status of subcommunities in legal theory, see the following articles by Christopher Eisgruber: "Birthright Citizenship and the Constitution," *New York University Law Review* 72 (April 1997): 54–96; "Reconstructing the Establishment Clause: The Case against Discretionary Accommodation of Religion," *University of Pennsylvania Law Review* 140 (December 1991): 555; and "Where Rights Begin: The Problem of Burdens on the Free Exercise of Religion," *Harvard Law Review* 102 (March 1989): 933. Also see Jonathan Boyarin, "Circumscribing Constitutional Identities in Kiryas Joel," *Yale Law Journal* 106, no. 5 (March 1997): 1537–70.

15. See Shane Phelan, *Identity Politics: Lesbian Feminism and the Limits of Community* (Philadelphia: Temple Univ. Press, 1989). Also see idem, "Democracy and Difference: Contesting the Boundaries of the Political," *Journal of Politics* 59 (November 1997): 1314–16; and idem, "The Shape of Queer: Assimilation and Articulation," *Women and Politics* 17 (1997): 55–73. The term "community without propinquity" is taken from sociologist Melvin Weber. (See Melvin Weber, "Order in Diversity: Community, City,

and Metropolis," in *Neighborhood, City, and Metropolis,* ed. R. Gutman and D. Popenoe [New York: Random House, 1970], 792–811.) Some theorists—such as Jean Francois Lyotard—heralded the end of modernity and liberalism as coinciding with the rise of new social movements.

16. See the works of Alain Touraine, Alberto Melucci, and Jean Cohen. Alain Touraine, *Critique of Modernity,* trans. David Macey (Oxford: Blackwell, 1995); idem, *Voice and the Eye: An Analysis of Social Movements,* trans. Alan Duff (Cambridge: Cambridge Univ. Press, 1981); idem, Michel Wieviorke, and François Dubet, eds., *Workers Movement* (Cambridge: Cambridge Univ. Press, 1987); Alberto Melucci, *Challenging Codes: Collective Action in the Information Age* (Cambridge: Cambridge Univ. Press, 1996); idem, *The Playing Self: Person and Meaning in a Planetary System* (London: Cambridge Univ. Press, 1996): idem, *Nomads of the Present: Social Movements and Individual Needs in Contemporary Society* (Philadelphia: Temple Univ. Press, 1989); Jean Cohen, *Class and Civil Society: The Limits of Marxian Critical Theory* (Amherst: Univ. of Massachusetts Press, 1982); and Jean Cohen and Andrew Arato, *Civil Society and Political Theory* (Cambridge, Mass.: MIT Press, 1992).

17. On identity politics see Shane Phelan, *Identity Politics: Lesbian Feminism and the Limits of Community* (Philadelphia: Temple Univ. Press), 1989. For a critique of identity politics see Martha Minow, *Not Only for Myself: Identity, Politics, and the Law* (New York: New Press, 1997). Also see Judith Butler, *Gender Trouble: Feminism and the Subversion of Identity* (New York: Routledge, 1990); and idem, *Bodies That Matter: On the Discursive Limits of "Sex"* (New York: Routledge, 1993).

18. Biddy Martin, "Sexual Practice and Changing Lesbian Identities," in *Destabilizing Theory: Contemporary Feminist Debates,* ed. Michèle Barrett and Anne Phillips (Stanford: Stanford Univ. Press, 1992).

19. Jodi Dean, *Solidarity of Strangers: Feminism after Identity Politics* (Berkeley: Univ. of California Press, 1996).

20. See Rosemarie Tong, *Feminine and Feminist Ethics* (Belmont, Calif.: Wadsworth, 1993).

21. For an excellent feminist summary of the debate, see Drucilla Cornel, "The Problem of Normative Authority in Legal Interpretation," and "In Defense of Dialogic Reciprocity," *Tennessee Law Review* 54 (1987): 327–43. Also see Elizabeth Frazer and Nicola Lacey, *The Politics of Community: A Feminist Critique of the Liberal-Communitarian Debate* (Toronto: Univ. of Toronto Press, 1993) and Christine Sypnowich, "Justice, Community and the Antinomies of Feminist Theory," *Political Theory* 21, no. 3 (August 1993): 484–506.

22. Frazer and Lacey, *Politics of Community,* 37. Also see Gisela Bock and Susan James, eds., *Beyond Equality and Difference: Citizenship, Feminist Politics, and Female Subjectivity* (New York: Routledge, 1992).

23. In feminist political theory, the usual target of their critiques of liberalism are the now classic texts of John Rawls, *A Theory of Justice* (Cambridge, Mass.: Belknap Press of Harvard Univ. Press, 1971); Ronald Dworkin, *Taking Right Seriously* (Cambridge, Mass.: Harvard Univ. Press, 1977); idem, *A Matter of Principle* (Cambridge, Mass.: Harvard Univ. Press, 1985); and Robert Nozick, *Anarchy, State and Utopia* (New York: Basic Books, 1974). Note that, in recent years, Rawls has made concessions toward social constructivism (Frazer and Lacey, *Politics of Community,* 58), but he still thinks there is a person prior to its particular ends and attachments, so he ultimately rejects constructivism of the strong variety.

24. Iris Marion Young, *Justice and the Politics of Difference* (Princeton, N.J.: Princeton Univ. Press, 1990), 45.

25. See Frazer and Lacey, *Politics of Community,* 48.

26. See Virginia Held, "Non-Contractual Society: A Feminist View," chap. 14 in Weiss and Friedman, *Feminism and Community,* 209. Also see Held's *Feminist Morality: Transforming Culture, Society, and Politics* (Chicago: Univ. of Chicago Press, 1993); *Rights and Goods: Justifying Social Action* (New York: Free Press/Macmillan, 1984); "Non-Contractual Society: A Feminist View," *Canadian Journal of Philosophy* 13 (1987): 111–37; and "The Meshing of Care and Justice," *Hypatia* 10 (spring 1995): 128ff. Also see Jane Mansbridge, *Beyond Adversary Democracy* (New York: Basic, 1980); idem, *Why We Lost the ERA?* (Chicago: Univ. of Chicago Press, 1986); idem, ed., *Beyond Self Interest* (Chicago: Univ. of Chicago Press, 1990); and idem and Susan Moller Okin, eds., *Feminism* (Aldershot, Hants, Eng.: Elgar, 1994).

27. This is the point at which one can distinguish democratic socialist liberals from free-market liberals. See Roberto Unger, *Politics: A Work in Constructive Social Theory,* 3 vols. (Cambridge: Cambridge Univ. Press, 1987); and idem, "The Critical Legal Studies Movement in America," *Harvard Law Review* 99 (1983): 561.

28. A recent attempt to argue for women's liberation within the liberal model of community is found in Susan Moller Okin's *Justice, Gender, and the Family* (New York: Basic, 1989), 101–9. Okin defends Rawls's early conception of the original position but expands the issue of gender. For more examples of liberal feminist theory, see Valerie Byson, *Feminist Political Theory,* 1992; Alison M. Jaggar, *Feminist Politics and Human Nature,* 1983; Janet Richards, *The Skeptical Feminist,* 1980. See also, Ann Ferguson, "Sex-War: The Debate between Radical and Libertarian Feminists," *Signs* 10 (1994): 106–12.

29. Carol Gould is an excellent model of this feminist defense of liberalism. See Carol Gould, *Rethinking Democracy: Freedom and Social Cooperation in Politics, Economy and Society* (Cambridge: Cambridge Univ. Press, 1988); idem, "Diversity and Democracy: Representing Difference," in *Democracy and Difference: Contesting Boundaries of the Political,* ed. Seyla Benhabib (Princeton: Princeton Univ. Press, 1996); and idem "Feminism and Democratic Community Revisited," Democratic Community, *Nomos* 35, ed. John Chapman and Ian Shapiro (New York: New York Univ. Press, 1993): 395–401.

30. See Carol Pateman's *The Sexual Contract* (Oxford: Polity, 1988); and *The Disorder of Women* (Oxford: Polity, 1989). Feminists point out that sexual violence as gender exploitation is connected to particular bodies. If the body is considered unimportant to the nature of the social contractor, then this kind of oppression will never be explicitly named.

31. Joan Scott, *Only Paradoxes to Offer: French Feminism and the Rights of Man* (Cambridge, Mass.: Harvard Univ. Press, 1996).

32. On liberalism's failure to monitor the activity of the "individual" in the "home" and the effects of this failure on women and children, see Catharine MacKinnon, *Toward a Feminist Theory of the State* (Cambridge, Mass.: Harvard Univ. Press, 1989); idem, *Feminism Unmodified: Discourses on Life and Law* (Cambridge, Mass.: Harvard Univ. Press, 1987); idem, "Feminism, Marxism, Method and the State," *Signs: Journal of Women in Culture and Society* 7 (1982): 515–44; and idem, *Sexual Harassment of Working Women* (New Haven: Yale Univ. Press, 1979).

33. Here the work of Virginia Held is important. See her "The Meshing of Care and Justice," 128. Drucilla Cornell also makes a similar argument. See Cornell, "What Is Ethical Feminism?" in *Feminist Contentions: A Philosophical Exchange,* ed. Seyla Benhabib,

Judith Butler, Drucilla Cornell, and Nancy Fraser (New York: Routledge, 1995), 75–106; idem, *Transformations: Recollective Imagination and Sexual Difference* (New York: Routledge, 1993); idem, *Beyond Accommodation: Ethical Feminism, Deconstruction, and the Law* (New York: Routledge, 1991); and idem, *Philosophy of the Limit* (New York: Routledge, 1992). Also see Robert Cover's article on affiliative ties: "Violence and the Word," *Yale Law Journal* 95 (1986): 1601–29. More of Cover's work can be found in Martha Minow, Michael Ryan, and Austin Sarat, eds., *Narrative, Violence, and the Law: The Essays of Robert Cover* (Ann Arbor: Univ. of Michigan Press, 1992).

34. Martha Minow, "Relational Rights and Responsibilities: Revisioning the Family in Liberal Political Theory and Law," *Hypatia* 11 (winter 1996): 4ff. Also see Minow's *Making All the Difference: Inclusion, Exclusion, and American Law* (Ithaca, N.Y.: Cornell Univ. Press, 1990). Feminists have also been concerned to promote parental leave policies that include men even though men do not physically bear children.

35. Lani Guinier, *Lift Every Voice: Turning a Civil Rights Setback into a Strong New Vision of Social Justice* (New York: Simon and Schuster, 1998); and idem, *The Tyranny of the Majority: Fundamental Fairness in Representative Democracy* (New York: Free Press, 1994).

36. See Susan Moller Okin, "Political Liberalism, Justice and Gender," *Ethics* 105 (1994): 23–43; Kate Nash, *Universal Difference: Feminism and the Liberal Undecidability of Women* (London: Macmillan Press, 1998); and Zillah Eisenstein, *The Radical Future of Liberal Feminism* (Boston: Northeastern Univ. Press, 1986).

37. As an example of this variety of feminism, see Mary Ann Glendon, *Rights Talk: The Impoverishment of Political Discourse* (New York: Free Press, 1991).

38. Nancy Fraser, *Justice Interruptus: Critical Reflections on the "Postsocialist" Condition* (New York: Routledge, 1997).

39. Vicki Schultz, "Women 'Before' the Law: Judicial Stories about Women, Work, and Sex Segregation on the Job," in *Feminists Theorize the Political*, ed. Judy Butler and Joan W. Scott (New York: Routledge, 1992). Also see Cynthia Epstein, "Work, Self, and Society: After Industrialization," *Sociological Inquiry* 67 (spring 1997): 250–52; and idem, "Gender in Practice: A Study of Lawyers' Lives," *Works and Occupations* 24 (February 1997): 122–25. Also see Nancy Levitt, *The Gender Line: Men, Women, and the Law* (New York: New York Univ. Press, 1998).

40. Rawls has recently tried to make this argument. See John Rawls, "The Idea of Public Reason Revisited," *University of Chicago Law Review* 64 (summer 1997): 765–807; and idem, "Reply to Habermas," *Journal of Philosophy* 92 (1995): 132–80.

41. See Michel Rosenfeld, *Affirmative Action and Justice: A Philosophical and Constitutional Inquiry* (New Haven: Yale Univ. Press, 1991); Kathanna Greene, *Affirmative Action and Principles of Justice* (New York: Greenwood, 1989); Albert Mosely and Nicholas Capaldi, *Affirmative Action: Social Justice or Unfair Preference?* (Lanham, Md.: Rowman & Littlefield, 1996); Nicolaus Mills, ed., *Debating Affirmative Action: Race, Gender, Ethnicity and the Politics of Inclusion* (New York: Delta, 1994); Allan P. Sindler, *Equal Opportunity: On the Policy and Politics of Compensatory Minority Preferences* (Washington, D.C.: American Enterprise Institute for Public Policy Research, 1983); Christopher Edley, *Not All Black and White: Affirmative Action, Race, and American Values* (New York: Hill and Wang, 1996); and Stephen Carter, *Reflection on the Affirmative Action Baby* (New York: Basic, 1991).

42. The principal theorists to whom I am referring as "communitarians" are Michael Walzer, *Spheres of Justice* (New York: Basic, 1983); Alisdair MacIntyre, *After Virtue* (London: Duckworth, 1981); Michael Sandel, *Liberalism and the Limits of Justice* (Cambridge:

Cambridge Univ. Press, 1982); Will Kymlicka, *Liberalism, Community and Culture* (Oxford: Clarendon, 1989). For overviews of communitarianism, see Haig Khatch-adourian, *Community and Communitarianism* (New York: Peter Lang, 1999); and Henry Benedict Tam, *Communitarianism: A New Agenda for Politics and Citizenship* (Hound-mills, Basingstoke, Hampshire: Macmillan Press, 1998). Also see Amy Gutmann, "Communitarian Critics of Liberalism," *Philosophy and Public Affairs* 14 (1985): 311; *Civic Repentance*, ed. Amitai Etzioni (Lanham: Rowman & Littlefield Publishers, 1999); and *New Communitarian Thinking: Persons, Virtues, Institutions, and Communities*, ed. Amitai Etzioni (Charlottesville: Univ. of Virginia Press, 1995).

The schools of thought typically referred to as "communitarianism" are quite diverse. There are civic republicanism and the new public-law theorists, who argue that we need a substantive conception of common life that is more than procedural. See John Dewey, *Individualism* (New York: Minton, Balch and Co., 1930); and idem, *Human Nature and Conduct* (New York: The Modern Library, 1930). Also see Hannah Arendt, *The Human Condition* (Chicago: Univ. of Chicago Press, 1958). There are also the interpretivists in legal theory, such as Stanley Fish and Ronald Dworkin. See Stanley Fish, *Doing What Comes Naturally: Change, Rhetoric, and the Practice of Theory in Literary and Legal Studies* (Durham, N.C.: Duke Univ. Press, 1989); and idem, *Is There a Text in This Class?: The Authority of Interpretive Communities* (Cambridge, Mass.: Harvard Univ. Press, 1980). Also referred to by some as "communitarians" are theorists grounded in the hermeneutic tradition, such as Hans Georg Gadamer, *Truth and Method*, trans. Garrett Barden and John Cumming (London: Sheed & Ward, 1975). Out of this tradition have emerged pragmatists, such as Richard Rorty and critical theory/discourse ethics philosophers like Jürgen Habermas, both of whom are sometimes described as having communitarian leanings.

43. Communitarians argue for normative values in different ways. Pragmatic relativist or functionalist communitarians shy away from the prescriptive project of normative politics. By remaining agnostic about specific social values, they argue, they are better able to avoid falsely universalizing principles and values. Examples of this position include thinkers such as Michael Sandel and Richard Rorty. See Richard Rorty, *Truth, Politics and Post-Modernism* (Assen: Van Gorcum, 1997). The second group of dialogical or deliberative communitarians believes it is necessary to create formal rules that will allow us to talk to each other, in respectful ways, about our differences and our shared interests. For this perspective, see the work of Jürgen Habermas in *The Habermas Reader*, ed. William Outhwaite (Cambridge, U.K.: Polity Press, 1996) and Benjamin Barber, *Strong Democracy: Participatory Politics for a New Age* (Berkeley: University of California Press, 1984). The third and perhaps best known group are the value communitarians, who argue openly and rigorously for the normative ideals that their traditions have bestowed upon them. On the left-wing side of this trajectory, we find the work of Michael Walzer and Roberto Unger, who share Marxist inclinations. See Roberto Mangabeira Unger, *Democracy Realized: The Progressive Alternative* (London; New York: Verso, 1998). On the neo-conservative side, see Alisdair MacIntyre, *After Virtue*, and Amitai Etzioni, *New Communitarian Thinking*.

44. The exceptions here are left-wing communitarians like Walzer and Unger and pluralists like Charles Taylor. Charles Taylor, *Sources of the Self* (Cambridge: Cambridge Univ. Press, 1989).

45. For feminists who stand in the liberal tradition, this understanding of community-oriented personhood is most likely rooted in a relational ontology, a weak

constructivism; feminists with more historicist inclinations hold a stronger version of constructivism.

46. Christine Pohl, *Making Room: Recovering Hospitality as a Christian Tradition* (Grand Rapids, Mich.: Eerdmans, 1999).

47. For feminists, this attention to particularity especially characterizes women's work of care. See Carol Gilligan and Ethics of Care literature: See Mary Jeanne Larrabee, ed., *An Ethic of Care: Feminist and Interdisciplinary Perspectives* (New York: Routledge, 1993); Nel Noddings, *Caring: A Feminine Approach to Ethics and Moral Education* (Berkeley: Univ. of California Press, 1984); and Martha Alberton Fineman, *The Neutered Mother* (New York: Routledge, 1995). Also see Eve Brown Cole and Susan Coultrap-McQuin, eds., *Explorations in Feminist Ethics: Theory and Practice* (Bloomington: Indiana Univ. Press, 1992). Also see Carol Gilligan, *In a Different Voice: A Psychological Theory of Women's Development* (Cambridge, Mass.: Harvard Univ. Press, 1982); idem, ed., *Mapping the Moral Domain: A Contribution of Women's Thinking to Psychological Theory and Education* (Cambridge, Mass.: Harvard Univ. Press, 1988); and Susan Hekman, *Moral Voices, Moral Selves: Carol Gilligan and Feminist Moral Theory* (Cambridge: Polity Press, 1995).

48. See Jean Bethke Elshtain, *Democracy on Trial* (New York: Basic Books, 1995); *Public Man, Private Woman: Women in Social and Political Thought* (Princeton, N.J.: Princeton Univ. Press, 1981).

49. Note that communitarians are almost as allergic to race as they are to gender. For a fuller discussion of these critiques of communitarianism, see Susan Bickford, "Why We Listen to Lunatics: Antifoundational Theories and Feminist Politics," *Hypatia* 8, no. 2 (spring 1993). Exceptions to this would be left-wing communitarians such as Walzer, *Spheres of Justice*; Unger, *Democracy Realized*; and Taylor, *Sources*. Theorists such as these gesture toward gender but nonetheless keep it undertheorized as a constitutive moment in communal identity.

50. Note again the place of left-wing communitarians.

51. See Jane Mansbridge, "Feminism and Democratic Community," *Democratic Community*, ed. John Chapman and Ian Shapiro (New York: New York Univ. Press, 1993), 365. Mansbridge, along with many feminist historians, maintains that in almost every historical social configuration, one can find subordinate groups or marginalized voices seeking to subvert the value systems of dominant culture and to advance their own values and moral systems.

52. See "The Communitarian Platform on the Family," Communitarian Network, The Communitarian Platform: Rights and Responsibilities, 2: Responsive Community: Rights and Responsibilities, 4 (1991–1992). Communitarians have in recent years given strong defenses of the value of the two-parent, heterosexual household, the need for society to care for the elderly and the sick as valued persons, the value of sexual monogamy, and the value of religious education and the nurturing of traditional religious sensibilities as the source for our understandings of virtue. For a feminist critique of this platform's position on the family, see Susan Apel, "Communitarianism and Feminism: The Case Against the Preference for the Two-Parent Family," *Wisconsin Law Journal* 10:1 (1995): 1–26.

53. Frazer and Lacey, *Politics of Community*, 137

54. Feminist critics of communitarianism do not apply this second critique to all communitarians. While they may fault socialist and Marxist communitarians for not taking gendered power relations seriously enough, these theorists do not fall prey to the problems of social conservatism discussed here.

55. Francis Olsen has wisely noted: "Our historical experience (as women) makes us assume, often without realizing it, that the only alternatives are patriarchy on the one hand, and atomistic individualism on the other" (Weiss and Friedman, eds., *Feminism and Community,* 25).

7. Church: Graced Community

1. See Avery Dulles, *Models of the Church* (Garden City, N.Y.: Image, 1974). Dulles describes the church as institution, mystical communion, sacrament, herald, and servant.

2. Shoshanna Felman and Dori Laub, M.D., *Testimony: The Crisis of Witnessing in Literature, Psychoanalysis and History* (New York: Routledge and Chapman and Hall, 1992).

3. This brief narrative is not meant to serve as an exhaustive account of the normative narrative frames operative in the Christian traditions of the West.

4. See René Girard's discussion of imitation, "The Victimage Mechanism as the Basis of Religion," chap. 1 in *Things Hidden since the Foundation of the World* (Stanford: Stanford Univ. Press, 1987).

5. On this particular point, my reflections have been informed by the work of Shannon Craigo-Snell and Ruthanna Hooke, both of whom have done extensive work on the theme of performance and theology. They have yet to write their books, however. We are waiting!

6. The term used in the tradition to describe this unusual status is "election." For a feminist discussion of election, see Judith Plaskow, *Standing Again at Sinai: Judaism from a Feminist Perspective* (New York: Harper & Row, 1990).

7. Also referred to as "visible/invisible" and "hidden/revealed church." See Philip Hefner, "Ninth Locus: The Church," in *Christian Dogmatics,* ed. Karl Braaten and Robert W. Jenson, vol. 2 (Philadelphia: Fortress Press, 1984), 99. Hefner has a good discussion of church as militant/triumphant, an image that illustrates church is not the kingdom of God; the kingdom represents God's ultimate purpose for creation, and the church anticipates the Kingdom.

8. Letty Russell, *Church in the Round: Feminist Interpretation of the Church* (Louisville, Ky.: Westminster John Knox, 1993); Rosemary Radford Ruether, *Women-Church: Theology and Practice of Feminist Liturgical Communities* (San Francisco: Harper & Row, 1985).

9. Rebecca Chopp, *The Power to Speak: Feminism, Language, God* (New York: Crossroads, 1989); Elisabeth Schüssler Fiorenza, *Discipleship of Equals: A Critical Feminist Ekklesia-logy of Liberation* (New York: Crossroads, 1993).

10. Starhawk, *The Spiral Dance: A Rebirth of the Ancient Religion of the Greek Goddess* (San Francisco: Harper & Row, 1979); Russell, *Church in the Round,* 80–81; Sharon Welch, *A Feminist Ethic of Risk* (Minneapolis: Fortress Press, 1990); Mud Flower Collective (Katie Cannon, Beverly Harrison, Carter Heyward, Ada Maria Isasi-Diaz, Bess Johnson, Mary Pelauer, and Nancy Richardson), *God's Fierce Whimsy: Christian Feminism and Theological Education* (New York: Pilgrim, 1985), xiii: "We offer *God's Fierce Whimsy* as a sign that—like a mud flower—women's power in the world/church grows only with difficulty and then only when well nourished and absolutely determined to grow sturdier and bigger and even more beautiful."

11. See Miriam Therese Winter, Adair Lummis, and Alison Stokes, eds., *Defecting in Place: Women Claiming Responsibility for Their Own Spiritual Lives* (New York: Crossroads, 1994).

12. In the Smalcald Articles, Luther writes, "a seven-year-old child knows what the church is, namely, holy believers and sheep who hear the voice of their Shepherd." See "The Smalcald Articles," *Martin Luther's Basic Theological Writings*, ed. Timothy Lull (Philadelphia: Fortress Press, 1989), 534. For a fuller discussion of the meaning of "church," see also "On the Councils and the Church," *Luther's Basic Writings*, 540–75. See also Walter Altmann's *Luther and Liberation: Latin American Perspective*, trans. Mary M. Solberg (Minneapolis: Fortress Press, 1992), 61 Altmann. Also see Gordon Rupp, *The Righteousness of God* (London: Hodder and Stoughton, 1953). Note that the following exploration of Luther's theology and the ecclesial force of justification is not intended as an exhaustive defense of Luther's position on this matter. I offer it here more as a thought-experiment which, I believe, is grounded in Luther's work while also moving imaginatively beyond it.

13. See Werner Elert, *The Structure of Lutheranism* (St. Louis: Concordia, 1962), 257.

14. See Paul Althaus's discussion of Luther's Small Catechism in *The Theology of Martin Luther*, trans. Robert Schultz (Philadelphia: Fortress Press, 1966), 288. See "The Small Catechism" in *Luther's Basic Writings*, 471–96.

15. Althaus, 61; John Headley, *Luther's View of Church History* (New Haven: Yale Univ. Press, 1963), 30.

16. Luther's most trenchantly anti-institutional attacks on the church come in his 1520 *Babylonian Captivity*, where he attacks the sacramental system as a set of works that we must do. ("The Babylonian Captivity of the Church, Part 1," *Martin Luther's Basic Writings*, ed. Timothy Lull [Philadelphia: Fortress Press, 1989], 267–313.) Luther gets more institutionally friendly in the 1530s as he begins to confront the real institutional challenges associated with being church.

17. Althaus summarizes this dimension of Luther's thought as follows: "Because the question of our salvation has been solved in justifying faith, and because man expects everything from God and nothing from himself, he is now completely free to use all he has, can do, and suffer to serve his brother. He no longer lives in any way for himself but rather completely for the community of saints," Paul Althaus, *The Theology of Martin Luther*, 308.

18. Luther captures this dynamic well in his claim that "it is the promises of God that make the church and not the church that makes the promises of God. For the Word of God is incomparably superior to the church, and in this Word, the church, being a creature, has nothing to decree, ordain or make, but only to be decreed, ordained, and made" by the Word of God. *Luther's Works* 36:107, cited by Altmann, *Luther and Liberation*, 61.

19. Luther says this: "Every man has been created and born for the sake of the other." WA 21, 346 (Cruciger's edition).

20. Altmann offers a nice summary of these last points, particularly the one about the church's drive for liberation from institutional tutelage (his words), 66. "The face of the church cannot be without suffering, persecution, and dying, yes, not without sin either" (WA 7, 684, 9). "The face of the church is the face of the one who is a sinner, troubled, forsaken, dying and full of distress" See Elert, 262.

21. This account of the justified church leaves many important issues in Luther's doctrine of the church unaddressed, such as his politically conservative "two kingdoms" doctrine, his vocal opposition to church involvement in political matters of his day, and his consistently (but not singularly) patriarchal assumptions about the gender of God and humanity.

22. See *John Calvin and the Church: A Prism of Reform*, ed. Timothy George (Louisville, Ky.: Westminster John Knox, 1990).

23. For an account of Calvin's theology and the role of the persecuted church, see David N. Wiley's discussion of election and persecution in "The Church of the Elect," *John Calvin and the Church,* 109ff.

24. Carlos Eire, "John Calvin's Attack on Idolatry," chap. 6 in *War Against the Idols: The Reformation of Worship from Erasmus to Calvin* (Cambridge: Cambridge Univ. Press, 1986).

25. Calvin, *Institutes,* 4.1.1, 1012.

26. Calvin tried studiously to avoid implying that church can function as a device for getting us grace. He rejects any mediatorial understanding of the church. It is rather a device that God uses to reach us. Calvin, *Institutes,* 4.1.1, 1011. For a more fully developed account of this stance, see his lengthy discussion of the sacraments in *Institutes,* Book 4.

27. For analysis of Calvin's mother imagery, see Amy Plantinga Pauw, "The Church as Mother and Bride: Rethinking the Reformed Heritage: Challenge and Promise" *Many Voices, One God: Being Faithful in a Pluralistic World,* ed. Walter Brueggemann and George Stroup (Louisville, Ky.: Westminster John Knox, 1998). Calvin borrows the mother image from Cyprian and Augustine; see François Wendel, *Calvin: The Origins and Development of His Religious Thought,* trans. Philip Mairet (New York: Harper & Row, 1950), 294.

28. Calvin, *Institutes,* 4.1.4, 1016.

29. See Brian Gerrish, *Grace and Gratitude: The Eucharistic Theology of John Calvin* (Minneapolis: Fortress Press, 1993), 119.

30. Embedded within this image of the church gestating and birthing are a number of important ecclesial claims. It is clear that the life the believer receives in the church is not earned but given. Just as a child does not choose to be conceived or born, so too, the faithful receive new life not only because of their own decision but also because of their proximity to a community that agrees to shape them through the power of the Spirit. In this regard, the church both predates and constitutes the agency and identity of the believer and not vice versa; it is the womb out of which the agentic, embodied self emerges into a gifted existence. This means that the process of becoming a Christian does not start with an individual who, in isolation from the church, has a private conversion experience that prompts her to join the church. To the contrary, the image of a gestating, birthing mother suggests that one becomes a Christian only by being first enveloped by the community, which shapes one through a series of practices and relationships that make up the patterns of Christian living. As one undertakes and is undertaken by these practices and is shaped by these relationships, one slowly becomes a self who is disposed to love God and neighbor in a manner that conforms to the image of Christ; and it is only after this shaping process begins that one may choose formally to become a member of the body that brought one to life.

31. Calvin, *Institutes,* 4.1.5, 1018.

32. Ibid., 4.1.7, 1017.

33. Ibid., 4.1.5, 1018; 4.1.2, 1013.

34. Ibid., 4.1.5, 1019. "It is especially to this end that, as I have said, in ancient times under the law all believers were commanded to assemble at the sanctuary."

35. A suggested image is of God as the father who is married to (and impregnates) the mother church, who then gives birth to believers. While this image captures Calvin's sense that the church has no power to save, it raises troubling questions about the underlying gender assumptions that drive his doctrine of the church as mother. Calvin's

description of the church as a womb raises a number of other questions as well. Each of these images requires more careful analysis, from a feminist perspective, than I have given here. I raise them in the hopes of provoking further work.

36. There are many themes in Calvin's ecclesiology I have left unaddressed, such as his understanding of church-state relations, his "theocratic" view of community life, and, most important, the sexist gender binarism inherent in his use of feminine, maternal imagery for the church.

37. Robert Cover refers to this kind of community as a "nomic community." See Martha Minow, Michael Ryan, and Austin Sarat, eds., *Narrative, Violence, and the Law: Essays by Robert Cover* (Ann Arbor, Mich.: Univ. of Michigan Press, 1993).

38. Amy Plantinga Pauw describes this well in "The Church as Mother and Bride."

39. Bass et al., *Practicing Our Faith: A Guide for Conversation, Learning, and Growth* (San Francisco: Jossey-Bass, 1997), 5. By practices, I mean the rather ordinary things that "people of faith do together, over time, in response to and in light of the grace of God."

40. Stephanie Paulsell, "Honoring the Body," *Practicing Our Faith*, 13–27.

41. Dorothy Bass, *Receiving the Day: Christian Practices for Opening the Gift of Time* (San Francisco: Jossey-Bass, 1999).

42. Letty Russell, *Household of Freedom: Authority in Biblical Theology* (Philadelphia: Westminster, 1987).

43. Catherine Keller describes "People in community with nature" in idem, "Postmodernism, Nature, Feminism, and Community" chap. 7 in *Theology for Earth Community: A Field Guide*, Ecology and Justice Series, ed. Dieter Hessel (Maryknoll, N.Y.: Orbis, 1996), 93–102.

44. This dynamic of giving a law to love is described beautifully by Margaret Farley in *Personal Commitments: Beginning, Keeping, Changing* (San Francisco: Harper & Row, 1986), 34–37. Also see Gene Outka, "Universal Love and Impartiality," in *The Love Commandments*, ed. Edmund N. Santurri and William Werpehowski (Washington, D.C.: Georgetown Univ. Press, 1992).

Index

CPSIA information can be obtained
at www.ICGtesting.com
Printed in the USA
LVHW052137160821
695425LV00003B/484